MILLION MAN MARCH/
DAY OF ABSENCE

MILLION MAN MARCH/
DAY OF ABSENCE

A COMMEMORATIVE ANTHOLOGY

SPEECHES, COMMENTARY, PHOTOGRAPHY, POETRY, ILLUSTRATIONS, DOCUMENTS

Edited by

Haki R. Madhubuti and Maulana Karenga

Third World Press
Chicago

University of Sankore Press
Los Angeles

Also by Haki R. Madhubuti

Claiming Earth: Race, Rage, Rape, Redemption (1994)
Black Men: Obsolete, Single, Dangerous? The Afrikan–American Family in Transition (1990)
From Plan to Planet: Life Studies: The Need for Afrikan Minds and Institutions (1973)
Enemies: The Clash of Races (1978)
Kwanzaa: A Progressive and Uplifting African–American Holiday (1972)
A Capsule Course in Black Poetry Writing
  (co-authored with Gwendolyn Brooks,
   Keorapetse Kgositsile and Dudley Randall) (1975)

Poetry
Killing Memory, Seeking Ancestors (1987)
Earthquakes and Sunrise Missions (1984)
Book of Life (1973)
Directionscore: New and Selected Poems (1971)
We Walk the Way of the New World (1970)
Don't Cry, Scream (1969)
Black Pride (1968)
Think Black (1966)
Heart Love: Essential Meditations of Commitment:
  Poetry Celebrating Marriage and Family (forthcoming)

Criticism
Dynamite Voices: Black Poets of the 1960's (1971)

Anthologies
Why L.A. Happened:
  Implications of the '92 Los Angeles Rebellion (ed. 1993)
Say That the River Turns:
  The Impact of Gwendolyn Brooks (1987)
To Gwen, With Love
  (co-edited with Pat Brown and Francis Ward)
Confusion by Any Other Name:
  Essays Exploring the Negative Impact of the Blackman's Guide to
  Understanding the Black Woman (ed. 1990)

Also by Maulana Karenga

The Book of Coming Forth By Day: The Ethics of the Declarations of Innocence (1990)
Reconstructing Kemetic Culture: Papers, Perspectives, Projects (ed.) (1990)
The African-American Holiday of Kwanzaa: A Celebration of Family, Community and Culture (1988)
Kemet and the African Worldview: Research, Rescue, and Restoration (ed.) (1986)
Selections from the Husia: Sacred Wisdom of Ancient Egypt (1984)
Introduction to Black Studies (1st Edition) (1982)
Kawaida Theory: An Introductory Outline (1980)
Essays on Struggle: Position and Analysis (1978)
Kwanzaa: Origins, Concepts, Practice (1977)
The Foundations of Kawaida Theory: An Essay in Communitarian African Philosophy (forthcoming)
Race, Ethnicity and Multiculturalism: Issues in Domination, Resistance and Diversity (forthcoming)

Third World Press books may be purchased for educational, business or solely promotional use. For information, please write: Sales Department, Third World Press, P.O. Box 19730, Chicago, Illinois 60619 (312) 651-0700

The University of Sankore Press books may be purchased for educational, business or solely promotional use. For information, please write: Sales Dept. The University of Sankore Press 2560 West 54th Street, Los Angeles, CA. 90043 (213) 295-9799

First Edition
January 1996

Library of Congress Cataloging-in-Publication Data
Million Man March/Day of Absence: A Commemorative Anthology
Edited by Haki R. Madhubuti and Maulana Karenga.-1st Edition

ISBN #: 0-88378-188-3
Text and cover design Angelo Williams
Cover photo by J.D. Howard

Manufactured in the United States of America

1. Black Studies-Photography-Literary Collection 2. Politics 3. Culture
African American Men

96 97 98 99 10 9 8 7 6 5 4 3 2 1

To our brothers who did not make the march
and for our sisters.

Haki Madhubuti
Maulana Karenga

Contents

Part 7
Media, Media, Media

Part 8
Documents

Illustrators:

Tom Feelings
Jon Lockard
Murry DePillars

Photographers:

J. D. Howard Cover Photo
Brian 6X Jackson
Roy Lewis
Richard Muhammad
Robert Sengstacke
Robert L. Thorton
James Wethers
Kenneth Wright

ACKNOWLEDGMENTS

A project the size and complexity of the *Million Man March/Day of Absence: Commemorative Anthology* is by no means the work of just the editors. The MMM/DOA took place on October 16, 1995 and we are publishing our anthology on January 16, 1996, three months after that earth shaking event.

This work would not be in your hands today if it was not for the generosity, commitment, professionalism and determination of a good many people. We cannot thank our contributors enough; the writers, poets, photographers and illustrators took a detour from their own "work in progress" and rallied to our call. They responded in the spirit of the MMM/DOA.

Our staff at Third World Press went far beyond the call of duty and must be given special thanks. Those staff members who worked directly on the project and the others who took on extra work so that we could complete the *MMM/DOA: Commemorative Anthology* three months before its scheduled publication date.

Finally, Angelo Williams, our graphic designer/consultant and Make No Mistake Editorial Services of Hazel Crest, Il. were indispensable. Special thanks also go out to my friend and colleague Dr. Donda West and my wife Safisha Madhubuti for giving their "fresh" eyes in the final stages of the book.

H. R. M.

DECLARATION

IN THE PRESENCE OF GOD WE HUMBLY DECLARE OUR EARNEST AND SINCERE COMMITMENT TO ATONE TO GOD FOR OUR SINS AND FOR THE SINS OF OUR PEOPLE IN OUR LONG STRUGGLE FOR LIBERATION.

AS RELIGIOUS AND SPIRITUAL LEADERS AND MINISTERS OF FAITH TO OUR PEOPLE, WE CALL UPON ALL OUR PEOPLE TO REPENT, TO ATONE AND RECONCILE OURSELVES TO THE GOD OF OUR CREATION AND SALVATION.

*WE SOLEMNLY DECLARE OCTOBER 16, 1995 AS A **"HOLY DAY OF ATONEMENT AND RECONCILIATION."***

WE CALL UPON ALL OUR PEOPLE TO BE IN PRAYER AND SOLIDARITY ON THIS HOLY DAY. THERE IS TO BE NO WORK, NO SCHOOL, NO SPORT OR PLAY, NO ENTERTAINMENT, AND NOTHING PROFANE ON THIS HOLY DAY. FOR THOSE WHO ARE ABLE, THERE SHOULD BE FASTING FROM SUNDOWN ON THE DAY BEFORE UNTIL SUNDOWN ON THE DAY OF THIS HOLY DAY.

LET US ALL BE IN UNITY WITH GOD AND WITH ONE ANOTHER AS WE RECOMMIT AND RENEW OUR DETERMINATION TO DO GOD'S WILL AND SEEK JUSTICE, FREEDOM, AND EMPOWERMENT FOR OUR PEOPLE.

Photo by RoyLewis

WHO CAN BE BORN BLACK

Who
can be born black
and not
sing
the wonder of it
the joy
the
challenge

And/to come together
in a coming togetherness
vibrating with the fires of pure knowing
reeling with power
ringing with the sound above sound above sound
to explode/in the majesty of our oneness
our comingtogether
in a comingtogetherness

Who
can be born
black
and not exult!

—Mari Evans

Photo by Brian Jackson

Part 1
Aftershocks: Introduction, Comments, Possibilities

Photo by Robert Sengstacke

TOOK BACK OUR TEARS, LAUGHTER, LOVE AND LEFT A BIG DENT IN THE EARTH

Haki R. Madhubuti

If one closely followed the commentary and comments that appeared in the media prior to the Million Man March/Day of Absence (MMM/DOA), it was assumed by most that the Black community, specifically Black men, had to make a choice between the "messenger and the message." Time and time again the Julian Bonds, Roger Wilkins, Angela Davis' and their white and Black imitators were allotted prime television, radio and print space to denounce Minister Farrakhan, Reverend Benjamin Chavis, the Nation of Islam and the MMM/DOA Organizing Committee as if they, and only they, were solely responsible for the largest, most peaceful assembly of folks ever to grace the grounds of the nation's capital in a single day of spiritual sharing and political debate. Lies sell quickly when people want to believe them.

Early in June, 1995, it was clear to me, as one of the thousand or so organizers and as a member of the Executive Council MMM/DOA Organizing Committee, that the idea of men, Black men, men of African ancestry making a collective statement about race, our space in America and the world was overly needed. The need for spiritual renewal and a discussion about the economic, social and political state of African Americans focusing on solutions had to be on the agenda. During 1994 and 1995, Minister Farrakhan had been filling stadiums, auditoriums and churches across the nation demanding that Black men stand up.

Black men had been painted and brushed by those in power as somehow deficient, irresponsible, lacking in moral and ethical character, unable to speak truth to power or themselves. If anything was needed, it must be an action—collective in nature—that would resound around the nation and the world that stated without doubt or hesitation that Black men cared, that we hurt and needed healing, that we needed each other, that we do have money, resources and an independent spirit and mindset, that we are family-based, and that we do have fire in our bellies for that which is right, correct and good. We also needed to make clear that we are not ignorant simpletons, lock-stepped behind people who do not like us or our children. And yes, for the great majority of men, the choice was *never* between a man or a movement; it was about having a *voice* and being *listened* to.

The earth shook on October 16, 1995, and left a large dent in the capital. And, to try and separate Minister Farrakhan from the shared spirit and renewed energy of the million-plus men who walked, ran, drove, flew, took trains and buses to the nation's capital from most parts of the Black Diaspora is to encourage dishonesty and to deny reality and history. We did not buy into the white lie that suggested if we joined hands with Minister Farrakhan, Reverend Benjamin Chavis and others that we would somehow relinquish all critical faculties and negate our ability to think or function independently or collectively at the local, national and international levels. If we had, that would only have branded us what many of our sworn enemies wished us to be: weak-minded and irrelevant. To most of us, such irrational thought contradicts the complexity of the *human spirit under siege* which, if observed with any sensitivity or seriousness, does rise at appropriate times to re-write history and the brain-dead white supremacist assumptions of our detractors. This was our time and it will not stop in Washington, D.C.

That Minister Farrakhan had the vision, organization, money, independence and spiritual strength to stand up against gangsta odds and say, "let's meet in Washington," and to reach out to the Black church, Black fraternal organizations, Black professional organizations, Black women organizations, Black Nationalists and Pan-Africans, Black college students and Black street people all across the country was definitely an act of humility, spiritual growth, inclusion and political insight. Regardless of his contradictions—many would say hypocrisy—Minister Farrakhan had earned a *part* of our *trust* and one-twentieth of the Black male population responded with a fired-up yes to the MMM/DOA call and mission statement (see documents).

Of the million or so men who traveled to Washington, D.C., another two or three million wanted to come, but could not make it due to family or employment responsibilities, lack of financial resources, incarceration in the nation's prisons, and some remained home because of *fear*. I'm sure that General Colin Powell wanted to be there, but he had locked himself into a cultural and political community that if he came he would have put at risk both his political and financial future. The risk was too great for him and thousands of others to be seen at such an historic Black gathering.

Could the Nation of Islam (NOI) and Minister Farrakhan have pulled the MMM/DOA off on their own? Probably not. They knew as early as May of 1995 that they had assigned themselves an awesome task; and in order not to fall flat on their collective faces, and also in the new spirit of inclusion that undercurrents Minister Farrakhan's national message, they reached out to the broad heterogeneous Black community. This strategy of inclusion *worked*. At that point, people not in the Nation of Islam joined the organizing efforts, from Reverend Benjamin Chavis to Chicago's Reverend Jeremiah Wright, from Washington D.C.'s Reverend Willie Wilson to New York's Bob Law, from Louisville's Reverend Kelvin Crosby to New York City's Ron Daniels, from Los Angeles' Maulana Karenga to New York City's Reverend Johnny Youngblood, from Newark's Danny Bakewell to New Orleans' Dr. Morris Jeff, from Chicago's Conrad Worrill to Baltimore's Reverend Frank Reid. The list, including Cornell West, Jesse Jackson, Dick Gregory, Stevie Wonder, Reverend Wendell Anthony, Bob Brown, Eddie Reid, and Craig Hodges, is unending.

The great majority of men focused on themselves and each other rather than the speaker's platform. Due to the numbers and the inadequate video and audio systems, it was just about impossible to hear or see all that was coming from the speaker's platform. Therefore, the men and boys communed, touched, shared, laughed, cried, introduced themselves to strangers, formed new relationships, testified to sons, grandsons, great-grandsons, confessed, rejoiced, wrote notes and letters to their wives, girlfriends, and mates. These brothers on that day of atonement, reconciliation, and responsibility subordinated their superficial differences and for *many for the first time* began to truly *listen* to and *touch* each other's hearts.

Whether one was straight or gay; old or young; democratic, republican, or independent; Christian, Muslim, Buddhist, Yoruba, Akan, or non-sectarian; poor, rich, or sliding somewhere in between; single, married, divorced, or thinking about each; lay worker or professional; famous or trying to attain fame; illiterate or super-educated; employed or unemployed; saved or looking for spiritual resolution— it was clear that each man came for *different* and for the *same* reasons. And, to a man/boy they (we) left with not only a better understanding and feeling about ourselves and our future—we left *knowing that we could do something about both.*

Few of the men at the MMM/DOA could give a detailed analysis of the comments emanating from the speaker's platform. Most of the men—after three to eight hours of commuting there and standing there—chose to bathe in the *joy* of being there. Around 4:30 p.m. or so, Minister Farrakhan arrived and partially compromised his place in history with a two-and-one-half hour speech that should have been shorted by, at the minimum an hour and a half. He and his advisors blew a major opportunity to speak, clearly and definitively, truth to the world via *Black College*

Satellite, CNN, C-Span, BET, and Black radio—by *not* taking into consideration the length of time that the men had been there—many for as long as twelve hours. A crisp, politically astute, culturally detailed, and inspirational message of forty to fifty minutes would have been the crowning achievement of the day and his life. Be as it was, he was able to make several points around the theme that undoubtedly will encourage and stimulate Black men to local action: a) all men should maintain their families; b) join churches, mosques, temples, and organizations; c) register to vote; d) become politically and culturally active; e) support a national African American Development Fund; f) respect Self and Black women, etc.

If a million-plus white men led by Jesse Helms or Pat Robertson had marched into Washington, D.C., you could be sure that press coverage would have been a lot more insightful and less biased. The ineptitude of the major white media was obvious in its racist and insulting coverage—this was both prior to and after the march. One of the reasons for this book is to tell our own story. And to tell it in all of its diversity, love, contradictions, and conflicts, as well as highlight the utter, undeniable unity and concerns of the MMM/DOA and the indispensable role Minister Farrakhan and the Nation of Islam played in order to make it possible.

However, we are all back in our respective cities, towns, and villages; and if the MMM/DOA is to have a lasting importance and meaning, it must translate into day-to-day activities at the street, home, farm, employment, political, economic, and institutional levels. If nothing else, we must understand that there are *no simplistic* answers to the mess that we are in. To that end, I would conclude by offering a number of suggestions:

1) In all of our homes, there needs to be a renewal of respect for ideas, information, and knowledge. Obviously, I believe that African-centered cultural knowledge needs to be at the top of the list, but by no means do I feel that having received life-giving and life-saving African/Black history, psychology, sociology, literature, and spiritual substance is enough. Our knowledge base must be expanded and expandsive. We live in a world where illiteracy is the norm and all too often the students who excel intellectually are ostracized and made to feel unwanted by their peers. Also, television has become the fact giver for too many of us. The acquisition of pertinent information is not easy and requires more effort on our part than turning on a television, radio, or browsing newspapers and magazines (see Bill McKibbeh's, *The Age of Missing Information* and Sven Birkerts, *The Gutenberg Elegies*).

2) We need to check our *egos* and *negative* personalities at the door of the meeting, seminar, classroom, workplace, and conferences, and believe we are not more important than our people or the problems we face. We have to not just *hear* each other, we have to *listen* to each other and progressively act on the listening. We all have to rise above the limited expectations of others as well as ourselves.

3) We are not in this condition just because of the breakdown of Black families. We must go to the heart of why many of our families are not working, but also understand why many are working. What roles do social policy, economics, political policy, white supremacy, educational policy, and funding, housing, employment, the loss of boys and men to imprisonment, acute ignorance, and sexist-homophobic acculturation play in our powerlessness? Dr. Andrew Billingsley gives us some insight into this in his remarkable book, *Climbing Jacob's Ladder*. Also, see Nathan and Julia Hare's, *The Endangered Black Family*, and Chancellor Williams', *The Destruction of Black Civilization*.

4) If, indeed Black folk have a GDP of $400 billion and growing—where does the money come from and where do we spend it? We now live in what Charles A. Reich in his book, *Opposing the System* defines as economic government: "a combination of two kinds of government—public government and private economic government, functioning together. This combined system has escaped all traditional limits and control. It has circumvented the constitution, nullified democracy, and overridden the free market. It usurps our power and dominates our lives. Yet we cannot see it or describe it. It is new to human history. It is immensely powerful and without brakes, it is indifferent to the effect of its actions on human beings." The point here is that we must not think that just starting businesses—which I advocate—is enough to come to grips with this international money system that only benefits the few at the expense of the working majority. The call for a national African American Development Trust is only a first step in this gigantic game of money, where our conversation must not only examine our self-worth, but also our net worth.

5) We have to be a part of the national health care debate. The Nation of Islam and others are offering a health plan that needs to be studied and considered. However, health is much, much larger than a plan or HMO. It is about individual health maintenance, preventive care and where we place our priorities in how we eat, exercise, rest, seek and maintain inner peace, share love and familyhood, organize our lives around work, play, and study. The problem of AIDS needs to be on the lips of our children as a life/death disease. The largest number of AIDS cases are in the African community—here and abroad.

6) It has been noted many times that there is no culture without agriculture. What is our relationship to land and food production? Wendell Berry continues to point out how farming is being reduced to machines and money and the human, community factors are being overshadowed by profit and greed. Local agriculture is critical for any people who are serious about a healthy and sane tomorrow. Being close to the earth (nature) on a daily basis has a way of humbling and humanizing the most arrogant of us (see Berry's,

Another Turn of the Crank and Sex, Economy, Freedom and Community).

7) There is a lot that is positive and progressive in Black communities that we need to build upon. Three national summits need to be considered:

a) A national economic summit where our leading minds, practitioners, and activists in the economic front come to share ideas, plan local, national, and international strategies and just hang out and share war stories. However, the soul of such a summit would be to offer us a national plan to first harvest part or most of the 90% of African American money that is spent outside of our community; to develop a national economic plan that would include a savings and investment component.

b) A national political summit—prior to a Black political convention—to work through and come out with suggestions regarding: 1) a third party, 2) political education for our people, and 3) funding of the convention.

c) The leadership and governing boards of all of our professional organizations should convene a national summit. They would include Black psychologists, doctors, dentists, historians, political scientists, social scientists, social workers, lawyers, nurses, educators, bankers, small business owners, health practitioners, farmers, national trade unions, journalists and media people, etc. They need to start talking to each other.

In reading Hedrick Smith's, *Rethinking America*, he makes it absolutely clear that much of the western world is changing about as fast as the speed of light. Not that all of this is positive or necessary, but we do need to know what is happening in our own country. Few of us are migrating elsewhere—we have life-time duty in America and it is our responsibility to make the United States better and more responsive to us and others. Smith's critique of education for "a new global game" is must reading. Finally, I would balance his assessment with that of Theodore Roszak's, *The Voice of the Earth*, C. Owen Paepke's, *The Evolution of Progress*, and the works of Norm Chomsky and Cheikh Anta Diop.

I would offer this final assessment of the Million Man March/Day of Absence; it was our most current introduction of Black men to the world and our collective giant step into the 21st century. It was a profound statement acknowledging that we can and we must stand together, learn from each other, love each other, protect each other, and refuse to come to anybody's table as beggar or buyer, but as an equal participant in contributing to a better tomorrow for all, including the children of our sworn enemies.

Haki R. Madhubuti: Haki Madhubuti is an award-winning poet, the publisher and editor of Third World Press. Mr. Madhubuti is also a professor of English and Director of the Gwendolyn Brooks Center at Chicago State University. He also served as a member of the Executive Committee for the Million Man March.

The March, The Day of Absence and the Movement:

Maulana Karenga

Photo by Robert Sengstacke

The Million Man March and Day of Absence marks a decisive phase in the history of our struggle. They form a joint project of raising a necessary challenge to ourselves and the country in a critical time of the country's jerk to the right, deteriorating social and environmental conditions, and a resultant need for transformative leadership. Moreover, the project reaffirmed our self-understanding that we are our own liberators, expressed our commitment to operational unity and above all reinforced our commitment to our ancient and continuing moral tradition dedicated to speaking truth, doing justice and always seeking the good. Certainly, the MMM/DOA also re-focused and expanded discussion on critical issues as those addressed in the Mission Statement (see documents). And it produced a galvanizing, mobilizing and organizing process which raised consciousness, cultivated a commitment to act and thus laid an important groundwork for increased membership in organizations and heightened positive social, political and economic activity.

Especially important was the challenge to ourselves framed in the three focal themes of "atonement, reconciliation and responsibility." My task in the Mission Statement,

as I understood it, was to expand the concept of atonement from simply an internal posture of spiritual purification and a public posture of confession to a personal and social posture of self-criticism and self-correction around issues of social/ ethical practice. Thus atonement was tied to social practice which not only revealed spiritual and ethical concern with the quality of human life and human environmental integrity and social justice, but the quality of our commitment to struggle and building moral community. Likewise, reconciliation in the Mission Statement speaks to the social practice of overcoming conflict, practicing operational unity, ending character assassination and choosing sisterhood and brotherhood, rejecting communal family and personal violence and building and sustaining loving, respectful and reciprocal relations.

Responsibility also was posed in terms of standing up and standing together as partners in equality, struggle and pursuit of the good and the challenge to ourselves, the government and corporations this requires. In a word, the MMM/DOA was in the final analysis about thought and practice to improve and push our lives forward in a meaningful way. And inherent in each and every call for an empowered community, a just society and a better world was the challenge to engage in practice which would bring these into being.

It is at this point that one realizes that if the MMM/DOA is to be more than another episodic public expression of pain and angry announcement of intention, there is no alternative to ongoing activity which continues the momentum. In a word, the March will remain an awesome event, but soon becomes just a memory if it is not made part of a living tradition of struggle. And I say here "March" because, in spite of the clear significance and massive mobilization and political education process the DOA represents, the March has assumed the preeminent place in the joint venture. Its name, its leaders and organizers, its focus in the capital, its concentration of forces in a single spot, the media generated from this and even the established order's opposition to it, all contributed to its overshadowing the Day of Absence. It became the single event of reference in most quarters and in this lies its vulnerability to mere symbolism. For it often represents over focus on the event as opposed to the massive organizing, mobilizing and political education process involved in both making the March and the DOA a success. A typical example of this is the tendency by some to make the March a God-determined event without acknowledging the work that went into it. Thus, we say to the faith communities, "Give God the glory, and praise to the people." For we say: is it not the teachings of your faiths "that faith without work is dead," (Bible) that "the righteous one is one who prays and works," (Kuran) and that "that which exists is that which was created." (Husia)

In the midst of remembrance of October 16, then, is the challenge to reaffirm through ongoing practice the sense of renewedness and possibility and the commitment to action framed and forged in the process. In a word, sustained momentum requires a program and practice to harness and direct the energy and ideas generated by this historical moment and turn it into a liberation project. In the final analysis, only work works and practice proves and makes possible everything. What is required is nothing less than the rebuilding of the liberation movement. And that is a long, difficult and disciplined practice. Furthermore, it must be clear that the struggle itself is even more difficult and will of necessity be a protracted one. Therefore, as Amilcar Cabral says, we must along the way "mask no difficulties, tell no lies and claim no easy victories."

Kawaida Theory argues that there are at least five fundamental things necessary to build and sustain a movement: 1) philosophy; 2) structure; 3) program; 4) communications; and 5) resources. And it is how we are able to institute, develop and maintain these that will dictate whether the March and Day of Absence remains a single awesome event or the basis for an ongoing collective practice. In the beginning, there must be the word, to focus on fundamen-

tals and to carve out of the rock of reality, through building on the best of tradition and reason, a vision of possibility and framework for self, social and world understanding and practice. Certainly, the Mission Statement offers such a vision and framework. And it must be read, taught, studied and discussed not only in local organizing committees (LOC's), but also in the community and public sphere. For it is the core of common concerns and principles around which we organize ourselves, understand ourselves and our tasks and introduce ourselves to others.

It is in this context that I stressed in writing the Mission Statement that we were, in both our thought and practice, reaffirming the best of what it means to be African and human. And this means "reaffirming the best values of our social justice tradition which require respect for the dignity and rights of the human person, economic justice, meaningful political participation, shared power, cultural integrity, mutual respect for all peoples and uncompromising resistance to social forces which deny or limit these." In addition to the Mission Statement's being an important moral vision of community and society, its significance lies also in the fact that it represents the first time nationalist groups have offered such a communal and public vision which ranged from respect for the human person and right relations with the environment, to mutually respectful, complementary and equal male/female relations and insistence on government and corporate responsibility. Clearly, we must embrace and build on this common ground document which represents not only a summary of dialogue around the MMM/DOA but also a serious and sustained dialogue over a long period of time across the country—in a word, a continuation of a legacy of concern with the quality and direction of human life and parallel ethical concern for the environment which sustains us.

The second challenge is to build and sustain a structure or series of structures that house our aspirations and aid us in our defining, defending and promoting our interests. In our initial discussion on the Executive Council, we had agreed that the MMM/DOA should be used to build the National African American Leadership Summit (NAALS) and to encourage strengthening of local and national organizations and institutions. NAALS is thus challenged to consolidate itself, to expand the dialogue process and to establish an effective and equitable decision-making process for its members. Moreover, a serious issue which must be resolved is whether NAALS will be able to or should absorb the LOC's or urge them to become chapters of the National Black United Front. This is an issue because NAALS by its very conception and functioning is for national organizations, i.e., NOI, NAACP, SCLC, NAKO (Us), NBUF, et al. Thus, integrating the local organizing committees would change the nature of the organization. At this stage, when NAALS is essentially forming itself, its fluid structure allows for the kind of dialogue it now conducts. But as decision-making and practical engagement become more of a focus, a tighter structure will be required. The option of integrating the LOC's into NBUF must be explored seriously and soon. For it not only has the capacity for such absorption of local organizations, but its chapters also become LOC's and play key roles in others.

A third challenge is program. Again, we repeat: in the final analysis, practice proves and makes possible everything. The projects cited and promised in the Mission Statement must be pursued vigorously and in a sustained manner. At the top of the agenda must be the follow-up development of an expanded Black political agenda and the holding of a Black Political Convention to forge this agenda for serious political change and a progressive independent politics.

Also important are the establishment of a Black Economic Development Fund or Trust without neglect to other things; the struggle for public admission, apology and recognition of the Holocaust of Enslavement and appropriate compensation; family strengthening measures; the struggle against police abuse and in support of political prisoners; the building of a solid wall against drugs and communal, family and personal violence; the struggle for full employment, quality public education and increased support for independent African schools; the battle for a positive and an independent media; strengthening Black organizations and institutions; standing in solidarity with other African peoples and other people of color in their struggle to free themselves and harness their human and material resources for a better life; building appropriate alliances and coalitions in mutually beneficial activities to create and sustain a just and good society and challenging our faith communities to give the best of what we have to offer to build a moral and empowered community, a just society and a better world.

Building a communications network is the fourth challenge for a movement. We must speak our own truth, present ourselves to each other, our allies and the world. On one hand, it is good to be attacked by the oppressor for it draws a clear line between us and them and reaffirms our opposition to him. But we must answer him in our own terms. Thus, we must, as the Mission Statement stated, support Black independent media and develop new ways to speak our position. We also must begin the use of talk radio and TV more systematically and move our people and their discourse away from those established-order spectacles of mutual degradation we see so often on TV. Our challenge is to reestablish a discourse of social justice in contrast and in opposition to the pathological portrait being painted of us by the established order and its allies. Also, we must expand the concept and practice of town-hall meetings which NAALS and NBUF use regularly. And we must develop serious and regular position papers on the critical social and public policy issues confronting us, society and

the world. Especially should we in using the established-order media, avoid premature, excessive, unnecessary and counterproductive press conferences and limit ourselves as far as possible to announcing things done as opposed to the things we are again going to do.

To build and sustain a network of resources is the fifth major challenge of a movement. From a Kawaida standpoint, resources are essentially four types: money, material, skilled personnel and the masses. In terms of money, the challenge is to create a financing process beyond simple membership dues and to meticulously expend and account for the funds and a network of consistent donors, large and small, is key here. Moreover, an exploration and use of the payroll deduction process is important as well as regular local and national kinds of fundraising. Likewise, a network of skilled personnel who volunteer and a network of sources for donation of materials are an unavoidable requirement for a successful movement.

Finally, the ultimate resource of any movement is the masses of our people who, organized and conscious of themselves and their oppressor and oppression, cannot be defeated. They represent an unlimited source of energy and insight and we must harness their energy, and build on their insight and in the tradition of transformative leadership aid them in becoming self-conscious agents of their own liberation and life. Thus, as Nkrumah says, we must "go to the masses; start with what they know and build on what they have." In a word, we must organize, mobilize and politically educate them around their interests, learn from them and serve them.

Let me end here with a quote from the Mission Statement which speaks to our need to understand ourselves through our ethical tradition, work and struggle for a moral and empowered community, a just society and a better world. It is indeed true that if we dare accomplish this, we will "always know and introduce ourselves to history and humanity as a people who are spiritually and ethically grounded; who speak truth, do justice, respect our ancestors and elders, cherish, support and challenge our children, care for the vulnerable, relate rightfully to the environment, struggle for what is right and resist what is wrong, honor our past, willingly engage our present and self-consciously plan for and welcome our future."

Dr. Maulana Karenga is professor and chair of the Department of Black Studies at California State University, Long Beach; member, Executive Council, Million Man March/Day of Absence and author of the MMM/DOA Mission Statement; chairman of The Organization Us; and executive director of the Kawaida Institute of Pan-African Studies and African American Cultural Center (Us), Los Angeles. Dr. Karenga is the creator of Kwanzaa and the Nguzo Saba and author of numerous scholarly articles and books including, *The African American Holiday of Kwanzaa: A Celebration of Family, Community and Culture and Introduction to Black Studies* and *Selections From the Husia: Sacred Wisdom of Ancient Egypt.*

7

Part 2
Speeches: Atonement, Reconciliation, Responsibility

Illustration by Tom Feelings

DAY OF ATONEMENT

Minister Louis Farrakhan

In the name of Allah, the beneficent, the merciful. We thank Him for His prophets, and the scriptures which they brought. We thank Him for Moses and the Torah. We thank Him for Jesus and the Gospel. We thank Him for Muhammad and the Koran. Peace be upon these worthy servants of Allah.

I am so grateful to Allah for his intervention in our affairs in the person of Master Farad Muhammad the Great Madi, who came among us and raised from among us a divine leader, teacher and guide, his messenger to us, the Most Honorable Elijah Muhammad. I greet all of you, my dear and wonderful brothers, with the greeting words of peace. We say it in the Arabic language, As–Salaamalaikum.

I would like to thank all of those known and unknown persons who worked to make this day of atonement and reconciliation a reality. My thanks and my extreme gratitude to the Reverend Benjamin Chavis and to all of the members of the national organizing committees.

To all of the local organizing committees, to Dr. Dorothy Height and the National Council of Negro Women, and all of the sisters who were involved in the planning of the Million Man March. Of course, if I named all those persons whom I know helped to make this event a reality, it would take a tremendous amount of time. But suffice it to say that we are grateful to all who made this day possible.

I'm looking at the Washington Monument and beyond it to the Lincoln Memorial. And, beyond that, to the left, to your right, the Jefferson Memorial. Abraham Lincoln was the 16th President of these United States and he was the man who allegedly freed us.

Abraham Lincoln saw in his day, what President Clinton sees in this day. He saw the great divide between Black and White. Abraham Lincoln and Bill Clinton see what the Kerner Commission saw 30 years ago when they said that this nation was moving toward two Americas--one Black, one White, separate and unequal. And the Kerner Commission revisited their findings 25 years later and saw that America was worse today than it was in the time of Martin Luther King, Jr. There's still two Americas, one Black, one White, separate and unequal.

Abraham Lincoln, when he saw this great divide, pondered a solution of separation. Abraham Lincoln said he never was in favor of our being jurors or having equal status with the Whites of this nation. Abraham Lincoln said that if there were to be a superior or inferior, he would

Photo by Brian Jackson

9

rather the superior position be assigned to the White race.

There, in the middle of this mall is the Washington Monument, 555 feet high. But if we put a 1 in front of that 555 feet, we get 1555, the year that our first fathers landed on the shores of Jamestown, Virginia as slaves. In the background are the Jefferson and Lincoln Memorials. Each one of these monuments is 19 feet high.

Abraham Lincoln is the 16th president. Thomas Jefferson is the third president. 16 and 3 make 19 again. What is so deep about this number 19? Why are we standing on the Capitol steps today? That number 19! When you have a nine, you have a womb that is pregnant. And when you have a one standing by the nine, it means that there's something secret that has to be unfolded.

Right here on this mall where we are standing, according to books written on Washington, D.C., slaves used to be brought right here on this mall in chains to be sold up and down the eastern seabroad.

Right along this mall, going over to the White House, our fathers were sold into slavery. But, George Washington, the first president of the United States, said he feared that before too many years passed over his head, this slave would prove to become a most troublesome species of property.

Thomas Jefferson said he trembled for this country when he reflected that God was just and that His justice could not sleep forever.

Well, the day that these presidents feared has now come to pass, for on this mall, here we stand in the capital of America, and the layout of this great city, laid out by a Black man, Benjamin Banneker. This is all placed and based in a secret Masonic ritual. And at the core of the secret of that ritual is the Black man. Not far from here is the White House.

And the first president of this land, George Washington, who was a grand master of the Masonic order, laid the foundation, the cornerstone of this capitol building where we stand. George was a slave owner. George was a slave owner. Now, the President spoke today and he wanted to heal the great divide. But I respectfully suggest to the President, you did not dig deep enough at the malady that divides Black and White in order to affect a solution to the problem. And so, today, we have to deal with the root, so that perhaps a healing can take place.

Now, this obelisk at the Washington Monument is Egyptian and this whole layout is reminiscent of our great historic past, Egypt. And, if you look at the original Seal of the

United States, published by the Department of State in 1909. Gaylord Hunt wrote that late in the afternoon of July 4, 1776, the Continental Congress resolved that Dr. Benjamin Franklin, Mr. John Adams, and Mr. Thomas Jefferson be a committee to prepare a device for a Seal of the United States of America.

In the design proposed by the first committee, the face of the Seal was a coat of arms measured in six quarters. That number is significant: six quarters, with emblems representing England, Scotland, Ireland, France, Germany and Holland, the countries from which the new nation had been peopled. The eye of providence in a radiant triangle and the motto, "E Pluribus Unum" were also proposed for the face of the Seal. Even though the country was populated by so-called Indians and Black slaves were brought to build the country, the official Seal of the country was never designed to reflect our presence, only that of the European immigrants.

The Seal and the Constitution reflect the thinking of the founding fathers, that this was to be a nation by White people and for White people. Native Americans, Blacks, and all other non-White people were to be the burden bearers for the real citizens of this nation.

For the back of the Seal, the committee suggested a picture of Pharaoh sitting in an open chariot with a crown on his head and a sword in his hand, passing through the divided waters of the Red Sea, in pursuit of the Israelites. And, hovering over the sea was to be shown a pillar of fire in a cloud, expressive of the divine presence and command.

And raised from this pillar of fire, beaming down, was to be shown, Moses standing on the shore, extending his hand over the sea, causing it to overwhelm Pharaoh. The

Photo by Third World Press

motto for the reverse of the seal was "Rebellion to Tyrants is Obedience to God." Let me say it again. Rebellion is obedience to God. Now, why did they mention Pharaoh? I heard the President say today "E Pluribus Unum"--out of many, one.

But in the past, out of many comes one meant out of many Europeans come one people. The question today is, out of the many Asians, the many Arabs, the many Native Americans, the many Blacks, the many people of color who populate this country, do you mean for them to be made into the one?

If so, truth has to be spoken to justice. We can't cover things up, cover them over, give it a pretty sound to make people feel good. We have to go to the root of the problem. Now, why have you come today?

Photo by Robert A. Sengstacke

When you say "Farrakhan, you ain't no Moses, you ain't no Jesus, and you're not no Muhammad. You have a defect in your character."

Well, that certainly may be so. However, according to the way the Bible reads, there is no prophet of God written of in the Bible that did not have a defect in his character. But, I have never heard any member of the faith of Judaism separate David from the Psalms, because of what happened in David's life and you've never separated Solomon from the building of the Temple because they say he had a thousand concubines, and you never separated any of the Great Servants of God.

So today, whether you like it or not, God brought the idea through me and He didn't bring it through me because my heart was dark with hatred and anti-semitism, He

You came not at the call of Louis Farrakhan, but you have gathered here at the call of God. For it is only the call of Almighty God, no matter through whom that call came, that could generate this kind of outpouring. God called us here to this place, at this time, for a very specific reason.

And now, I want to say, my brothers, this is a very pregnant moment, pregnant with the possibility of tremendous change in our status in America and in the world. And although the call was made through me, many have tried to distance the beauty of this idea from the person through whom the idea and the call was made.

Some have done it mistakenly. And others have done it in a malicious and vicious manner. Brothers and sisters, there is no human being through whom God brings an idea where history doesn't marry the idea with that human being no matter what defect was in that human being's character.

You can't separate Newton from the law that Newton discovered, nor can you separate Einstein from the theory of relativity. It would be silly to try to separate Moses from the Torah or Jesus from the Gospel or Muhammad from the Koran.

didn't bring it through me because my heart was dark and I'm filled with hatred for White people and for the human family of the planet. If my heart were that dark, how is the message so bright, the message so clear, the response so magnificent?

(applause)

So, we stand here today at this historic moment. We are standing in the place of those who couldn't make it here today. We are standing on the blood of our ancestors. We are standing on the blood of those who died in the Middle Passage, who died in the fields and swamps of America, who died hanging from trees in the South, who died in the cells of their jailers, who died on the highways and who died in the fratricidal conflict that rages within our community.

We are standing on the sacrifice of the lives of those heroes, our great men and women that we today may accept the responsibility that life imposes upon each traveler who comes this way.

We must accept the responsibility that God has put upon us, not only to be good husbands and fathers and builders of our community, but God is now calling upon the despised and the rejected to become the cornerstone and the builders of a new world.

And so, our brief subject today is taken from the American Constitution. In these words, toward a more perfect union, toward a more perfect union.

Now, when you use the word "more" with "perfect," that which is perfect is that which has been brought to completion. So, when you use "more perfect," you're either saying that what you call "perfect" is "perfect" for that stage of its development but not yet "complete." When Jefferson said, "toward a more perfect union," he was admitting that the union was not perfect, that it was not finished, that work had to be done.

And so we are gathered here today not to bash somebody else. We're not gathered here to say all of the evils of this nation. But we are gathered here to collect ourselves for a responsibility that God is placing on our shoulders to move this nation toward a more perfect union. Now, when you look at the word "toward," "toward," it means in the direction of, in furtherance or partial fulfillment of, with the view to obtaining, or having shortly before, coming soon, eminent, going on in progress. Well, that's right. We're in progress toward a perfect union. Union means bringing elements or components into unity.

It is something formed by uniting two or more things. It is a number of persons, states, etcetera, which are joined or associated together for some common purpose. We're not here to tear down America.

America is tearing itself down. We are here to rebuild the wasted cities. What we have in the world is motion. The Honorable Elijah Muhammad taught us that motion is the first law of the universe.

This motion which takes us from one point to another shows that we are evolving and we are a part of a universe that is ever evolving. We are on an evolutionary course that will bring us to perfect or completion of the process toward a perfect union with God. In the word "toward" there is a law and that law is everything that is created is in harmony with the law of evolution, change. Nothing is standing still.

It is either moving toward perfection or moving toward disintegration, or under certain circumstances doing both things at the same time. The word for this evolutionary changing, affecting stage after stage until we reach perfection, in Arabic, it is called Rhab. And from the word Rhab you get the Rhaby, or teacher, one who nourishes a people from one stage and brings them to another stage. Well, if we are in motion, and we are, motion toward perfection, and we are, there can be no motion toward perfection without the Lord, who created the law of evolution, and is the master of the changes.

Our first motion then must be toward the God, who created the law of the evolution of our being. And if our motion toward him is right and proper, then our motion toward a perfect union with each other and government and with the peoples of the world will be perfected. So, let us start with a process leading to that perfect union must first be seen. Now, brothers and sisters, the day of atonement is established by God to help us achieve a closer tie with the source of wisdom, knowledge, understanding and power.

For it is only through a closer union or tie with Him, who created us all, with Him who has power over all things that we can draw power, knowledge, wisdom and understanding from Him, that we maybe enable to change the realities of our life. A perfect union with God is the idea at the base of atonement. Now, atonement demands of us eight steps, in fact, atonement is the fifth step in an eight stage process.

Look at our division, not here, out there. We are a people, who have been fractured, divided and destroyed, and because of our division we now must move toward a perfect union. But let's look at a speech delivered by a White slave holder on the banks of the James River in 1712, Sixty-eight years before our former slave masters permitted us to join the Christian faith. Listen to what he said. He said, "In my bag I have a fool proof method of controlling black slaves. I guarantee everyone of you, if installed correctly, it will control the slaves for at least 300 years. My method is simple. Any member of your family or your overseer can use it. I have outlined a number of differences among the slaves and I take these differences and I make them bigger. I use fear, distrust, and envy for control purposes."

I want you to listen. What are those three things? Fear, envy, distrust. For what purpose? Control. To control who? The slave. Who is the slave? Us. Listen, he said, "These methods have worked on my modest plantation in the West Indies and they will work throughout the south."

"Now, take this simple little list and think about it. On the top of my list is age. But it's only there because it starts with an "A". And the second is color or shade. There's intelligence, sex, size of plantation, status of plantation, attitude of owners, whether the slaves live in the valley or on a hill, north, east, south or west, have fine hair or course hair, or is tall or short.

Now that you have a list of differences I shall give you an outline of action. But before that, I shall assure you that distrust is stronger than trust. And envy is stronger than adulation, respect, or admiration.

The black slave after receiving this indoctrination shall carry it on and will become self-refueling and self-generating for hundreds of years. Maybe thousands of years. Now don't forget, you must pitch the old black male against the young black male. And the young black male against the old black male.

Photo by Brian Jackson

You must use the female against the male. And you must use the male against the female. You must use the dark-skinned slave against the light–skinned slave. And the light skinned slave against the dark-skinned slave.

You must also have your white servants and overseers distrust all blacks. But it is necessary that your slaves trust and depend on us. They must love, respect, and trust only us.

Gentlemen, these keys are your keys to control. Use them. Never miss an opportunity. And if used intensely for one year, the slaves themselves will remain perpetually distrustful. Thank you, gentlemen." –End of quote–So spoke Willie Lynch 283 years ago.

And so, as a consequence, we as a people now have been fractured, divided and destroyed, filled with fear, distrust and envy. Therefore, because of fear, envy and distrust of one another, many of us as leaders, teachers, educators, pastors and persons are still under the control mechanism of our former slave masters and their children.

And now, in spite of all that division, in spite of all that divisiveness, we responded to a call and look at what is present here today. We have here those brothers with means and those who have no means.

Those who are light and those who are dark. Those who are educated, those who are uneducated. Those who are business people, those who don't know anything about business. Those who are young, those who are old. Those who are scientific, those who know nothing of science. Those who are religious and those who are irreligious. Those who are Christian, those who are Muslim, those who are Baptist, those who are Methodist, those who are Episcopalian, those of traditional African religion. We've

got them all here today.

And why did we come? We came because we want to move toward a more perfect union. And if you notice, the press triggered every one of those divisions. You shouldn't come, you're a Christian. That's a Muslim thing. You shouldn't come, you're too intelligent to follow hate! You shouldn't come, look at what they did, they excluded women, you see? They played all the cards, they pulled all the strings.

Oh, but you better look again, Willie. There's a new Black man in America today. A new Black woman in America today. Now brothers, there's a social benefit of our gathering here today. That is, that from this day forward, we can never again see ourselves through the narrow eyes of the limitation of the boundaries of our own fraternal, civic, political, religious, street organization or professional organization. We are forced by the magnitude of what we see here today, that whenever you return to your cities and you see a Black man, a Black woman, don't ask him what is your social, political or religious affiliation, or what is your status? Know that he is your brother.

You must live beyond the narrow restrictions of the divisions that have been imposed upon us. Well, some of us are here because it's history making. Some of us are here because it's a march through which we can express anger and rage with America for what she has and is doing to us. So, we're here for many reasons but the basic reason while this was called was for atonement and reconciliation. So, it is necessary for me in as short of time as possible to give as full an explanation of atonement as possible.

As I said earlier, atonement is the fifth stage in an eight stage process. So, let's go back to the first stage of the process that brings us into perfect union with God. And the first stage is the most difficult of all because when we are wrong, and we are not aware of it, someone has to point out the wrong. I want to, I want to say this again, but I want to say it slowly. And I really want each one of these points to sink in. How many of us in this audience, at some time or another have been wrong? Would we just raise our hands?

O.K. Now, when we are wrong, Lord knows we want to be right. The most difficult thing is when somebody points it out do we accept it, do we reject it, do we hate the person who pointed out our wrong?

How do we treat the person who points out our wrong? Now, I want you to follow me. When you go to a doctor, you're not feeling well, the doctor says, what's wrong? Well, I don't know, doc. Well, where is the pain? Tell me

13

something about the symptoms. You want the doctor to make a correct diagnosis. You don't smack the doctor when he points out what's wrong.

You don't hate the doctor when he points out what's wrong. You say, thank you, doctor. What's my prescription for healing? We all right? Now, look, whoever is entrusted with the task of pointing out wrong, depending on the nature of the circumstances, is not always loved.

In fact, more than likely, that person is going to be hated and misunderstood. Such persons are generally hated because no one wants to be shown as being wrong. Particularly when you're dealing with governments, with principalities, with powers, with rulers, with administrations. When you're dealing with forces which have become entrenched in their evil, intractable and unyielding their power produces an arrogance. And their arrogance produces a blindness. And out of that evil state of mind, they will do all manner of evil to the person who points out their wrong. Even though you're doing good for them by pointing out where America when wrong.

Now, Martin Luther King, Jr. was probably the most patriotic American. More patriotic than George Washington. More patriotic than Thomas Jefferson. More patriotic than many of the presidents because he had the courage to point out what was wrong in the society. And because he pointed out what was wrong, he was ill-spoken of, vilified, maligned, hated and eventually, murdered.

Brother Malcolm had that same road to travel. He pointed out what was wrong in the society and he had to suffer for pointing out what was wrong and he ultimately died on the altar for pointing out what was wrong. Inside the nation, outside the nation, to the greater nation and to

Photo by Brian Jackson

the smaller nation.

We're talking about moving toward a perfect union. Well, pointing out fault, pointing out our wrongs is the first step.

The second step is to acknowledge. Oh, thank you. Oh, man, I'm wrong. To acknowledge means to admit the existence, the reality or the truth of some reality. It is to recognize as being valid. Or having force and power. It is to express thanks, appreciation, or gratitude. So in this context, the word acknowledgement to be in a state of recognition of the truth of the fact that we have been wrong. This is the second step.

Well, the third step is that after you know you're wrong and you acknowledge it to yourself, who else knows it except you confess it. You say, well, yeah, all right. But who should I confess to? And why should I confess?

And why should I confess? The Bible says confession is good for the soul. Now, brothers I know, I don't have a lot of time, but the soul is the essence of a person's being. And when the soul is covered with guilt from sin and wrongdoing, the mind and the actions of the person reflect the condition of the soul. So, to free the soul or the essence of man from its burden, one must acknowledge one's wrong, but then one must confess.

The Holy Koran says it like this: I've been greatly unjust to myself, and I confess my faults. So grant me protection against all my faults, for none grants protection against faults but Thee. It is only through confession that we can be granted protection from the consequences of our faults.

For every deed has a consequence. And we can never be granted protection against the faults that we refuse to acknowledge or that we are unwilling to confess. So, look. Who should you confess to? I don't want to confess. Who

14

should you confess to? Who should I confess to? Who should we confess to? First, you confess to God. And everyone of us that are here today, that knows that we have done wrong, we have to go to God and speak to Him in the privacy of our rooms and confess. He already knows, but when you confess, you're relieving your soul of the burden that it bears.

But, then, the hardest part is to go to the person or persons whom your faults have ill-affected and confess to them. That's hard. That's hard. But, if we want a perfect union, we have to confess the fault. Well, what happens after confession? There must be repentance. When you repent, you feel remorse or contrition or shame for the past conduct which was and is wrong and sinful. It means to feel contrition or self-reproach for what one has done or failed to do.

And, it is the experiencing of such regret for past conduct that involves the changing of our mind toward that sin. So, until we repent and feel sick, sorry over what we have done, we can never, never, change our minds toward that thing. And if you don't repent, you'll do it over and over and over again. But to stop it where it is, and Black men, we got to stop what we're doing where it is. We cannot continue the destruction of our lives and the destruction of our community. But that change can't come until we feel sorry.

I heard my brother from the West Coast say today, I atone to the mothers for the death of the babies caused by our senseless slaughter of one another. See, when he feels sorry deep down inside, he's going to make a change.

That man has a change in his mind. That man has a change in his heart. His soul has been unburdened and released from the pain of that sin, but you got to go one step further, because after you've acknowledged it, confessed it, repented, you're comes to the fifth stage. Now you've got to do something about it.

Now, look brothers, sisters. Some people don't mind confessing. Some people don't mind making some slight repentance. But, when it comes to doing something about the evil that we've done we fall short.

But atonement means satisfaction or reparation for a wrong or injury. It means to make amends. It means penance, expiation, compensation and recompense made or done for an injury or wrong.

So, atonement means we must be willing to do something in expiation of our sins so we can't just have a good time today, and say we made history in Washington. We've got to resolve today that we're going back home to do something about what's going on in our lives and in our families and in our communities.

15

Now, we all right? Can you hang with me a few more? Now, brothers and sisters, if we make atonement it leads to the sixth stage. And the sixth stage is forgiveness. Now, so many of us want forgiveness, but we don't want to go through the process that leads to it. And so, when we say we forgive, we forgive from our lips, but we have never pardoned in the heart.

So, the injury still remains. My dear family. My dear brothers. We need forgiveness. God is always ready to forgive us for our sins. Forgiveness means to grant pardon for, or remission of, an offense or sin. It is to absolve, to clear, to exonerate and to liberate. Boy, that's something!

See, you're not liberated until you can forgive. You're not liberated from the evil effect of our own sin until we can ask God for forgiveness and then forgive others, and this is why in the Lord's Prayer you say, forgive us our trespasses as we forgive those who trespass against us.

So, it means to cease to feel offense and resentment against another for the harm done by an offender. It means to wipe the slate clean. And then, that leads to the seventh stage. You know, I like to liken this to music. Because in music, the seventh note is called a leading tone. Do, re, me, fa, so, la, te.... You can't stop there. Te.

It leaves you hung up, te. What you got to get back to? Do. So, whatever you started with when you reach the eighth note, you're back to where you started only at a higher vibration. Now, look, at this. The seventh tone, the leading tone that leads to the perfect union with God is reconciliation and restoration because after forgiveness, now, we are going to be restored to what? To our original position. To restore, to reconcile means to become friendly, peaceable again, to put hostile persons into a state of agreement or harmony, to make compatible or to compose or settle what it was that made for division.

It means to resolve differences. It can mean to establish or re-establish a close relationship between previously hostile persons. So, restoration means the act of returning something to an original or un-impaired condition. Now, when you're backed to an impaired position, you have reached the eighth stage, which is perfect union. And when we go through all these steps, there is no difference between us, that we can't heal. There's a bomb in Gilead to heal the sin sick soul. There is a bomb in Gilead to make the wounded whole.

We are a wounded people but we're being healed, but President Clinton, American is also wounded. And there's hostility now in the great divide between the people. Socially the fabric of America is being torn apart and it's Black against Black, Black against White, White against White, White against Black, Yellow against Brown, Brown against Yellow. We are being torn apart. And we can't gloss it over with nice speeches, my dear, Mr. President.

Sir, with all due respect, that was a great speech you made today. And you praised the marchers and they're worthy of praise. You honored the marchers and they are worthy of honor. But of course, you spoke ill indirectly of me, as a purveyor of malice and hatred.

I must hasten to tell you, Mr. President, that I'm not a malicious person, and I'm not filled with malice. But, I must tell you that I come in the tradition of the doctor who has to point out, with truth, what's wrong. And the pain is that power has made America arrogant. Power and wealth has made America spiritually blind and the power and the arrogance of America makes you refuse to hear a child of your slaves pointing out the wrong in your society.

But, I think if you could clear the scales from your eyes, sir, and give ear to what we say, perhaps, oh perhaps, what these great speakers who spoke before me said, and my great and wonderful brother, the Reverend Jesse Jackson said, and perhaps, just perhaps from the children of slaves might come a solution to this Pharaoh and this Egypt as it was with Joseph when they had to get him out of prison and wash him up and clean him up because Pharaoh had some troubling dreams that he didn't have any answer to. And he called his soothsayers and he called the people that read the stars and he called all his advisors, but nobody could help him to solve the problem. But he had to go to the children of slaves, because he heard that there was one in prison who knew the interpretation of dreams. And he said bring him, bring him and let me hear what he has to say.

God has put it for you in the scriptures, Mr. President. Balshasar and Nebuchadnezer couldn't read the handwriting on the wall. But, Daniel had to read the handwriting for him. Manne, manne tek elauhu phossen (PH) (your kingdom has been weighed in the balance and has been found wanting).

Do you want a solution to the dilemma that America faces? Then, don't look at our skin color, because racism will cause you to reject salvation if it comes in the skin of a Black person. Don't look at the kinkiness of our hair and the broadness of our nose and the thickness of our lips, but listen to the beat of our hearts and the pulsating rhythm of the truth. Perhaps, perhaps, you might be as wise as that Pharaoh and save this great nation.

And so, the eighth stage is perfect union with God. And in the Koran, it reads. "Oh soul that is at rest, well pleased with thy Lord and well pleasing." Oh, brothers, brothers, brothers, you don't know what its like to be free. Freedom can't come from white folks. Freedom can't come from staying here and petitioning this great government. We're here to make a statement to the great government, but not to beg them. And this is why Jesus said "come unto me," not some who are heavy laden, "but all that are heavy laden, and I will give you rest."

But listen, all of these eight steps take place in a process called time. And whenever a nation is involved in sin to the point that God intends to judge and destroy that nation, he always sends someone to make that nation or people know their sins, to reflect on it, to acknowledge, to confess, to repent and to atone that they might find forgiveness with

God. America, oh America. This great city of Washington is like Jerusalem. And the Bible says, "Jerusalem, oh Jerusalem, you that stoneth and killith the prophets of God."

Right from this beautiful Capitol and from the beautiful White House have come commands to kill the prophets. David's trouble came from this house. Martin Luther King's trouble came from this house. Malcolm's trouble came from this house. W.E.B. Dubois' trouble came form this house. And from this house, you stoned and killed the prophets of God that would have liberated Black people, liberated America.

But I stand here today knowing, knowing that you are angry. That my people have validated me. I don't need you to validate me. I don't need to be in any mainstream. I want to wash in the river of Jordan and the river that you see and the sea that is before us and behind us and around us.

It's validation. That's the mainstream. You're out of touch with reality. A few of you in a few smoke-filled rooms, calling that the mainstream while the masses of the people, White and Black, Red, Yellow, and Brown, poor and vulnerable are suffering in this nation.

Well, America, great America. Like Jerusalem that stoned and killed the prophets of God. That a work has been done in you today unlike any work that's ever been done in this great city. I wonder what you'll say tomorrow?

I wonder what you'll write in your newspapers and magazines, tomorrow. Will you give God the glory? Will you give God the glory? Will you respect the beauty of this day? All of these Black men that the world sees as savage, maniacal, and bestial. Look at them. A sea of peace. A sea of tranquility. A sea of men ready to come back to God. Settle their differences and go back home to turn our communities into decent and safe places to live.

America. America, the beautiful. There's no country like this on the earth. And certainly if I lived in another country, I might never have had the opportunity to speak as I speak today. I probably would have been shot outright and so would my brother, Jesse, and so would Maulana Karenga, and so would Dr. Ben Chavis and Reverend Al Sampson and the wonderful people that are here.

But because this is America you allow me to speak even though you don't like what I may say. Because this is America, that provision in the constitution for freedom of speech and freedom of assembly and freedom of religion, that is your saving grace. Because what you're under right now is grace. And grace is the expression of divine love and protection which God bestows freely on people.

God is angry, America. He's angry, but His mercy is still present. Brothers and sisters look at the afflictions that have come upon us in the Black community. Do you know why we're being afflicted? God wants us to humble ourselves to the message that will make us atone and come back to Him and make ourselves whole again. But why is God afflicting America? Why is God afflicting the world?

Why did Jesus say there would be wars and rumors of wars, and earthquakes in diverse places and pestilence and famine, and why did He say that these were just the beginning of sorrows?

In the last ten years America has experienced more calamities than at any other time period in American history. Why America? God is angry. He's not angry because you're right. He's angry because you're wrong and you want to stone and kill the people who want to make you see you're wrong. And so, the Bible says Elijah must first come. Why should Elijah come? Elijah has the job of turning the hearts of the children back to their fathers, and the father's heart back to the children. Elijah becomes an axis upon which people turn back to God and God turns back to the people. And that's why it said Elijah must first come. And so, here we are, 400 years, fulfilling Abraham's prophecy.

Some of our friends in the religious community have said, why should you take atonement? That was for the children of Israel. I say yes, it was. But atonement of the children of Israel prefigured our suffering here in America. Israel was in bondage to Pharaoh 400 years. We've been in America 440 years. They were under affliction. We're under affliction. They were under oppression. We're under oppression.

God said that nation which they shall serve, I will judge. Judgement means God is making a decision against systems, against institutions, against principalities and pow-

> "Well, America, great America. Like Jerusalem that stoned and killed the prophets of God. That a work has been done in you today unlike any work that's ever been done in this great city. I wonder what you'll say tomorrow?"

ers. And that's why Paul said, we war not against flesh and blood, but against principalities and powers, and the rulers of the darkness of this world and spiritual wickedness in high places. God is sending His decision. I can't help it. If I've got to make the decision known. You don't understand me. My people love me.

And yet, I point out the evils of Black people like no other leader does, but my people don't call me anti-Black, because they know I must love them in order to point out what's wrong so we can get it right to come back into the favor of God!

But, let me say in truth, you can't point out wrong with malice. You can't point out wrong with hatred. Because, if we point out wrong with bitterness and

hatred, then the bitterness and the hatred become a barrier between you and the person whom you hope to get right, so that they might come into the favor of God.

So, we ask Muslims who, in our first stage, yeah, we pointed out the wrong of America, but we didn't point it out with love, we pointed it out with the pain of our hurt. The pain of our suffering. The bitterness of our life story. But, we have grown beyond our bitterness. We have transcended beyond our pain. Why? It's easy for us to say, the White man did this, the White man did that, the White man did the other, he deprived us of that. He killed the Indians. He did this. Yes, he did all of that.

But, why did God let him do that? That's the bigger question. And since we are not man enough to question God, we start beating up on the agent who is fulfilling prophesy. But, if we can transcend our pain to get up into God's mind, and ask God, "God, why did you let our fathers come into bondage? God, why did you let us die in the Middle Passage? God, why did you suffer us to be in the hull of ships? God, why did you let him lash us, why did you let him beat us, why did you let him castrate us? Why did you let him hang us? Why did you let him hurt us? Why, God, why, why, why?"

We got a right to question God. That's the only way we can become wise. And if we question him like Job did, God may bring you up into His own thinking.

And if God were to answer us today he would say to Black people, yes, I allowed this to happen. And I know you suffered, but Martin King, my servant, said it, undeserved suffering is redemptive.

A whole world is lost, not just you Black people. A whole world has gone out of the way, not just you Black people. You the lost sheep, but the whole world is lost. You the bottom rail, but the one that put you on the bottom is in

the bottom with you holding you down. He's in the bottomless pit himself.

He said, Black Man, I love you. He said, but God, I mean, that's a heck of a way to show me you love me. He said, but I love my son.

I love Jesus more than I love any of our servants. But I had a cross for him. I had nails for him. I had him to be rejected and despised. I had him falsely accused and brought before the courts of men. I had them spit on him. I had them to pierce his side. But, I loved him more than anybody else. Why, God?! Why did you do it? Why?

He said, I did it that I might be glorified because like Job, no matter what I did to him, he never cursed me, he never said my God ain't no good. He said whatever your will is, that's what I want to do and that's why, even though he descended into Hell, I have raised him to the limitless heights of Heaven, because only those who know the depths of Hell can appreciate the limitless heights of Heaven.

And so, my children, I caused you to suffer in the furnace of affliction so that I might purify you and resurrect you from a grave of death and ignorance. I, God, put in your soul, not a law written on stone, but I have written the law on the tablets of your heart.

So, I'm going to make a new covenant with you. Oh, Black man. The secret of the Masonic Order is the secret of Hirem Obid. The secret of the Masonic Order is a master builder that was hit in the head. The secret of the Masonic Order is a master that ruffians roughed up.

I think one of the ruffians was named Jubilo Furhman. And another was named Jubilah Bilbow. And another one was named Juilum Jesse Helms. These racists hit him in his head and carried him on a westerly course and buried him in the north country, in a shallow grave. Many tried to raise him up but they didn't have the master grip. It would take a master to come after him.

And this is why Matthew said, "as lightening shines from the east, even unto the west, so shall the coming of the son of man be for wheresoever the eagles are gathered together, there shall the carcass be." Here's the carcass, the remains of a once mighty people, dry bones in the valley, a people slain from the foundation of the world.

But God has sent the winds to blow on the bones. One of those winds is named Gingrich. And the companion wind is named Dole.

And the other is called Supreme Court decision. The other is fratricidal conflict, drugs and dope and violence and crime. But we've had enough now. This is why you're in Washington today. We've had enough.

We've had enough distress, enough affliction. We're ready to bow down now. If my people, who are called by my name, would just humble themselves and pray, and seek my face, and turn from their wicked ways, then will I hear from heaven, forgive their sins, heal their land.

You are ready now to climb out of your furnace of affliction. You are ready now to accept the responsibility, oh, not just of the ghetto. God wants to purify you and lift you up, that you may call America and the world to repentance. Black man, you are a master builder, but you got hit in the head.

Black men, you're the descendants of the builders of the pyramids. But you have amnesia now. You can't remember how you did it. But the Master has come. You know, pastors, I love that scripture where Jesus told his disciples, go there and you'll see an ass and a colt tied with her. Untie them and bring them to me. If anybody asks you what you're doing, because it may look like you're stealing and you know they are going to accuse you of stealing, tell them the Master got need of these. And Jesus rode into Jerusalem on an ass.

The Democratic Party has for its symbol, a donkey. The donkey stands for the unlearned masses of the people. But the Democratic Party can't call them asses no more. You got them all tied up, but you're not using them. The donkey is tied up. But can you get off today? No, I can't get off, I'm tied up. Somebody on your donkey? Well, yeah. I got a master. He rides me like the Master rode Balem's (ph) ass, you know. But, hail, the ass is now talking with a man's voice. And the ass wants to throw the rider off, because he got a new rider today.

If anybody asks you, tell them the Master has need. Look at you. Oh, I don't know what the number is. It's too much for me to count.

But I think they said it's a million and a half, or two. I don't know how many. But you know, I called for a million. When I saw the word go out my mouth, I looked at it. I said, "Oh my God!" It just came out of my mouth. I didn't know. And after it came out, I said, "Well I got to go with it." And, I'm so glad I did. People told me you better change that figure to one more realistic. And I should have changed it to the Three Million Man March.

Now, we're almost finished. I want to take one last look at the word "atonement."

The first four letters of the word form the foundation: "a-t-o-n"...."a-ton," "a-ton." Since this obelisk in front of us is representative of Egypt. In the 18th dynasty, a Pharaoh named Akhenaton, was the first man of this history period to destroy the pantheon of many gods and bring the people to the worship of one god. And that one god was symboled by a sun disk with 19 rays coming out of that sun with hands holding the Egyptian Ankh-the cross of life. A-ton. The name for the one god in ancient Egypt. A-ton, the one god. 19 rays. Look at your scripture.

A woman, remember the nine means somebody pregnant, with an idea. But, in this case, its a woman pregnant with a male child destined to rule the nations with a rod of iron. God is standing over her womb, and this child will be like the day sun, and He will say "I am the light of the world." Hands coming out of that sun, come unto me all ye that are heavy laden. I'm gonna give you rest, but I'm gonna give you life, because I am the resurrection and the life and if you believe in me, though you are dead, yet shall you live again.

You're dead, Black man. But if you believe in the God who created this sun of truth and of light with 19 rays, meaning he's pregnant with God's spirit, God's life, God's wisdom. Abraham Lincoln's statue, 19 feet high, 19 feet wide. Jefferson, 19 feet high 16 feet wide (off mike) and the third president, 19. Standing on the steps of the Capitol, in the light of the sun. Offering life to a people who are dead.

Black man, the a-ton represents the one God. In the Koran, Muhammad is called a light giving son. So if you look at the aton, add an "e" to it, and separate the "a" from the next four letters and you get the word a tone.

A "tone" means sound. And "a," the first letter of the alphabet and the first letter of the numerical system is one. So "a" equals one.

So "a" sound means when you hear the "a" tone, you will hear the right sound. And when you hear the right sound from the one God calling you to divine life, you will respond. So what is the "a" tone? In music, a equals 440 vibrations. How long have we been in America? Four hundred and forty years.

Well, in the 440th year, from the one God, the aton will come the a tone and all of us got to tune up our lives by the sound of the a tone. Because we've got to atone for all that we have done wrong.

And when you atone, if you take the "t" and couple it with the "a" and hyphenate it, you get "at one." So when you atone you become at one. At one with who? The aton or the one God. Because you heard the a tone and you tuned up your life and now you're ready to make a new beginning.

So when you get at one, you get the next two letters. It is "m" "e." Me.

Who is it that has to atone?
Audience:
Me.
Farrakhan:
Who went wrong?
Audience :
Me.
Farrakhan:
Who got to fix it?
Audience:
Me.
Farrakhan:
Who should we look to?
Audience:
Me.
Farrakhan:
Yes! And then if you add, if you add another letter to "me" you get an "n." What does that say?
Audience:
Men.

Farrakhan: So Farrakhan called men. Why did you call men? Because in the beginning, God made man. And if we are at a new beginning, we got to make a man all over again, but make him in the image and the likeness of God.

Now if you add the "t" on, you get the suffix "ment." Ment means action, process. The instrument or agent of an action or process. So when you say I'm atoning, you got to act on it. You got to get in the process. You got to acknowledge your wrong, confess your wrong. Repent of your wrong. Atone for your wrong.

Then you'll get forgiveness, then reconciliation, and restoration. And then you're back to the aton. Oh, Lord.

Now brothers, let's close it out. Don't move. Don't move. Don't move. Now you know the Bible says in the 430th year of this sojourn they went out.

That's in a book called Exodus. Now the word exodus means departure--a going out. A way out. What did we come to Washington for? We didn't come to Washington to petition the government for a way out of her. But to find a way out of our affliction. But a way out from something bigger than our affliction. Oh, man. When you say come out, what do you mean? You've got to come out from under the mind of a slave. We've got to come out from a mind that is self-afflicted with the evil of Black inferiority. We've got to come into a new way of thinking.

Now brothers, sisters, I want to close this lecture with a special message to our President and to the Congress. There is a great divide, but the real evil in America is not white flesh, or black flesh. The real evil in America is the idea that undergirds the set up of the western world. And that idea is called white supremacy.

Now wait, wait, wait. Before you get angry. Those of you listening by television. You don't even know why you behave the way you behave.

Photo by Brian Jackson

20

I'm not telling you I'm a psychiatrist, but I do want to operate on your head. White supremacy is the enemy of both White people and Black people because the idea of White supremacy means you should rule because you're White, that makes you sick. And you've produced a sick society and a sick world. The founding fathers meant well, but they said, "toward a more perfect union."

So, the Bible says, we know in part, we prophesy in part, but when that which is perfect is come, that which is in part shall be done away with.

So either, Mr. Clinton, we're going to do away with the mind-set of the founding fathers. You don't have to repudiate them like you've asked my brothers to do me. You don't have to say they were malicious, hate filled people. But you must evolve out of their mind-set.

You see their minds were limited to those six European nations out of which this country was founded. But you've got Asians here. How are you going to handle that? You've got children of Africa here. How are you going to handle that?

You've got Arabs here. You've got Hispanics here. I know you call them illegal aliens, but hell, you took Texas from them by flooding Texas with people that got your mind. And how they're coming back across the border to what is Northern Mexico, Texas, Arizona, New Mexico, and California. They don't see themselves as illegal aliens. I think they might see you as an illegal alien. You have to be careful how you talk to people. You have to be careful how you deal with people. The Native American is suffering today. He's suffering almost complete extinction. Now, he learned about bingo. You taught him. He learned about black jack. You taught him. He learned about playing roulette. You taught him. Now, he's making a lot of money.

You're upset with him because he's adopted your ways. What makes you like this? See, you're like this because you're not well. You're not well. And in the light of today's global village, you can never harmonize with the Asians. You can't harmonize with the islands of the Pacific. You can't harmonize with the dark people of the world who outnumber you eleven to one, if you're going to stand in the mind of

White supremacy. White supremacy has to die in order for humanity to live.

(applause)

Now, oh, I know. I know. I know it's painful, but we have to operate now, just, just take a little of this morphine and you won't feel the pain as much. You just need to bite down on something, as I stop this last few minutes, just bite down on your finger. Listen, listen, listen, listen White supremacy caused you all, not you all, some White folk to try to rewrite history and write us out. White supremacy caused Napoleon to blow the nose off of the Sphinx because it reminded you too much of the Black man's majesty.

White supremacy caused you to take Jesus, a man with hair like lambs wool and feet like burnished brass and make him White. So that you could worship him because you could never see yourself honoring somebody Black because of the state of your mind. You see, you, you really need help. You'll be all right. You'll be all right. You will be all right. Now, now, now you painted the Last Supper, everybody there White.

My mother asked the man that came to bring her the Bible about black people. He said, look there, the pictures in the Bible. You see, Jesus and all his disciples are at the Last Supper--my mother in her West Indian accent said, You mean ain't nobody Black was at the Last Supper?

(laughter)

And the man said, "Yes, but they was in the kitchen." So now you've whitened up everything.

Any great invention we made you put white on it, because you didn't want to admit that a Black person had that intelligence, that genius. You try to color everything to make it satisfactory to the sickness of our mind.

So you whitened up religion, Farrakhan didn't do that. You locked the Bible from us, Farrakhan didn't do that. Your sick mind wouldn't even let you bury us in the same ground that both of us came out of. We had to be buried somewhere

21

else. That's sick. Some of us died just to drink water out of a fountain marked White. That's sick. Isn't it sick?

You poisoned religion. And in all the churches, until recently, the master was painted white. So, you had us bowing down to your image. Which ill-effected our minds. You gave us your version of history. And you whitened that up. Yes, you did. Yes, you did.

You are a White Shriner. The Black Shriner don't integrate the shrine. Why don't you Black Shriners integrate the shrine? Because in the shrine, you are the essence of the secret. They don't want you there. They'll have to tell the world, it's you we been thinking about all along.

Now, White folks see the reason you could look at the O.J. Simpson trial, in horror, and the reason black folk rejoiced, had nothing to do with the horror of the tragedy. Black folk would never rejoice over the slaughter of Ron Goldman and Nicole Brown Simpson.

Black folk saw that with compassion. Many Black folk grieve over that reality. You say, "O.J. sold out." Now, he didn't sell out. He was drawn out.

Black folk that got talent, they all grow up in the "hood." When we first sing, we sing in these old raunchy night clubs in the "hood."

When we play sandlot ball, we play it in the "hood." But when you spot us, you draw us out. You say "that Negro can run. Look at how high he jumps." So you give us a scholarship to your university. But the Blacks who are in college, who play basketball for you, who play football for you, who run track for you, you disallow them to get involved with Black students and the suffering of Black students on all-White campuses. You hide them away. Give them privileges.

Then they find themselves with your daughter.

Then you take them into the NBA, the NFL, and they become megastars. Or in the entertainment field and when they become megastars, their association is no longer Black. They may not have a Black manager, a Black agent, a Black accountant. They meet in parties, in posh neighborhoods that Black folk don't come into. So their association becomes White women, White men, and association breeds assimilation.

And if you have a slave mentality, you feel you have arrived now because you can jump over cars, running in airports, playing in films.

I'm not degrading, my brother, I love him. But he was drawn out. He didn't sell out, he was drawn out. Michael Jackson is drawn out.

Most of our top stars are drawn out. And then, when you get them, you imprison them with fear and distrust. You don't want them to speak out on the issues that are political, that are social. They must shut their mouths or you threaten to take away their fame, take away their fortune because you're sick. And the president is not gonna

point this out. He's trying to get well. But he's a physician that can't heal himself.

I'm almost finished. White supremacy has poisoned the bloodstream of religion, education, politics, jurisprudence, economics, social ethics and morality.

And there is no way that we can integrate into White supremacy and hold our dignity as human beings because if we integrate into that, we become subservient to that. And to become subservient to that is to make the slave master comfortable with his slave.

So, we got to come out of here my people. Come out of a system and a world that is built on the wrong idea. An idea that never can create a perfect union with God.

The false idea of White supremacy prevents anyone from becoming one with God. White people have to come out of that idea, which has poisoned them into a false attitude of superiority based on the color of their skins. The doctrine of White supremacy disallows Whites to grow to their full potential. It forces White people to see themselves as the law or above the law. And that's why Furhman could say that he is like a god. See, he thinks like that, but the idea is pervasive in police departments across the country. And it's getting worse and not better because White supremacy is not being challenged.

And I say to all of us who are leaders, all of us who are preachers, we must not shrink from the responsibility of pointing out wrong, so that we can be comfortable and keep White people comfortable in their alienation from God. And so, White folks are having heart attacks today because their world is coming down. And if you look at the Asians, the Asians have the fastest growing economies in the world. The Asians are not saying, bashing White people. You don't find the Asians saying the White man is this, the White man is that, the White man is the other.

He don't talk like that. You know what he does? He just relocates the top banks from Wall Street to Tokyo. He don't say, "I'm better than the White man." He just starts building his world and building his economy and challenging White supremacy. I saw a young 14-year-old Chinese girl the other day play the violin.

Sarah Chang is her name. She was magnificent. I saw a young Japanese girl, Midori, play the violin. She was magnificent. They don't have to say to White people, "I'm better than you." They just do their thing. And White folk have to readjust their thinking, because they thought that they could master all of these instruments and nobody else could, but the Chinese are mastering it, the Japanese are mastering it. All these things are breaking up the mind of White supremacy.

Black man, you don't have to bash White people, all we gotta do is go back home and turn out communities into productive places. All we gotta do is go back home and make our communities a decent and safe place to live. And if we start dotting the Black community with businesses, opening up factories, challenging ourselves to be better than we are, White folk, instead of driving by, using the "N" word, they'll say, "Look, look at them. Oh my God. They're marvelous. They're wonderful. We can't, we can't say they're inferior anymore. " But every time we drive-by shoot, every time we carjack, every time we use foul, filthy language, every time we produce culturally degenerate films and tapes, putting a string in our

Photo by Robert A. Sengstacke

women's backside and parading them before the world, every time we do things like this we are feeding the degenerate mind of White supremacy and I want us to stop feeding that mind and let that mind die a natural death.

And so, to all the artists that are present, you wonderful gifted artists, remember that your gift comes from God. And David the Psalmist said, "praise Him on the tumbrel, praise Him on the lute, praise Him on the harp, praise Him in the sultry, praise Him in the song, praise Him in the dance, let everything be a praise of God."

So, when you sing, you don't have to get naked to sing. Demonstrate your gift, not your breast. Demonstrate your gift, not what is between your legs. Clean up, Black man, and the world will respect and honor you. But, you have fallen down like the prodigal son and you're husking corn and feeding swine.

Filthy jokes. We can't bring our children to the television.

We can't bring our families to the movies because the American people have an appetite like a swine. And you are feeding the swine with the filth of degenerate culture. We got to stop it.

We're not putting you down, brothers, we want to pick you up so with your rap, you can pick up the world. With your song, you can pick up the world. With your dance, with your music, you can pick up the world.

And so America, if your conscience is afflicted because God is lashing you, don't just start with the constitution, Mr. President. Start with the evil of slavery because that's the root of the problem.

And you can't solve the problem, Mr. President, unless we expose the root. For when you expose the root to the light, then the root will die. The tree will die. And something new can come to birth. And so to the Whites of this nation, except you be born again, you can not see the kingdom of God. But can I return back into my mother's womb for the second time? No. You can't do that. But this old mind of White supremacy has to die in order that a new mind might come to birth.

Black man. You can't see the kingdom of God unless we be born again. Must I enter back into my mother's womb for a second time? No. You can't do that Black man. But the mind of White supremacy is repulsive to God. And the mind of Black inferiority is repulsive to God. And any mind of Black supremacy is repulsive to God. But the only mind that God will accept is a mind stayed on him and on righteousness.

Black had to be taught to give us root in loving ourselves again. But that was a medicine, a prescription. But after health is restored we can't keep taking the medicine. We've got to move onto something else. Higher and better.

So, my beloved brothers and sister, here's what we would like you to do. Everyone of you, my dear brothers, when you go home, here's what I want you to do. We must belong to some organization that is working for and in the interest of the uplift and the liberation of our people.

Go back, join the NAACP if you want to, join the Urban League, join the All African People's Revolutionary Party, join us, join the Nation of Islam, join PUSH, join the Congress of Racial Equality, join SCLC, the Southern

Christian Leadership Conference, but we must become a totally organized people and the only way we can do that is to become a part of some organization that is working for the uplift of our people. We must keep the local organizing committees that made this event possible, we must keep them together. And then all of us, as leaders, must stay together and make the National African American Leadership Summit inclusive of all of us.

I know that the NAACP did not officially endorse this march. Neither did the Urban League. But, so what? So what? Many of the members are here anyway. I know that Dr. Lyons, of the National Baptist Association USA did not endorse the march, nor did the Reverend Dr. B. W. Smith, nor did Bishop Chandler Owens, but so what? These are our brothers and we're not going to stop reaching out for them simply because we feel there was a misunderstanding. We still want to talk to our brothers because we cannot let artificial barriers divide us. Remember the letter of Willie Lynch and let's not let Willie Lynch lynch our new spirit and our new attitude and our new mind.

No, we must continue to reach out for those that have condemned this, and make them to see that this was not evil; it was not intended for evil, it was intended for good. Now, brothers, moral and spiritual renewal is a necessity. Every one of you must go back home and join some church, synagogue or temple or mosque that is teaching spiritual and moral uplift. I want you, brothers, there's no men in the church, in the mosque.

The men are in the streets and we got to get back to the houses of God. But preachers, we have to revive religion in America.

We have to revive the houses of God that they're not

personal thiefdoms of those of us who are their preachers and pastors. But we got to be more like Jesus, more like Mohammed, more like Moses and become servants of the people in fulfilling their needs.

Brothers, when you go home, we've got to register eight million, eligible but unregistered brothers and sisters. So you go home and find eight more like yourself. You register and get them to register.

Should I register as Democrat? Should I register as a Republican? Should I register as independent?

If you're an independent, that's fine. If you're a Democrat, that's fine. If you're a Republican, that's OK. Because in local elections you have to do that which is in the best interest of your local community. But what we want is not necessarily a third party, but a third force.

Which means that we're going to collect Democrats, Republicans and independents around an agenda that is in the best interest of our people. And then all of us can stand on that agenda and in 1996, whoever the standard bearer is for the Democratic, the Republican, or the independent party should one come into existence. They've got to speak to our agenda.

We're no longer going to vote for somebody just because they're Black. We tried that. We wish we could. But we got to vote for you, if you are compatible with our agenda.

Now many of the people that's in this House right here are put there by the margin of the Black vote. So in the next election,we want to see who's in here that we want to stay and who in here do we want to go.

And we want to show them that never again will they ever disrespect the Black community. We must make them

Photo by Robert A. Sengstacke

afraid to do evil to us and think they can get away with it.

We must be prepared to help them if they are with us or to punish them if they're against us. And when they are against us, I'm not talking about color. I'm talking about an agenda that's into best interest of the Black, the poor and the vulnerable in this society.

Now atonement goes beyond us. I don't like this squabble with the members of the Jewish community. I don't like it. The honorable Elijah Muhammad said in one of his writings that he believed that we would work out some kind of an accord. Maybe so. Reverend Jackson has talked to the 12 presidents of Jewish organizations and perhaps in the light of what we see today, maybe it's time to sit down and talk. Not with any preconditions. You got pain. Well, we've got pain, too. You hurt. We hurt, too.

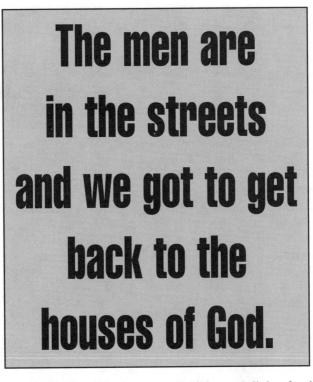

The men are in the streets and we got to get back to the houses of God.

since so many of us have been there already, we know what they suffer. Let's help our brothers and sisters who are locked down.

Did anybody mention the political prisons? Brother Conrad Worrell mentioned our political prisoners, never forget them. And now, brothers, there are 25,000 Black children in need of adoption. This is our brother Eason (ph) who is the president of Blacks in Government. I'm sorry, brother Dunston, the president of the Black Social Workers. He has 25,000 children in need of adoption. Out of this vast audience, there must be 25,000 men who will take one of these children and take them through life and make life worth living for those children.

The question is: if the dialogue is proper then we might be able to end the pain. And ending the pain may be good for both and ultimately good for the nation. We're not opposed to sitting down. And I guess if you can sit down with Arafat where there are rivers of blood between you-- why can't you sit down with us and there's no blood between us. You don't make sense not to dialogue. It doesn't make sense.

Well, brothers, I hope Father Clemons spoke today. Is Father Clemons here? Do you know father Clemons? He is one of the great pastors. Father Clemons, I wanted him to speak today because he has a program that he wants everyone of us when we leave here to go to some jail or prison and adapt one inmate for the rest of his and your life to make them your personal friend--to help them through their incarceration, to be encouragement for them. The brothers who are locked down inside the walls need us on the outside and we need them on the inside.

So if every one of us will pick out one inmate, Father Clemons will do the work of guiding this development, because it is his idea, and it is a good idea and the national African-American leadership summit adapts that idea.

Thank you, Father Clemons. Will you do that, brothers?

How many of you will adopt one Black man in prison and make him your pal, your brother for life. Help him through the incarceration. Well, go to the chaplain of that jail and say, you want to adopt one inmate. Start writing to that person, visiting that person, helping that person. And

In this vast audience, is there anyone one, two, ten, twenty-five, hundred, a thousand, 25 thousand who would be willing to adopt a Black brother or sister, bring them into your home and rear them properly? How many of you think you would like to do that, would you just raise your hand, let me take a look. Raise them high. That's a wonderful expression. Where should they go, what should they do, who should they see.

"They should see booth 26 north"

Booth 26 north is where you should go. It is to my right, your left. Or you should call 1-800-419-1999. Now brothers, the last thing we want to say, we want to develop an economic development fund. Suppose, the nearly 2 million here, and 10 million more back home that support us gave $10 a month to a national economic development fund.

Inside of one month, we would have over $100 million. And in one, year, we would have $1.2 billion. What will we do with that? I would love for the leadership up here to form a board and call in Myrley Evers Williams and ask her, what is the budget of the NAACP for this year? It's $13 million. It's $15 million, write a check. Now, next year you have to become accountable to the board, and the members of the NAACP will be on the board too, which means that no Black organization will be accountable to anybody outside of us.

But accountable to us and we will free the NAACP, the Urban League and all Black organizations to work in the best interest of our people. Now many of you would like to see all our Black organizations free?

Now, look brothers, an economic development fund for $10 a month is not a big price to ask to begin to build an economic infrastructure to nurture businesses within the Black community. Soon the leadership is going to meet and work out details of an Exodus, Exodus Economic Fund.

And we're going to get back to you. This is not a one day thing. A task force will be formed right out of this leadership to make sure that the things that we say today will be implemented so that next year of the day of atonement, which this will take place each and every year from now on until God says, well done. Now, you saw the money that was taken up today, didn't you? How many of you gave some money today? I see some hands that wanted to give, but didn't get that box to them.

Well, let me tell you something brothers, we want an outside accounting firm to come in and scrutinize every dollar that was raised from your pockets to make the Million Man March a success. And if there is any overage, it will not be spent. We will come back to this board of leadership and we will account for every nickel, every dime every dollar.

Do you know why? We want Willie Lynch to die a natural death. And the only way we can kill the idea of Willie Lynch, we have to build trust in each other. And the only way we can build trust is to open up the coat and show that you don't have a hidden agenda. All of us will be looking at the same thing, for the same purpose.

Photo by Robert A. Sengstacke

And then we'll come back to you and make a full accounting for every nickel, every dime and every dollar so that you can trust. I put my life on this. To rob you is a sin. To use you and abuse you is a sin. To make mockery of your love and your trust is a sin.

And we repent of all sin and we refuse to do sin anymore.

Is that agreeable, Black man? Now, brothers, I want you to take this pledge. When I say I, I want you to say your name. I know that there's so many names, but I want you to shout your name out so that the ancestors can hear it.

Take this pledge with me. Say with me please, I, say your name, pledge that from this day forward I will strive to love my brother as I love myself. I, say your name, from this day forward will strive to improve myself spiritually, morally, mentally, socially, politically, and economically for the benefit of myself, my family and my people.

I, say your name, pledge from this day forward I will never abuse my wife by striking her, disrespecting her for she is the mother of my children and the producer of my future. I, say your name, pledge that from this day forward, I will never engage in the abuse of children, little boys, or little girls for sexual gratification.

But I will let them grow in peace to be strong men and women for the future of our people. I, say your name, will never again use the B word to describe my female, but particularly my own Black sister.

I, say your name, pledge from this day forward that I will not poison my body with drugs or that which is destructive to my health and my well-being. I, say your name, pledge from this day forward, I will support Black newspapers, Black radio, Black television. I will support Black artists, who clean up their acts to show respect for themselves and respect for their people, and respect for the ears of the human family.

I, say your name, will do all of this so help me God. Well, I think we all should hold hands now. And I want somebody to sing "To God be the Glory."

And the reason I want this song sung is because I don't want anybody to take the credit for a day like this. I didn't do it. Reverend Chavis didn't do it. Reverend Jackson didn't do it. Reverend Sharpton didn't do it. Conrad Worrill or Maulana Karenga (ph) didn't do it. Dr. Cornell West didn't do it. But all of us worked together to do the best that we could but it's bigger than all of us.

So since we can't take the praise, then we have to give all the glory, all the honor, all the praise to Him to whom it rightfully belongs.

So in closing, we want to thank Mayor Barry and Mrs. Barry for opening this great city to us. And out of every dollar that was collected, 10 percent of it we're going to leave here in Washington that Mayor Barry may aid some institution, some good cause in the city. We want to set a good example.

This was a beautiful and peaceful meeting. Probably one of the best that ever was held in Washington held by Black men who want to atone to God and clear our slate. Beautiful Black brothers. Beautiful brothers, I'm going to say a prayer and I want to thank Phi Beta Sigma and its wonderful, wonderful president and all the Greet letter organizations but Phi Beta Sigma especially because they opened their door to the Million Man March and made it possible. I want to thank the Reverend Dr. Benjamin Chavis who did a wonderful, wonderful job.

I thank his wife for her sacrifice and my wife for hers. I thank Dorothy Height and the National Council of Negro Women. I thank Dr. Betty Shabazz who came in the name of her husband and I thank God for allowing the negative thing to be turned into a positive that she and I might start a process of reconciling 30-year-old differences.

Lord knows if we could do it with blood between us, God knows that Bloods and Crips have done it and

what we have done to one another, don't let the sun set before saying to your brother, I love you and I'm sorry. And after the prayer is said and the song is sung, I want you all to just embrace each other and say to each other, I love you my brother and thank you for making this holy day of atonement real in my life.

Don't do it now, wait till after prayer and the song. Will you bow your heads, please? Oh, before we say that prayer, the brother of my leader and teacher, the honorable Elijah Muhammad, is here with me and with us. He's like my father in the absence of my father. He knows this history of the Nation of Islam better than any man in America and I thank God that he lived long enough to see the day that he suffered and worked for, for now 65 years. The brother of the honorable Elijah Muhammad, brother John Muhammad.

(applause)

And so now
Muhammad: Dar Selim Eloahim! (ph)
Farrakhan: Dar Eloahim Salaam (ph). He looks just like my daddy! And oh, Reverend Jackson, where is that great man? He had to go! Didn't he preach today? And now, with your heads bowed,

(sings in Arabic)

In the name of Allah the beneficent, the merciful, praise be to Allah the Lord of the world, the beneficent, the merciful master of the day of requital.

Photo by Roy Lewis

27

Thee do we worship. Thine aid we seek. Guide us on the right path. The path of those upon whom you have bestowed favors, not the path of those upon whom wrath is brought down. Nor those who go astray. Oh, Allah. We thank you for this holy day of Atonement and Reconciliation.

We thank you for putting your spirit and your calm in Washington, D.C. and over the heads of this nearly two million of your servants. We thank you for letting us set a new example, not only for our people but for America and the world.

We thank you, oh Allah, for bringing us safely over the highways and we beg you to take us safely back to our wives and our children and our loved ones, who saw us off earlier or a few days ago.

And as we leave this place, let us be resolved to go home to work out this Atonement and make our communities a decent, whole, and safe place to live. And oh, Allah, we beg your blessings on all who participated, all who came that presented their bodies as a living sacrifice, holy and acceptable as their reasonable service.

Now, let us not be conformed to this world, but let us go home transformed by the renewing of our minds and let the idea of atonement ring throughout America.

That America may see that the slave has come up with power. The slave has been resorted, delivered, and redeemed. And now call this nation to repentance. To acknowledge her wrongs. To confess, not in secret documents called classified, but to come before the world and the American people as the Japanese prime minister did and confess her faults before the world because her sins have affected the whole world. And perhaps, she may do some act of atonement, that you may forgive and those ill-affected may forgive, that reconciliation and restoration may lead us to the perfect union with thee and with each other. We ask all of this in your Holy and Righteous Name, Allah, akbar (Prayer in Arabic). Allah, akbar. Allah, akbar. That means God is great.

And now Gregory Hopkins to sing To God Be the Glory. Keep holding each other's hands, brothers. And after the song is sung, let us embrace each other.

(performance of song)

Farrakhan: Turn to your brother and hug your brother and tell your brother you love him and let's carry this love all the way back to our cities and towns and never let it die, brothers. Never let it die.

MILLION MAN MARCH PLEDGE
WASHINGTON, D.C.
OCTOBER 16, 1995

I, (say your name), pledge that from this day forward I will strive to love my brother as I love myself.

I, _____, from this day forward will strive to improve myself spiritually, morally, mentally, socially, politically, and economically for the benefit of myself, my family and my people.

I, _____, pledge that I will strive to build businesses, build houses, build hospitals, build factories and enter into international trade for the good of myself, my family and my people.

I, _____, pledge that from this day forward I will never raise my hand with a knife or a gun to beat, cut, or shoot any member of my family or any human being except in self-defense.

I, _____, pledge from this day forward I will never abuse my wife by striking her or disrespecting her, for she is the mother of my children and the producer of my future.

I _____, pledge from this day forward I will never engage in the abuse of children, little boys or little girls, for sexual gratification; I will let them grow in peace to be strong men and women for the future of our people.

I, _____, will never again use the "B" word to describe any female, but particularly, my own Black sister.

I, _____, pledge from this day forward that I will not poison my body with drugs or that which is destructive to my health and my well-being.

I, _____, pledge from this day forward I will support Black newspapers, Black radio, Black television; I will support Black artists who clean up their act to show respect for themselves and respect for their people and respect for the heirs of the human family.

I, _____, will do all of this, so help me God.

FROM A BLACK WOMAN TO A BLACK MAN

Maya Angelou

The night has been long
The wounds have been deep
The pit has been dark
The walls have been steep

Beneath a blue sky
On a golden beach
I was dragged by braids
Beyond your reach

Your hands were tied
Your feet were bound
You couldn't save me
From the selling ground

We lay in the slave hold
Air thickened with cries
You lowered your head
Evading my eyes

The night has been long
The wounds have been deep
The pit has been dark
The walls have been steep

We stood on the block
Clothed only in shame
Then someone whispered
That we were to blame

If our skin had been pale
And our hair had been straight
We would have escaped
Our devilish fate

Our lives have been shaped
By that crippling lie
Yet, you were not guilty
And neither was I

The night has been long
The wounds have been deep
The pit has been dark
The walls have been steep

Today we declare
This a guilt free season
Greed was the culprit
Greed was the reason

Voices of old, spirit sound
Speak to us in words profound
Across the years and centuries
Across the oceans and roiling seas

"Draw near to each other
Value your race
You were paid for dearly
In another place.

The hell you have lived through
And live through still
Has sharpened your senses
And toughened your will."

I look through your anguish
Down into your soul
And know that together
We can be made whole.

I look through the posture
And past your disguise
And see pride of race
In your big brown eyes.

Clap hands
Together at this meeting ground

Clap hands
We have dallied over long
On the low road of indifference

Clap hands
Let us come together
And reveal our hearts

Clap hands
Let us revive our spirits

Clap hands
Let us cleanse our souls
Let us leave the preening as
Impostors in our own history

Clap hands
And call our spirits back from the ledge

Clap hands
Call joy back into our conversation

Clap hands
Call laughter back into our dialogue

Clap hands
Call nurturing back into our nurseries
And romance back into our bedrooms

The ancestors tell us
Through a history of pain
We're a going on people
On the rise again

Make a vow of friendship
Let us take each other's hand
Shout Hurray for the Black Woman
Shout Hurray for the Black Man

The night has been long
The wounds have been deep
The pit has been dark
The walls have been steep

Photo by Roy Lewis

Maya Angelou is one of the best known and admired writers/artists in this country. As a writer, poet, dancer, singer, director and now Reynolds Professor of American Studies at Wake Forest University, Ms. Angelou has touched the heart of this nation with her lyrical, stirring prose and poetry. Ms. Angelou is the recipient of numerous awards and honorary degrees. Her autobiography has been written through six books; her poetry collections include *Just Give Me a Cool Drink of Water 'Fore I Die, Shaker, Why Don't You Sing?, I Shall Not Be Moved,* and *On The Pulse of Morning,* which was presented as the inaugural poem for President Clinton in 1993.

REMARKS BEFORE ONE MILLION MEN BY REVEREND JESSE L. JACKSON, SR. MONDAY, OCTOBER 16, 1995

To Minister Farrakhan, members of the Organizing Committee, Support Committees, Host Mayor Marion Barry, Preachers of the Gospel, The Women Organizers, you have organized a great historical event. You have helped to unleash a great spiritual power of a great people. How good it is to hear the sounds of chains and shackles breaking from the ankles and minds of men. How beautiful it is to see the rejected stones stand up to become the cornerstones of a new spiritual and social order.

Let us pray. Repeat these words: In the spirit of atonement, healing and recovery "Dear God, accept our petition. Forgive us for our sins against thee and toward one another. Forgive us for the foolishness of our ways. Empower us to be better and never bitter. Make us fit for the fight to rebuild the walls that we might go from disgrace to amazing grace. Empower us to do justice, love mercy, and walk humbly before thee." Repeat these words: "In the spirit of atonement and healing and recovery, dear God accept our petition. We want to make our families secure and give our children a legacy of hope. We want to forgive each other and move on. We have before us miles to walk, mountains to climb, much work to do, and we cannot take the burdens of hatred and jealousy and fear or meanness on this journey. We must not allow fear, pride nor ambition to stand between us and your will. We just want to do your will and to you, our God, be the glory. Amen."

The idea of the Million Man March has touched a nerve deep in the hearts of people yearning to breathe free. Big meetings were never allowed, they were illegal, on the plantation. We have always yearned for a big meeting. A raw nerve of ancient longings for dignity has been touched. I wish that Dr. King and Mr. Muhammad and Malcolm and Floyd McKissick and Medgar and Fannie Lou Hamer and Daisy Bates and Bayard Rustin and Paul Robeson, and Cleve Robinson and Mr. Micheaux and Whitney Young and Clarence Mitchell and Roy Wilkins and Thurgood Marshall could see us now.

America will benefit and ultimately be grateful for this day. When a rising tide for racial justice and gender equality and family stability and inclusion and fairness lifts the boats stuck at the bottom, all boats benefit.

We are under attack by the courts, legislators, and mass media with despise; racists attack us for sport to win votes. We are attacked for sport to win votes, to make money. But I tell you today, rabbit hunting ain't fun when the rabbits stop running. Here we are in 1995, trying to stop 1996 from becoming like 1896, the end of the second Reconstruction. DuBois said, "the color line will be the problem of this century." He was right. Mr. Muhammad said, "when we come into ourselves and know our truer selves, we will achieve

Photo by Roy Lewis

Photo by Robert Sengstacke

our place in the sun." Fannie Lou Hamer said, "I am sick and tired of being sick and tired." Sojourner Truth said to the feminist movement as she sought an even playing field between white and black women, "ain't I too a woman." And Martin Luther King, Jr. said when he went to rescue Rosa Parks, "it is better we walk in dignity than ride in shame."

We are here because we will not surrender to the forces of evil, hostility, hate and hurt. Something deep within us says stand up less we perish. Choose life, but if we must die, let it be nobly and not like dogs, Claude McKay said. We come because there is a structural malfunction in America. Two Americas. It was structured into the constitution that determined us to be three-fifths of a human being legally. It is why there is a crack in the liberty bell in Philadelphia. The Kerner Commission Report warned us of the cost and immorality of two Americas, one essentially white and have, and one essentially black and brown and have not. Lincoln said "we can't exist as a nation half slave and half free." The reaction to the verdict of the O.J. Simpson trial exposed wounds unhealed. There is more vile and venom toward an integrated jury with a unanimous verdict that a racist policeman who perjured himself. How could blacks and whites see the verdict so differently. One man looking at an apple from the top down sees a shiny apple. Another man on the bottom up sees the worm, the rot. We all have

a right to eat the fruit. None of us should have to eat the worms and the rot. We are all God's children.

Why march? In 1963 Dr. King said, "because of the shameful condition of the Negro." Today, it is a disgraceful condition. We are under attack by the Supreme Court, the Congress, state legislatures, the police. Why do we march? Our babies are dying earlier for lack of prenatal care. Inner-city hospitals are closing. Why do we march? Inferior primary and secondary education compared with the suburbs. A two-track system codified by law. Why do we march? We are less able to go to college. Two hundred thousand more blacks in the jail industrial complex than in college. Why do we march? Media stereotypes. The media projects us as less intelligent than we are, less hard working than we work, less universal than we are, less patriotic than we are and more violent than we are. They reinforce the fear and the big lie. Why do we march? We are less able to borrow money in a system built on credit and risk. In San Diego a report came out — 30,000 mortgage loans, only 29 for Blacks. We are objects of hate and scapegoating. Economic downsizing is the cause of economic fear. Capital merging going upward; jobs going outward; middle class coming downward angrily; poverty base expanding; affirmative action the diversion, and race becomes the bait. We are culturally conditioned to hate Blacks and get away with it. We are conditioned to attack each other quickly, and viciously. When Blacks kill Whites the call is for capital punishment. When Whites kill Blacks we want to riot. When Blacks kill Blacks we shrug our shoulders. We have adjusted. Nobody has the right to kill anybody. For that sin we must atone.

Why do we march? Because the House of Representatives cut $1.1 billion from the nation's poorest public schools, about $5,000 per classroom; because they cut $137 million from head start, eliminating 45,000 preschoolers from the budget. Because they cut $871 million from youth summer jobs, eliminating 600,000 jobs for youth. Why do we march? In every major city the two newest buildings are a sports stadium and a new jail. The fastest growing industry in urban America are jails. The stadium industry is a substitute for real manufacturing and the jail is the catch basin for the maladjusted. Half of all public housing built in the last 10 years has been jails. The fastest growing industry in urban America are jails. When there are two mountains and nothing in between there is a canyon. In that canyon fierce winds blow. It's a double sucking sound— sucking jobs out, destroying the family means of survival and sucking youth up. It's a negative urban policy. Chastisement for the mothers, chasing the fathers, and locking up the children. They say three strikes and you're out is a solution. Many of our youth are born with three strikes against them and never held a bat. A

33

young mother without prenatal care, inferior education and a parent without a job. We need four balls and you're on. Prenatal and head start, ball one. Adequately funded public education, ball two. A marketable skill and access to college, ball three. And a job, ball four. We know prenatal care, head start and day care on the front side of life makes more sense than jail care and welfare on the backside. We want a humane welfare plan, but our struggle is not for welfare, it's for equal opportunity and for justice. We want one set of rules. Why is it to spend five years in jail you must possess $45,000 worth of marijuana, $8,000 powder cocaine and $29.00 worth of crack. If you are caught with 5 grams of crack cocaine in a first time nonviolent offense, 5 years in jail is mandatory. If you are caught with 500 grams of powder, you can get probation, because it is not mandatory. What's wrong with this picture? Powder is wholesale, crack is retail. You strike a match to powder, it becomes crack. Ninety-four percent of those in jail for the $5.00 high are young Black and brown males. Fifty-five percent of the crack users are white. Seventy-five percent in possession of powder are white. The

Fifty-five percent of the crack users are white. Seventy-five percent in possession of powder are white.

U.S. sentencing commission has said that the crime does not correspond with the time, and that it is racist and there is disparity. And yet, this justice department has not moved to change the ratio. By 1998, the prison labor force will be making $9 billion worth of products, supplanting 400,000 private sector jobs. In Illinois, alone, prisoners are making 280 products. How can we see a chip in the eye of the Chinese and protest prison labor, while we have a log in our own eye? We must protest prison labor and chain gangs. Our youth are being locked up for sport and industry. Rural legislators are now fighting to get a new jail (1500 cells) in their county. They can then inflate the price of land and sell it for an inflated price. Then, a construction contract. Then, a maintenance contract. Then, a contract for uniforms and food. Once they get the new jail, they then build new roads, restaurants, hotels, incorporate the town and build the town around the jail. It's called a Jail Industrial Complex. And now as they privatize the jails, the new investors are Smith Barney, American Express, GE, Prudential Insurance, Merrill Lynch, Goldman-Sachs. Maybe the follow-up march has to be to Wall Street. Many of the same firms that we had to picket out of South Africa now see the new Jail Industrial Complex as attractive. Blacks who work in those firms should meet and address those indignities.

One-third of Black males aged 20-29 are in the Jail Industrial Complex at a cost of $6 billion a year. There is an 828% increase in Black women in jail during the last five years, not because behavior worsened; the regulations and traps have fed the appetite for the new Jail Industrial Complex. Treatment centers are closing. Recovery centers for addicted babies are closing. Legal assistance for the poor is cut off. The media is obsessed with who has organized this march. Try Clarence Thomas and Newt Gingrich for starters.

Why do we march? We march because our dignity and our destiny are at stake. What must we do? We cannot wallow in our pain. We must turn pain to power. We can't get a victim's complex, a central message of Jesus the Christ who was born in the slum, but the slum was not born in him. He was born to a young mother with a neighborhood debate about who his father was. Mary rode a donkey or walked 35 miles, nine months pregnant. Herod did not provide adequate housing, but they had to pay taxes and didn't have the right to vote while living under occupation. He was born outdoors, homeless, in the wintertime. He could have developed a victim's complex and become a local Bethlehem bum. But one day he heard a voice saying you are my beloved son, with whom I am well pleased. There is a higher voice available to us. It is the voice of our God. Victims have to turn pain into power. Slave masters never retire. The victims must become abolitionists. Pimps never retire. Prostitutes have to regain their character. Oppressors never retire. The oppressed must change their minds. Victims have power— the power to choose, the power to stand up. When you stand up, your head is closer to heaven and further from hell. When you stand up, the world has to adjust.

What must a million men do? A million men must honor their God with all their hearts and souls; must affirm their wives as co-partners. God made both Eve and Adam. It was a statement about a common substance, a common necessity, not about inferiority or subservience. It takes both to procreate, to produce and build.

What must a million men do? We can reduce divorce rates, stop self-destructive behavior, drive out guns and drugs, see the ten ethical commandments as the keys to educational and economic empowerment. We can pay alimony where there is no matrimony and become upbeat dads rather than deadbeat dads. The recently freed people in the journey of Moses needed more than new land and the defeat of Pharaoh. They needed a higher ethical standard than the oppressor from whom they escaped. A million men can lead the charge to stop domestic violence, to stop wife battering, to spare our children from seeing the trauma of a pleading mother and a mad and abusive father. A million men can joint venture with their children's teachers and do six things:

1. Take a child to school;

2. Meet your child's teacher;

3. Exchange home telephone numbers;

4. Turn off the television three hours each night;

5. Pick up a report card every nine weeks;

6. Initial report cards.

You can go back and meet with judges and become mentors and nurturers, alternatives to unnecessary jailings. A million men can use selective boycotts. It worked with Dr. King in Montgomery and Mandela in South Africa to demand corporate accountability. A million men can register five voters and change the national equation. Kennedy beat Nixon by 112,000 votes. Nixon beat Humphrey by 500,000 votes. The Gingrich forces won by a cumulative score by 19,000 votes. In 1994, 6 million _fewer_ people voted, not more. After all the bloodshed and lives lost, 8 million Blacks are unregistered to vote. We must atone for that sin and rebuild and fight for new public policy. It is not that their water was high, our walls were low.

We must build independent lines on ballots all across the nation. We must expand our political options and create greater competition for the progressive vote. There is a way out. A million men can build coalitions. Blacks need not bear this cross alone. Every survival program being cut now — medicare, medicaid, food stamps, scholarships, legal support for battered women, affirmative action— all affect more Whites, numerically, than Blacks. The poor are mostly White, female and young. They put a Black face on poverty and it's open season for all in that class, Black or White. Dr. King's last effort was organizing garbage workers in the collective bargaining units. There is power in worker organizing.

A million men could set a moral tone for the whole nation. We must have a quality of ethics, responsibility, character and justice—greater than the cultural norm. We come not to conform, but to transform. We affirm race pride, but not race idolatry. Cain and Abel were of the same race, but Cain killed Abel, a character crisis. Color we inherit, character we develop. Racism is the great sin of our culture. Racism is harmful to the body and damaging to the soul. Racism is morally wrong. Racism is socially distasteful. Racism is emotionally unsettling. Racism is polit-

ically destabilizing. As Dr. King said, "Racism is an ontological affirmation that God made a creative mistake." Racism unbridled drove the institution of slavery for 250 years. That same spirit called fascism led to 55 million deaths in World War II. It was pillars of apartheid in South Africa. Racism, sexism, anti-Semitism, anti-Arabism, Asian bashing, homophobia, xenophobia are the stuff of which fascism is made. A great people must go another way. Today, I say to you my brother, it is not enough to say, Pharaoh, let my people go. My people, let Pharaoh go. Let his values, his violence, his drugs, let them go.

What do we want? We want a new deal with corporate America and the government. Our government set up with our tax assistance a Polish-American development bank. We made to Poland a 40-year loan at 3/4 of one percent interest, first payment due in 10 years, with $4 trillion in private and public pension funds. Ten percent of that money ($400 billion), government secured or a one cent gas tax, could build a series of development banks around the country and wipe out slums and expand our economy.

We want a white house conference on urban policy and economic development. We must review the foreign and domestic industries of food and autos and mass media and beverage and clothing which offer franchises and distributorships. We want our share.

In conclusion:

Don't let these forces of oppression break your spirit. It's been a long journey from slave ship to championship, from disgrace to dignity. You may be unemployed, overworked, underpaid, unskilled, burdened with compromised dreams, who have been bloodied but must now bow.

When you leave here they will ask you where did you go. Just tell them I took a trip from pain to power to promise. Tell them I saw a number like John saw — No man can number. They were in the trees, they were in cars, they were in the hospitals, they were in office buildings, they were in the parks. For a moment the world stood still. They will ask you who are you? I didn't see you in Washington. Tell them you are one in a million. Tell them that you have a light and you will let it shine. Tell them I am one in a million. They will ask who organized this march. Tell them Clarence Thomas and Newt Gingrich. Tell them you are a dreamer, that your dream is bigger than the circumference of your jail cell. That your dream is bigger than the ghetto that you have been assigned to. Tell them like John on the Isle of Patmos, locked away and left to perish, you still dream of a new heaven and a new earth. The old world will pass away and the new one will surely appear. Tell them you are flying on the wings of faith and, like Job, through all your suffering, you are a survivor, and you still trust God. Tell them you are one in a million and, tell them you will turn stripes of suffering into hope and healing, and not hurt and hate. Tell them like Joseph, you

are a minority with a majority dream. We were not brought here by mean men to be slaves. We were sent here by God to help save the human race. Our oppressors meant it for evil; God meant it for good. There is another view of history.

Dream bigger than one race, dream as big as the human race. Dream bigger, from one side of town to citizens of the world. Students study diligently. There is power in a developed mind and strong character. Tell them you are somebody. Tell them God has a place for us. Mandela, the jailed, paradoxically had to free South Africa. Twenty-seven years in jail, Robbins Island, cut off from humanity, couldn't see a newspaper for 15 years, couldn't see a television for 22 years. But because of a dream and faith early one Sunday morning, he emerged in a kind of second resurrection. Mr. prisoner without a gun, a knife, with a mind of steel, backbone erect, and a heart of love, became Mr. President. Our vision and our abilities and our values are not limited by color. We will heal and lead the whole nation. We will be Balm in Gilead and make the nation whole. Tell them the White House is not off-limits. It is within reach. We may not be there yet, but we are qualified; we are on our way.

Tell them I am somebody. Down with dope; up with hope.

I am, somebody.

Keep hope alive!

WHY I'M MARCHING IN WASHINGTON

Cornel West

On Monday, maybe a million black men will march on Washington. Coming after the O.J. Simpson verdict, the march promises to be a pivotal moment in our nation's life. As the writer Greg Tate has rightly noted, the verdict "may represent the first time in history that a majority black jury has wielded an apparatus of state power against the will of the nation's white citizenry."

Our fragile civic and legal order, with its precious jury system that does not guarantee justice, must now contend with a level of white rage unprecedented in American history. Needless to say, black rage has risen exponentially since bullets ripped through the Rev. Dr. Martin Luther King, Jr. in 1968. Can our deeply divided society wrestle with this challenge without exploding?

For most whites, the Million Man March called by Minister Louis Farrakhan can only worsen race matters. For them, he not only embodies black rage, but also black hatred and contempt for whites, Jews, women, gay men and lesbians. Building on a long and diverse tradition of black nationalism–Marcus Garvey, Elijah Muhammad, Queen Mother Moore, Malcolm X–Minister Farrakhan is white America's worst nightmare.

Why am I supporting the march? After all, I am a radical democrat devoted to a downward redistribution of wealth and a Christian freedom-fighter in the King legacy, which condemns any xenophobia, including patriarchy, homophobia and anti-Semitism.

First, unlike "color-blind" neo-liberals and conservatives who cheaply invoke Dr. King's words even as they kill the substance and spirit of his radical message, I take his last efforts seriously. When Dr. King was killed, not only was he working on the multiracial poor people's campaign, he was also meeting with Elijah Muhammad and Amiri Baraka–black nationalists demonized by the white media–to promote black operational unity.

Dr. King sought to use moral and political means to transform the capitalist structure of society while deepening its democratic one. But he realistically assessed the true depth of white supremacy. In short, Dr. King, the integrationist, had no fear of a black united front and no hatred of black nationalists.

The second reason I march: Although Minister Farrakhan, with whom I have deep disagreements, initiated the demonstration, the demonstration is about matters much bigger than he is. I have in mind the general invisibility of, and indifference to, black sadness, sorrow and social misery, and the disrespect in which blacks are held in America and abroad. We agree on highlighting black suffering.

In casting the demonstration as "Farrakhan's march," the mainstream media want to shift the focus from black pain to white anxiety. The media distort and disparage the

Photo by Robert L. Thornton III

motivations of most blacks who will march–men who are deeply concerned about black suffering and are outraged at the nation's right-wing turn yet are neither Nation of Islam members nor Farrakhan followers. No one man is the leader of black America–and most of its best leaders are black women.

Third, I must march because the next major battle in the struggle for black freedom involves moral and political channeling of the overwhelming black rage and despair. To stand on the sidelines and yield the terrain to Minister Farrakhan and other black nationalists would be to forsake not only my King legacy, but more importantly, my love for black people. Young blacks are hungry for vision, analysis and action; radical democrats must go to them and be with them.

I believe that if white supremacy can be reduced to a minimum, then patriarchy, homophobia and anti-Semitism can be lessened in black America.

If I am wrong, America has no desirable future. If I am right, black operational unity need not preclude multiracial democratic movements that target all forms of racism and corporate power. Whether right or wrong, I must fight. So I march.

Cornel West is an activist, writer and scholar of national renown. He is the author of numerous publications about the tenuous relationships between the races, including the seminal work *Race Matters*. Dr. West teaches in the Department of Religion, at Harvard University.

Illustration by Murry DePillars

STANDING AS AN AFRICAN MAN
Black men in a Sea of Whiteness

Haki R. Madhubuti

Where do I belong and what is the price I have to pay for being where and who I am?

Study the faces of children who look like you. Walk your streets. Count the smiles and bright eyes, and make a mental note of their ages. At what age do our children cease to smile naturally, smile full-teeth, uninhibited, expecting full life? At what age will memory of lost friends, and lost relatives, deaden their eyes? Where does childhood stop in much of our community? At seven, eight? How many killings, rapes, beatings, verbal and mental abuse, hustles, get-over programs, drug infestations, drive-by shootings/drive-by leaders must they witness before their eyes dry up for good and their only thought is : "Will I make it to the age of twenty-five?" When the life in the eyes of our children does not gleam brightly with future and hope, we cease being nurturers and become repairers of broken spirits and stolen souls. This is the state we are now in and too often it is too late.

Where do I belong and what is the price I have to pay for being where and who I am?

If you don't know, you can't do.

From whom do we buy our food? From whom do we rent our apartments? From whom do we buy our clothes, furniture, cars, and life bettering needs? On whose land do we walk, sleep, live, play, work, get high, chase women, lie, steal, produce children and die? Why is it that 800,000 Black men and 50,000 Black women populate the nation's prisons? Is race a factor in a land where white people control most things of value? Is race a factor in a country where young Black boys and men are dying quicker than their birth rate? When do we declare war on our own destruction? Why is it that the Blacker one is the worse it is? Who taught Black people that killing Black people is alright and sometimes honorable?

This is Our Charge!

Study the landscape. Read the music in your hearts. Remember the beauty of mothers, sisters, and the women in our lives who talked good about us. Remember when we talked good about us. Remember when we talked good about them. Understand the importance of ideas.

This is Our Mission!

Pick up a book. Challenge the you in you. Rise above the limited expectations of people who do not like you and never will like you. Rise above the self-hatred that slowly eats your heart, mind, and spirit away. Find like-minded brothers. Study together. Talk together. Find each others' hearts. Ask the right questions. Why are we poor? Why

Photo by Roy Lewis

are our children not educated? Why are our children dying at such an unbelievable rate? Why are we landless? What does land ownership have to do with race? What does wealth have to do with race? Why do we hate being called African and Black? What does Africa mean to me, us? Why is Africa in a state of confusion and civil war? Why is there no work in our communities? What is the difference between a producer and a consumer? What do we produce that is sold and used world-wide? Whose knowledge is most valuable for the development of Black (African) people? Would I kill myself and others who look like me if I loved myself and those who look like me? From where does self-love come? Who taught me, us, self-hatred? Is self-hatred an idea? Is self-love an idea? To whose ideas do we tap-dance? With whose ideas do we impress each other? Are African (Black) ideas crucial to our discourse and development? Can a Black person be multi-cultural if he/she does not have his/her culture first? When do we declare war on ignorance, intellectual betrayal, self-destruction, pimpism, weakening pleasures, European worldviews, beggar mentalities, and white world supremacy? Is race an idea? When will we use the race idea to benefit us?

Where do I belong and what is the price I have to pay for being where and who I am?

We belong among the people worldwide who look like us. We belong to a world where we produce rather than consume. We belong to a world where the measurement of Black beauty and worth is internal and cultural.

We belong where our education is not anti-us.
We belong among African men who are brothers and brothers who are Africans. How will we recognize them?

You will recognize your brothers
by the way they act and move throughout the world.
there will be a strange force about them,
there will be unspoken answers in them.
this will be obvious not only to you but to many.
the confidence they have in themselves and in
their people will be evident in their quiet sameness.
the way they relate to women will be
clean, complimentary, responsible, with honesty and as partners.
the way they relate to children will be
strong and soft full of positive direction and as example.
the way they relate to men
will be that of questioning our position in this world,
will be one of planning for movement and change,
will be one of working for their people,
will be one of gaining and maintaining trust within the culture.
these men at first will seem strange and unusual but
this will not be the case for long.
they will train others and the discipline they display
will be a way of life for many.
they know that this is difficult
but this is the life that they have chosen
for themselves, for us, for life:
they will be the examples,
they will be the answers, they will be the first line builders,
they will be the creators,
they will be the first to give up the weakening pleasures,
they will be the first to share a black value system,
they will be the workers,
they will be the scholars,
they will be the providers,
they will be the historians,
they will be the doctors, lawyers, farmers, priests
and all that is needed for development and growth.
you will recognize these brothers
and
they will not betray you.

Haki Madhubuti *is an award-winning poet, the publisher and editor of Third World Press, co-founder and current board member of the Institute of Positive Education/New Concept School in Chicago. Mr. Madhubuti is also a professor of English and Director of the Gwendolyn Brooks Center at Chicago State University. He also served as a member of the Executive Committee for the Million Man March.*

Part 3
Celebrations of the Spirit

Illustration by Jon Lockard

WHAT THAT DAY WAS LIKE FOR ME: THE MILLION MAN MARCH OCTOBER 16, 1995 FOR MY NEW BROTHER, HAKI

Alice Walker

In order to watch the Million Man March I had my tv repaired. It had been on the blink for six or seven months. Because I allow myself only two hours of television a week and because I often forget to use those two hours, I hadn't particularly missed it. However, the moment I learned there was to be a march, I knew I wanted to see it. I felt whatever happened would be exciting, instructive, hopeful and *different*. Television worth watching. Black men have a tradition after all of being very interesting.

Lucky for me a distant neighbor installs dishes (of which I needed a new one) and though complaining that it was a weekend and that he'd promised to take his son to play soccer, he managed to get everything installed - except for actually digging the trench in which the cable would be laid - within about five hours.

The morning of the march I made my usual bowl of oatmeal and prepared to camp out in front of the tv. I don't remember who was speaking when I sat down, but pretty soon there was a young man who reminded me of John Lewis (years ago, of SNCC*), who was exhorting his brothers to "go home" and take on the ills of violence and cocaine. It was a refrain that took me back to the March on Washington of 1963. At that march I sat in a tree listening to Martin Luther King, Jr. asking us to return to the South. I thought then, as I do now, that to ask anyone to go home and work on the problems, there is the most revolutionary advice that can be given. Hearing King's words, I packed up and went back to the South, from which I'd fled, like my brothers and sisters before me, and remained there, writing books, teaching, and doing Movement related work for seven years. It was an invaluable time. But one I'm not sure I would have had the courage to give myself if Martin had not spoken so emphatically in favor of it.

Oatmeal finished, still cozy in my jammies, I realized I wanted to hear what every speaker had to say, even if it took the entire day, which of course it did.

What stands out? The children, most of all. The articulate, poised and impassioned young boy, and the brave, thoughtful and serious young girl, who asked fervently to be <u>seen</u> as children: protected, respected and affirmed by black men. Queen Mother Moore, too old and weary by now even to talk, but still reminding us that, for our suffering and the stolen centuries of our lives, we deserve reparations. Rosa Parks. Jesse Jackson, a major

Photo by Robert L. Thornton III

42

teacher for this period. Clear, courageous, brilliant in his ability to use words to illuminate rather than obfuscate. Making connections. Naming names. Radiating a compassionate wrathfulness. Then, disappearing. Which was its own magic. Farrakhan. Who would have thought he'd try to teach us American history using numerology? I was intrigued. Who even suspected that his mother was West Indian, and that he could honor her not only by recalling her wry humor, but could share her spirit with us by uttering her Jamaican folk speech? This was the man nobody wanted black leaders to talk to? It seemed bizarre.

I can't imagine becoming Muslim. As a religion whose male Semitic God demands submission and whose spread, historically, has been primarily through conquest, I consider it unsafe. Anyone who considers converting to Islam should first investigate its traditional application in the Middle East and Africa, and its negative impact on women and children in particular, and also on the environment. They should also read the work of Taslima Nasrin, recently threatened with death for suggesting changes in Islamic law in Bangladesh, and *Why I Am Not a Muslim* by Ibn Warraq. However, I did not think Farrakhan was proselytizing. I thought he spoke as a black man with a following, and therefore some independence and power, and that the urge to do <u>something</u> in these grim and perilous times in which we risk being re-enslaved—by drugs, television, violence and the seductive traffic on the super-information highway along which most of us will have only a footpath—propelled him. If he is homophobic, as many of my friends believe, this is a great pity, and I assume he was asking forgiveness for that, knowing how black-male phobic society can be, and how wretched that feels. If he is anti-Semitic (and I thought his son quite beautiful denouncing this charge), he definitely needed to be forgiven, in front of the whole world, and that is what I felt he was asking for. I was moved by his apparent humility; and underneath all the trappings of Islam, which I personally find frightening, I glimpsed a man of humor, a persuasive teacher and someone unafraid to speak truth to power, a virtue that makes it easier to be patient as he struggles to subdue his flaws. His speech was long, but I think this is a result of having always been respectfully listened to by his Muslim congregation. As was clear from the presence of young women in the march, who had been asked to stay home, and that of gay men too, in the larger world, outside the Muslim community, it is only the part of his message that embraces us all that is likely to be heard.

In any event, as someone who has been thrown out of "the black community" several times in my life, and someone who blesses my flaws for all I've learned from them, it was heart-warming to see Jesse, Ben (Chavis) and Louis assert their right to stand together on issues so large that every one of us will have to strain to keep the race's raggedy boat afloat. I did not feel left out at all. I think it is absolutely necessary that black men regroup as black men; until they can talk to each other, cry with each other, hug and kiss each other, they will never know how to do those things with me. I know whole black men can exist, and I want to see and enjoy them.

I loved the flags! Each one a thrilling testament to our deep feeling of being people of many different nations, capable of coming together for the common good. The beauty of the men themselves was striking. This is the beauty of soul-searching, of spiritual seeking, and yes, also of recognizing you are lost. It is the beauty all human beings have when they give up the act, and settle down to work on the amazing and problematic stuff of life.

After the march ended, and while still thinking of the powerful pledge to change lives, directions, communities, Farrakhan led a million (or two million) black men through, I knew I needed to take a walk, to put my feet on the earth, to see late-flowering shrubs, and to stand among tall trees. I have known black men in my life who are flexible like the grass and sheltering like the trees. But many black men have themselves forgotten they can be this way. It is their own nature that they miss. And they have tried to find it again in drugs, sex, information overload, oppression of women and children, and violence. As I see it, black men have a deep desire to relearn their own loveliness, as Galway Kinnell expresses it in these lines:

for everything flowers, from within, of self-blessing;
though sometimes it is necessary
to reteach a thing its loveliness,
to put a hand on a brow
of the flower,
and retell it in words and in touch,
it is lovely
until it flowers again from within, of self-blessing**

Standing in a forest near my house that was once ravaged by poorly paid loggers intent on making a profit for rich thieves who do not respect the planet, and finding it still, in its ravaged, struggling-to-recover state, miraculous, I send a prayer to my brothers: that you continue to open to each other and to bless yourselves. Continue to let go of fear. Continue to insist on truth and trust. Our time is short on this earth, but that it can be rich and joyous in spite of oppression, white madness and black confusion is undeniable. Be each other's "hand on the brow." Don't miss your time.

*SNCC: Student Nonviolent Coordinating Committee, a student civil rights organization of the 1960s.

**I first encountered this poem in Sharon Salzberg's wonderful book <u>LOVINGKINDNESS, The Revolutionary Art of Happiness</u>. It is from "<u>St. Francis and the Sow</u>," by Galway Kinnell, from Mortal Acts, Mortal Words, 1980. Houghton Mifflin Co. and Jonathan Cape, Ltd.

Alice Walker is poet, novelist, short story writer, essayist and biographer. She is author of two collections of short stories, four volumes of poetry, two collections of essays, two children's books, a biography of Langston Hughes, and five novels. She is the recipient of both a Pulitzer Prize and an American Book Award. Recently Alice Walker served as executive producer of the independent film, *Warrior Marks*, a documentary on the subject of female genital mutilation. She and the film's director, Pratibha Parmar, also collaborated on a book companion volume entitled *Warrior Marks*, published in 1993. Ms. Walker currently lives in Northern California.

CAN THESE DRY BONES LIVE? A SPIRITUAL PERSPECTIVE ON THE MILLION MAN MARCH

Rev. Frank M. Reid, III

I saw a great many bones in the floor of the valley, bones that were very dry.
God asked me, "Son of man can these bones live?"

(Ezekiel 37:3)

It is no secret that the oppressor of African-American people developed a theology of white supremacy to keep African-Americans divided, docile, and dominated. To implement this strategy required a whitewashing of the Bible so that any and all positive and powerful references to African people and personalities were Europeanized. The second part of the strategy was to take the focus off of any spiritual themes that dealt with the deliverance and development of oppressed people. The goal of the spirituality of white supremacy was and is to create African-Americans who were and are spiritually enslaved and dependent.

It should also be no secret, however, that many African-Americans revolted against the spirituality of white supremacy. Seeing beyond the oppressors' theology of dependence gave birth to a rich African rooted spirituality of resistance, recovery, reconciliation, reformation and restoration. The Black and unknown bards who wrote songs like:

Go down Moses, way down in Egypt land, tell ole
Pharaoh let my people go
and
O Freedom! O Freedom over me
and before I'll be a slave
I'll be buried in my
grave and go home to my
Lord and be free.

One of the recurring themes in African-American liberation theology is rooted in the story of the prophet Ezekiel in the valley of dry bones. (Ezekiel, Chapter 37). The essence of the story is that the bones represent a divided, lifeless, dry, dominated and powerless people. God asks Ezekiel can these bones, can this community live? God responds by giving Ezekiel empowering directions and as their dialogue continues we find the following results:

So I prophesied as I was commanded. And as I was prophesying, there was a noise, a rattling sound and the bones came together, bone to bone. I looked and tendons and flesh appeared on them and skin covered them but there was no breath in them. Then God said to me, Prophesy to the breath (spirit)...so I prophesied as God commanded me, and breath entered them; they came to life and stood up on their feet a vast army.

(Ezekiel 37: 7-10)

It is not difficult to see how African and African-American people could and can see past and present realities in the valley of dry bones. The Million Man march represents our movement from being divided and dry in the valley to standing up as a vast army. If we look closely at what happened in the valley of dry bones and reflect deeply upon what happened on October 16, 1995 at the march, there can emerge a deeper understanding of what happened and what the possibilities are before us. From my own reflection, I would like to submit to you the following for your consideration:

I. Speak

The dry bones came together because of dialogue. God and Ezekiel spoke together. From the dialogue Ezekiel was commanded to speak (prophesy) to dry bones. The success of the March was rooted in the fact that groups and individuals who normally did not speak to each other began to communicate across political, theological, economic, gender and generational boundaries. The inclusive nature of the March was the foundational organizing secret of its success.

If we are going to build on the success of the Million Man March, it is imperative that this commitment to communication beyond boundaries and differences continue.

II. Structure

When Ezekiel spoke to the bones, there was noise, there was rattling, but the bones came together. There was structure. When Minister Louis Farrakhan called the March and Rev. Ben Chavis began to organize the march, they both emphasized that the goal of the Million Man March was to get every man/woman who attended to make a commitment to join and work with an organization that would empower and transform our community. From the beginning, the Million Man March was not about show, but about structure.

The organizing, development and reformation of new and already existing structures for the liberation of our people is an essential outgrowth of the Million Man March. Perhaps the African-American Leadership Summit is one of the new structures that can help us keep the dry bones together.

III. Spirit

Even after the dry bones had come together (structure), there was still no life, no breath, no spirit in the structure. (Ezekiel 37:8) Whatever the specific structures are that work for the transformation and empowerment of our community, is it essential that the structure be filled with a life giving spirit?

Many of our most effective organizations and movements have been derailed by the wrong spirit. Love, respect, integrity, trust and accountability must be the hallmarks of any individual or organization that would represent the best interests of our people. It is this type of spirit that will keep us focused and faithful to the liberating task that lies ahead. It is this kind of spirit that the marchers represented on October 16th.

Can these dry bones live? On October 16th a resounding cry that shook the world emanated from Washington, D.C.----Yes! Now that we have stood up together, it's imperative that we stay up together, because the struggle continues.

Rev. Dr. Frank Reid, III served as a member of the MMM/DOA Executive Council. He is also the Senior Pastor of Bethel African Methodist Episcopal Church in Baltimore, MD. Rev. Reid is the author of a book titled *The Nehemiah Plan: Preparing The Church to Build Broken Lives*. His ministry is nationally televised on BET.

Photo by Third World Press

LISTEN TO THE SOUND
OF THE GENUINE

Morris F.X. Jeff, Jr., D.S.W.

When I was in Booker T. Washington's Senior High Choir forty years ago, our choir director, the late Ms. Gladys Jones Hill, had us to sing a Black spiritual entitled, "Listen to the Lambs." The essence of this powerful spiritual was a call and cry to GOD, the Creator, to listen to His flock of suffering children plea for relief and redemption from their earthly trials and tribulation. We sang this plea: "Listen to the Lambs all are crying." And in the refrain, we sang this hope filled line "He shall feed His flock like a shepherd and carry the young lambs in His bosom." There in His bosom was salvation and peace and a sign that GOD had listened and will continue to listen.

Throughout the day on October 16th, I could not stop singing and humming the lines of this song as I looked out from the stage in front of the United States Capitol witnessing and unbelievable phenomenon of One Million Black Men. As the sun continued to rise and shine, as the numbers grew and swelled, and as I witness-ed the love and affection Brothers were unconditionally extending to one another, I knew that GOD was actively listening to the cry and plea of these ONE MILLION BLACK MEN who were living out of a history of not being listened to in America. Just as significant, I witnessed right before my eyes a protest movement transform itself from protestation to a true Brotherhood affirmation, and in that moment I knew that for once Black men were finally listening to themselves.

What with the newspaper headlines and television news stories and talk shows that focused on the so-called controversies, divisions, and character of the organizations, the focus on the negative rather than the positive, the gloom rather than the glow, the calculated miscount of the numbers, I knew that here again white America was not listening. What a

shame that America would not open her ears and hearts to the sound of the genuine of One Million Black Men.

The word listen means to pay attention to sound, to wait attentively for a special purposive sound, to hear with thoughtful attention, to heed and obey.

We African-Americans have historically voiced a special sound, not only to find relief from our pain, but to proffer balms to heal the sin sick soul of America. Shamefully, America would not pay attention, take heed, or obey the special message contained within.

During the epoch of slavery, America did not listen to our enslaved ancestors who cried "Sometimes I feel like a motherless child, a long ways from home." They did not listen as we sang "Everybody talking about heaven ain't going there, heaven." Nor did they listen as we sang "Pharaoh's army got drowned, ole Mary don 'cha weep." America did not take heed, nor listen to our suffering, our insights about oppression and redemption, our wisdom about the conse-

Photo by Third World Press

quential trauma and doom that comes to those systems and persons who oppress and degrade human life.

America did not listen to Frederick Douglas who informed America that "oppression makes wise men mad." This powerful, eloquent, and committed Black man who rose from the bowels of slavery warned America that slavery would leave a deleterious scar upon her soul. He chided America:

"Oh, be warned! Be warned! A horrible reptile is coiled up in your nation's bosom; the venomous creature is nursing at the tender breast of your youthful republic; for the love of GOD, tear away and fling from you the hideous monster, and let the weight of twenty millions crush and destroy it forever!

Eventually, America ended slavery but not because of the suffering of those Africans who helped her build America. She refused to listen to their pain and plea for equality.

America refused to listen to Sojourner Truth who questioned "Ain't I a woman?" as white women were fighting for suffrage rights just for white women alone. They refused to listen to Sojourner's cry for equality.

When in September of 1895 Booker T. Washington begged white America to not segregate the races as when he pleaded with them for economics and racial unity and cooperation as "a hand on a fist," White America refused to listen. One year later the Supreme Court gave its response to his request when it declared racial segregation the law of the land.

Like Langston Hughes, Malcolm X sounded the message" America never was America to me and yet it shall be," Langston died unhappy and unfulfilled. Malcolm was assassinated for sharing his painful view that America was a terrible nightmare.

Martin L. King, Jr. cried out for freedom and equality more eloquently than any other, either before or after him. Thirty-two years ago he urged America to fulfill the promises of freedom, justice and equality for all "now." He said that now is the time to make justice a reality for all of GOD's children, "that the legitimate discontent" of African-Americans "will not pass until there is invigorating freedom and equality for them." He warned that "If Western Civilization does not now respond constructively to the challenge to banish racism, some future historians will have to say that a great civilization died because it lacked the soul and commitment to make justice a reality for all men." Before America took heed to his healing call, he was soon assassinated. James Baldwin warned, "No more water, the fire next time." America did not listen.

All of these messengers are now a part of the living dead, and with them are thousands of our children who have now stopped climbing, onward upward. These, our children, have even stopped crying out in the wilderness, and in their frustration they have proceeded to kill themselves. America still is not listening attentively to their special cries of suffering, or to their pain and special healing sounds, but are wedded to responding to their own anxieties borne of their historical quilt.

Will America listen today to the sound of the genuine of the ONE MILLION BLACK MEN who have herded to herald a familiar but poignant message:

We Black men offer the world a love hued of compassion, borne of suffering and neglect. And in this love there is a fierce creative light that shines. And in that light, there is a unique vibration, a special glow and sound that spells hope. We are willing and ready to let our light shine for the salvation of America for we know that our Black historian Lerone Bennett is absolutely correct when he says that "the Black light that we are reflecting within us is the only light left to shine and save America from its own self destruction.

This is a powerful spiritual redemptive message. It is likely that white America will not listen again. But I am comforted by this reality, that Black men are finally united and listening to the sound of the genuine in themselves. For we know that we are the light, the salvation and the way. We also know that this truth affirmed for us sixty years ago by Dr. W.E.B. DuBois is still burning in our ears and hearts.

Again we offer it to America:

This the American Black man knows: Our fight here is a fight to the finish. Either we die or win. If we win, it will be by no subterfuge or evasion of amalgamation. We will enter modern civilization either in America as Black men on terms of perfect and unlimited equality with any white man, or we will enter not at all. Either extermination root and branch, or absolute equality. There can be no compromise. This is the last great battle of the West.

This is our cry. This is our plea. This is our unmitigated resolve.

Morris F.X. Jeff, Jr. is the Past President of the National Association of Black Social Workers (1986-1990). He currently serves as the Director of the New Orleans City Welfare Department.

"WE MUST GO TO THIS MARCH IN THE NAME OF GOD"

Earl K. Nelson, Jr.

Photo by Richard Muhammad

"I do not know what's going to happen to us but, I'm not turning back," I told my fraternity brother Calis and our brothers at Morgan State University, as we were eating dinner on Sunday night and anticipating what was going to take place at the Million Man March tomorrow. As we were sitting in our fraternity brother's home, at Morgan State University, a lot of questions crossed our minds. We were talking about whether we should attend this march or stay home. One brother said "it might be a trap". Another brother said, "they may be trying to bomb all the black men in one setting." I said, "what ever the government may try to do or do to us, it won't make our conditions as black men any worse than they already are." I told my brother, "we must not be afraid of man and his evil ways, we must go to this march in the name of God, for our women, our children, and black men all over this world." I'm tired of being mistreated just because I am a black man, and I know you are too." We stayed up almost half of the night talking about

the march. Was this march going to change the hearts and minds of man kind, or was this march going to start chaos throughout America? "Well, the only way we will know is to see what happens," I said as we all started to fall asleep.

We all woke up at about four o'clock on Monday morning and got ready for that special day we all had been waiting for, "The Day of Atonement." This was a day that African American men from all over the world would gather together in harmony to ask God to forgive us for our sins against our women, children, and each other. It was also to tell the government to give us what they owe us, and that injustice in this country toward African American people will not be tolerated anymore.

Well, this was it, we were showered and had changed our clothes for the big march. It was time to go. We drove down to the campus of Morgan State University and loaded up on the buses. When we arrived, there were about 250 people assembled outside. Black brothers and sisters were standing around singing songs of Zion and holding hands praying. This was the most emotional experience I have ever had in my life. Some sisters were crying because they did not know whether we were coming back or if we would be killed. Some were crying tears of joy, knowing that this march would be a successful one, because of their faith in God. The brothers were talking to each other and saying, "keep the peace, this march is focused on the black man." Black women on Morgan's campus were in full support of the march. They stayed up all night preparing lunches for the brothers and showing their love for all of us.

At 6:45 a.m., we loaded 14 buses and headed for Washington, D.C. When we arrived, there were approximately 800,000 black men assembled at Capitol Hill. We walked about 20 blocks from J.F.K. Stadium to Capitol Hill. When we arrived, people were shouting and chanting, "freedom for the black man." This was the most powerful movement I'd ever witnessed in my life. Never have I ever felt so proud to be a black man. Around ten o'clock that morning, the numbers had exceeded one million black men and more were still coming. The march was outstanding, powerful, and ordained by God. Who would have ever believed that over one million black men would assemble

together for a positive, common cause, despite all of the negative rhetoric that had been said about a black man and his behavior. There were not any fights or violent acts throughout the duration of the march. I believe that we raised almost $2 million that will go back into the black communities. This was without question, the largest and most powerful movement in America. I am so proud that I was a part of this history.

After the march, we had to wait about two hours before we could leave to go back to campus because of the mass traffic. So, the brothers started talking about how successful the march was. When we finally returned, we were welcomed by a group of African American women who were cheering, hugging and kissing us for a job well done. I never felt so good before in my life; this is truly an experience I will never forget.

Earl K. Nelson, Jr.: Earl Nelson is a twenty-seven year old college junior; he attends Richard Stockton College of New Jersey, located in Pomona, NJ. He is a member of Iota Phi Theta Fraternity, Inc. Alpha Alpha Chapter. He is currently enrolled in Introduction to African American Studies, which helped to serve as the inspiration for his attendance at the march. This article is reprinted from the *Argo Newspaper*.

Photo by Third World Press

VISIBLE GLORY IN A 'SEA OF PEACE'

Eugene B. Redmond

Photo by Kenneth Wright

ITEM: On October 14, 15 and 16, East Saint Louis, Illinois and Saint Louis, Missouri, which face each other across the River Mississippi, heaved up their fathers, grandfathers, great-grandfathers, sons, uncles, big-daddies, balladeers, workers, rappers, preachers and other 'Brothers'. Objective: The D.C. Hajj! East boogie—as East Saint is affectionately known—helped bolster a bi-state armada that launched wave after wave of carpools, convoys and flights. As the largest Black municipality in the United States, East Saint Louis was also the only city government to officially endorse the March, shut down its operations—

except for fire, police and emergency crews—and "March" en masse to the "Mecca." East Boogie Mayor Gordon Bush shared the Blacklight with Million Man March luminaries, including other "big" city mayors like Washington D.C.'s Marion Berry, Baltimore's Kurt Schmoke & Detroit's Dennis Archer.

I. MILLION MAN PLAN

It was a Million Years in the Making, that whopper-of-a Set: Million Man March. A "Monster Mash" that helped me—I gleaned during a Post-March Epiphany—re-"situate" myself among my Brothers, my People and my Pasts. Another "rupture" of Black Consciousness, as Clyde Taylor would pre-figure it during a Henry Dumas Panel at the 4th National Black Arts Festival in Atlanta. Another "healthy" rupture.......like *Sankofa* • *Daughters of the Dust* • Or *Boyz n the Hood*. Like the Sixties (Black Power/Black Hearts/Black Studies). The Twenties (W.E.B.) • Or the Thirties (Zora). Like a "Motherless Child." Or maybe Slavery. Like a Middle Passage. Like Goree Island & other "Castles." Like Wounded Knee. Or Wounded Love. Like Soyinka's *Mandela's Planet*. Or Masekela's *Sarafina!* Like Dye-Ommm-mite!

A Million Years in the Making: Yo, Black Men—& their Women—have been Marchin since the Beginning of the Species. Since Lucy, et. al. Check. Nubian Wrestlers. Ptahhotep & His Medu Netchers. Hannibal. The—Alps—Great. Marchin. Fistic Poet Muhammad Ali: The Greatest (!). Marchin. Out of Ife & IPE. Mansa Musa & His Hajj. Dred Scott. Scott Joplin. Scottsboro Boyz. Johnny Scott (prez of East Boogie NAACP). Marchin. Airmen out of Tuskegee. Benignly Neglected Syphilitic Victims out of Tuskegee. Freedom Riders out of Greensboro & Selma. SCLC out of Montgomery & Macon. James Brown out of *A Brand New Bag*. SNCC out of the Delta & D.C. Marchin. US out of South Central. Black Panthers out of Oakland, Chicago, New Haven & Harlem. Dick Gregory & Black Liberators out of Saint Loo. Eddie Robinson out of Grambling. Hudlin Brothers out of Virginia Place in East Boogie. Spike Lee out of Morehouse & Brooklyn.

Mumia out of the Fascist Clutches......

Marchin. "From Ethiopia to East Saint Louis" was how *Drumvoices Revue* metaphorized East Boogie's role in Renaissance III. Marchin......to the Mississippi's West Bank/Saint Louis: Mounds. Hollows. Canoes. Run-aways. Settlers. & a *First* Black Mayor!: "Freeman" Bosley Jr. Marchin. W.C. Handy's "Saint Louis Woman." Duke Ellington's "East Saint Louis Toodle-oo." Ike, Tina & The *Red Top*. Katherine Dunham's State Street, Choteau Street & East Boogie Ballets. [Anthro-Choreo-Empress "whose legs still straddle continents."] Marchin. Austin Black's *Tornado in My Mouth*. Sherman Fowler's dispatches from Ibadan—& Lagos—to East Saint Loo. Darlene Roy's "Black Bridge Blues"—'bout that "Signifyin'" & "woo-wooing" train that "took/my East St. Louis man from me."

Marchin. Local Daddies of Divine & Grace. Men of Foundations: Taylor Jones III & Clyde C. Jordan & Joe Lewis (& Joe Louis) & Judge Nathan Young & Nathaniel Sweets. Octogenarian/Cat-Daddy Homer Randolph matriculating at Langston U in '31. Malcolm X walking our own Piggott Street in '62. On to Miles Davis Elementary School! Or try MD Boulevard! Or Jackie Joyner/Kersee flying—from Lincoln Park & Lincoln High—into Olympic Sunrises. Marchin. Baraka blowin Trane & Diz & Langston at State Community College & SIUE. Yo, Gwen imparting Family Portraits in our Municipal Rotunda in '91.

II: LIFTED VOICES

Such were the dawns & pre-dawns of the Million Man March, "Rite" down to August 21 when the Memorable/Honorable/Minister Louis Farrakhan Songified Saint Louis' new Keil Center with his vision of the Million Man March. Or the October 12 Pre-MMM Rally at Harlem's Apollo Theater. Rite down to the *Monster Mash* itself, the "rest" of which remains/resides within the leg-works, mind-works, heart-works, prayer-works, soul-works and God-works of history. Marchin. Resides within October 16 Memories of buses, feet, planes, vans, bikes, carts, trucks, cars, horses' backs, boots. Within the echoes of The Minister. Maya Angelou [Phenomenal Woman!] Haki Madhubuti. [Positives!] Dorothy Height. [Heights!] Maulana Karenga. [O Kwanzaa-Father!] Rosa Parks. [Our Case Is Rested!] Jesse Jackson. [Endless Race Man! & Runner!] Betty Shabazz. [Preserver! Perseverer!] Benjamin F. Chavis. [Master-Blaster-Logistician!] Tynetta Muhammad. [Praisesong for the Widow!] AME Bishop H.H. Brookins. [Renew the Spirit!] Al Sharpton. [Direct Action Reverend!] Stevie Wonder. [Wondrous Spiritual "Vision!"] Marchin.......& drummers........Marchin......& poets-singers-orators-shakers-rattlers........& Masquerades from a Yoruba Village in South Carolina........& then, again & again & again, a Cool Mass/'Sea of Peace' that Created The Day.

III: POST-PERCUSSIVE PERFORMANCE

We went forth—multitudes of armadas—returning, as Sterling Brown's "Strong Men," to East Boogie and sundry other Black Ports. Proud, unjaundiced Brothers. With Agonies fore & aft. Determined Bubbles. Brightly re-Blackened by James Weldon Johnson's "star." The "star" of The Minister. The "stars" in ourselves. Sharp as Malcolm X. Cool as OJ. "In fact," a Sister said to me during Post-March debriefing, "the OJ Verdict & the Million Man March combined to re-align the Planets." Marchin.......On Wednesday, October 17, Sherman Fowler, Marcus Atkins & I met over lunch to discuss our "book project"—Visible Glory. From Pre-March soul-scrimmages, we evolved a Three-Man Plan which included interviewing Brothers—& some Sisters—before, during & after the March. We now had our interviews plus hundreds of photographs from the "spiritual belly" of the Hajj. We were "ready"—in the verse-force of Gwendolyn Brooks—"to be ready." Marchin.

On Thursday, October 18, I asked my English 342 Class—African-American Fiction—to salute the "returning warriors" who had left SIUE's campus for the March on Sunday, October 15, following a "Departure Celebration." Two of the 24 young men—Chicagoan Anthony Smith & Saint Louisan Christopher Nance—are members of the Fiction Class. Nance is also president of the Black Student Association.

A Benchmark, The March. A Million Years in the Making. And, still, we have our work "cut out" for us, as my grandmother Rosa A. Quinn used to say. So, yo—or lo!—the East Saint Louis Million Man March Committee meets—religiously—every Tuesday at 7 PM in the all-purpose room of Shiloh AME Church, 1900 Tudor, across the street from Dunbar Elementary School. Marchin.......& on Thursday, November 16, we held one of MANY Post-March Forums at SIUE. Entitled "Million Man March: Implications & Applications," the Standing Room Only event featured panelists Atkins, Sundiata Cha-Jua, Fowler, Nance & Smith. I served as moderator. The "Million Man March Drum Ensemble"—drumming out of East Boogie—included James Belk, Jared Brown & Montra Mumford. A headline in the next morning's Edwardsville Intelligener read: 'Million Man March Still Providing Inspiration.'

Before, during & following the March, an elaborate, though relaxed "grapevine", connected East Boogie to March ["nerve"] centers in Minneapolis-St. Paul, Cleveland, Sacramento, Atlanta, DC., New York, Chicago, Indianapolis, Denver, Dallas, Tucson, Philadelphia, & Toogaloo. Some Brothers & Sisters worked on the March and "other" projects (like "Free Mumia!") simultaneously. Examples: Sam E. Anderson in Harlem & Mahmoud El Kati in the Twin Cities. Everywhere there are summits, retreats, prayer-breakfasts, Million Man March re-enactments, conferences, workshops, conventions & special editions & supplements like the Sacramento Observer's "Real Brothers" and the Indianapolis Recorder's "Men." Building on the "Shoulders" of several millennia of love & struggle, Black Men—& Women—are opening newspaper columns, sermons, speeches, poems, lectures, family discussions, counseling sessions & dates with the phrase, "In the spirit of the Million Man March......"

At this writing—Thanksgiving Morning 1995—I am in Cleveland with Extended Family, where Black Men & Women are invoking the Million Man March as though it happened yesterday. During a lengthy phone conversation,

Edward Crosley informs me of Million Man March follow throughs in Akron & Kent. From here, I will travel South to Winston-Salem (via Greensboro) where, with Maya Angelou & more Extended Family, we will continue to "engage" the March. Along with the Beijing Women's Conference, the March has launched us into the Fall and early Winter. Now, on the eve of Kwanzaa, we have the "running" start needed to take us 'round the Year—-through Martin Luther King's Birthday, Carter G. Woodson's Black History Souljourn, Women's Month, Malcolm's Birthday, Black Music Month, Juneteenth, Atlanta's Black Arts Festival, Atlanta's Cultural Olympiad & Olympics &.......Marchin.

In East Boogie, the EBR Writers Club hosts an annual Pre-Kwanzaa Celebration—always on the third Tuesday of December—to pave the way for huge Saint Louis Area Kwanzaa Extravaganzas sponsored by Better Family Life (Oh yes, Malik & Deborah Ahmed!) & other organizations. On December 19, the Writers Club will re-visit the October 16 Pilgrimage with a Panel entitled "Parallels Between The Million Man March & The Current Renaissance in Black Culture, Politics & Literature." Speakers will be Atkins, Dallas Browne, Fowler, Darlene Roy, Evon Udoh & Andrea Wren. One aim of the Pre-Kwanzaa Panel is to draw connections between the Million Man March and the Fifth Annual Black Writers' Conference held at Chicago State University the weekend following the March.

Like August Wilson's Joe Turner, the Monster Mash has Come & Gone, though the Melodies & the Maladies linger on....A Million Years in the Marchin & A Million Years to Go.

*(A poetic preview of **Visible Glory**, a book coming out of East Saint Louis on the Million Man March. Writers, Compilers & Photographers: Eugene B. Redmond, Sherman L. Fowler & Marcus Atkins. Publishers: East Saint Louis Million Man March Committee. Due Date: Spring 1996. Other essentials: P.O. Box 6165, East Saint Louis, Illinois 62202.)*

Eugene Redmond: Teacher, poet and playwright, Eugene Redmond conducts poetry workshops and serves as a mentor for younger poets across this country. He is the author of three plays and seven collections of poetry. Mr. Redmond is the Poet Laureate of East St. Louis, Illinois, Professor of English at Southern Illinois University at Edwardsville, and founding editor of *Drumvoices Revue* and *Literai Internazionale: A Multicultural Journal of Literary and Visual Arts.*

A Tribute to the Million Man March

"Strong Men Keep Coming"

—Sterling Brown

Useni Eugene Perkins

We March
We March
In the Spirit of our Ancestors
who forged epic civilizations
across the bosom of Mother Afrika
and built ageless pyramids
that glorified the Nile Valley
erected academic cathedrals in Timbucktu
that attracted scholars from distant hamlets
and cultivated systems of government
that were replicated by other nations

Praise Hotep
Praise King Shaka
Praise Sonni Ali
Praise Queen Yaa Asantewa
Praise Queen Nzingha
Praise Piankhi
Praise those upon whose shoulders we stand
and drink from the fountain of their wisdom

We March
We March
In the Spirit of our Ancestors
who were uprooted from the traditions
that ordained their manhood and womanhood
and placed in the slave castles
of Ghana and the dungeons in Goree Island
before being transported across the perilous Middle Passage
where millions are buried
beneath the deep azure Atlantic waters
as the inhumane slave vessels
sailed to the Western Hemisphere
with cargoes of ebony bodies
Mandingo   Ebo
Fulani   Mendi
Yoruba   Massai

shackled in overcrowded pits of despair
to be seasoned and sold
to nations maligned with racism
and a self proclaimed Manifest Destiny
of imperialism and conquest

We March
We March
In the Spirit of our Ancestors
who endured the tribulations of slavery
but refused to yield to its tyranny
and waged struggles of resistance
from the sun-drenched island of Haiti
to the magnolia fields of South Carolina
Hail Prince Cinque
Hail Boukman
Hail L 'Ouverture, Dessalines and Christophe
Hail Harriet Tubman
Hail Nat Turner
Hail the thousands of brothers and
sisters whose graves have no markers
but their spirits are indelibly
etched in the archives of Black Liberation

We March
We March
In the spirit of our Ancestors
whose minds would not be contaminated
from the diatribe of Western Mythology
that denigrated our Blackness
and humiliated our culture
Revere Edward Blyden
Revere Marcus Garvey
Revere W.E.B. Du Bois
Revere Paul Robeson
Revere Ida B. Wells
Revere Carter G. Woodson
Revere Mary McCleod Bethune
Revere Honorable Elijah Muhammad

Revere Malcolm X
Revere Elkin Sithole
Revere Vivian Verdell Gordon

We March
We March
In the Spirit of our Ancestors
who remind us of our duty
as Afrikan men
as Black Men
as Muslim men
as Christian men
as Hebrew men
as men of color
who seek redemption
and empowerment
to serve our CREATOR
to atone for our sins
to care for our children
to preserve our families
to protect our communities
to reclaim our past greatness
to reconstruct our humanity
to respect our women
to sanctify our existence
and to resurrect our MANHOOD

Illustration by Tom Feelings

We March
We March
In the Spirit of our Ancestors
as we reach out to the Black Diaspora
where vestiges of our heritage
blossom throughout the Planet Earth
and to brothers who are incarcerated
in wretched prisons and urban cesspools
to brothers who are homeless
and incapacitated from drugs
to brothers who are dispirited
and have lost faith in the CREATOR

We pledge our honor
We pledge our love
We pledge our dedication
We pledge our unyielding commitment
to leave a legacy
for those not yet born
of hope, courage, perseverance
and spiritual reconstitution

We March
We March
to the drums of our Ancestors
whose crescendo can be heard
throughout the Cosmic Universe
Resounding hymns of declaration
that demand we be MEN
and leave our childhood behind
We can no longer procrastinate
and act like helpless dependents
We have arrived at our Moment of Truth
and we must respond
for time is not always eternal
nor each day a given
tomorrow was yesterday
and the future is today

AS BLACK MEN WE CAN DO NO LESS
AS BLACK MEN WE MUST DO MUCH MORE

A Luta Continua
in Brotherhood

Useni Eugene Perkins
October 16, 1995

Useni Perkins is a poet, playwright, and social practitioner. His published works include *Explosion of Chicago's Black Street Gangs, Harvesting New Generations, Home is a Dirty Street, Black Fairy and Other Plays, Afrocentric Self-Inventory and Discovery Workbook.* Mr. Perkins is also the editor of *Black Child Journal* and a professor of Social Work at Chicago State University. He is currently at work on *Beyond the Three Point Line,* which he is writing along with Craig Hodges.

The Miracle of The Million Man March

Rev. Willie F. Wilson

Pastor, Union Temple Baptist Church

As a local co-convener, National Committee member and executive producer of the Million Man March program on October 16, 1995, I have some special insight to share on the Million Man March.

Several years ago, there was a book on the best seller list titled *CHAOS.* The author of this book talked about certain human movements that are propelled by an unseen presence. Just as no one had to organize the students to sit in at a lunch counter in Greensboro, or tell the Chinese students to assemble at Tienneman Square or direct Rosa Parks to refuse to give up her seat on the bus in Montgomery, we really did not organize or orchestrate the Million Man March.

The now historic Million Man March is what theologians would classify as one of those "kairotic" points in history where forces are moved, people are assembled and aligned, in spite of undermanned, underfunded, unorganized efforts to make something happen.

Indeed, when we consider the absence of the type of organization and planning that it would ordinarily take to put forth such an effort, we must conclude that the Million Man March was nothing short of an act of God. When you add to that the ominous, organized opposition that we faced from the mainstream media, as well as within the African American community, this feat becomes even more astounding.

I speak first of the lack of organization. I say this not in a derogatory manner, but simply to point out the fact that Divine Intervention was operating at its best throughout this endeavor. Washington, D.C. was the national headquarters or base for the march, and more often than not, there was total chaos and confusion with regards to lines of authority and protocol; specific plans of action, as well as dissemination of basic information for people seeking to volunteer, was also difficult to obtain. People calling from across the nation found it difficult just to get simple details about the march. If this was the scene at "headquarters", I shudder to think what was happening at the various local organizing sites.

At weekly meetings, many volunteers and potential workers went away frustrated because of a lack of specific plans of action to work on. People came to meetings excited, enthused and ready to work, only to find organizers engaged in dialectical debate which often resulted in impotent, dissatisfying intellectual masturbation.

I personally felt that there was a need for less discussion and more doing. Therefore, I re-organized the men of Union Temple Baptist Church, along with a few men from other churches, to get out into the streets to sign up men for the march.

To my utter amazement, there was an electrifying enthusiasm out in the streets. We didn't have to prompt, cajole or beg anybody to sign up. Wives signed up their husbands, mothers signed up their sons and men joyfully signed up on their own. We went into barber shops, stood

Photo by Roy Lewis

at supermarkets and fast food entrances, went to street corners and stood in malls. Everywhere we went, the response was overwhelming. We signed up over 100,000 men in the Washington Metropolitan area!!

As I talked with other local organizers here in Washington, jointly lamenting the fast-approaching march while simultaneously observing our seeming ineptitude and inefficiency, this massive outpouring of positive support made it apparent to me that there was something at work in this situation greater than mortal man.

On one occasion, while talking to Cora Masters Barry, wife of D.C. Mayor Marion Barry as well as the coordinator of the Million Man March Voter Registration effort, I remember encouraging her to just keep working, because I was convinced, from the response of the people, that this march was going to be successful in spite of us.

In addition to the lack of organization, we faced a seemingly invincible task of counteracting the organized opposition which we faced. That opposition was based on several factors. Many outside of the African American community, because of the intense hatred for Minister Louis Farrakhan and the Nation of Islam, spent great sums of money to discourage African Americans from supporting the march. Within the African American community, the main opposition was centered around fear and jealousy. Several of the main African American religious organizations allied themselves to oppose the march. Their mutual opposition was based on two separate, but related concerns.

In the first group of those African American leaders opposed to the march, some of the Christian clergy hid behind "irreconcilable theological differences", while secretly harboring fear of the retribution of white America. They were really afraid because of deeply ingrained, conditioned fear, which is a product of the psychological conditioning of racism. An incident that occurred three months before the march (July 1995) best describes this phenomenon:

> I made a request to the largest Christian ministers' conference in Washington, D.C. to allow Minister Louis Farrakhan to speak to the several hundred pastors affiliated with that body to share the vision of the Million Man March.

Needless to say, the ministers were so impressed with Minister Farrakhan's grip on the Christian scriptures that they overwhelmingly voted to support the march. However, two weeks later, the Conference President explained their backpedaling this way: "Y'all don't want to say it, but we are scared!! I'm from down deep South and I know what white people will do to you. White people will kill you!! We are afraid of white folks! That's why we don't want to march." Sadly, I must report from among all these religious leaders who say God has all power, none rebutted the president's analysis of their reluctance to participate.

The second type of fear was based on protecting their turf and ensuring their survival. They were fearful that this was a "Farrakhan Led Muslim March," and that they would lose members to the Muslims. This feeling went well beyond the simple jealousy that came from the realization that they themselves did not come up with the idea of the march themselves. As Christians, they could not fathom the idea of Christians following and supporting an idea first given to a Muslim. If they had looked closely enough, such a notion would have been quickly dispelled. The ministers would have discovered that this march came not from "him" but from God through "us"! Minister Farrakhan related to many organizers how the idea for the march evolved. Gracious and humble spirit that he is, the Minister related how seriously complex the subconscious mind is. He reminded us how we can hear something and subtly take it in, and subsequently regurgitate it, and if we are not careful, think that it came solely from us, when in actuality, the seed for the idea came from another person at another time. Minister Farrakhan told us how Rev. Hycel Talor spoke at the mosque in Chicago and gave a message where he talked about how marvelous it would be to have a day in the African American community devoted entirely to God. Later, he said Rev. James Bevel came sharing the theology of Atonement. These two thoughts, along with the old Negro play *Day of Absence*, crystallized and came out of Minister Louis Farrakhan in a "call" for a Million Man March and Day of Atonement. Thus, God used several people, some no longer with us in the flesh, to make this Divine Call. God used two Christian ministers, a Muslim minister and a playwright to sound the clarion call for black men to come back to God.

And indeed, the words of the Negro spiritual "When He calls me, I will answer; I'll be somewhere listening for my name" rang out with the greatest and most profound realism. God did call and black men did answer. In spite of the fears, the jealousy, the hatred, the organized opposition and oftimes unclear direction–God called and black men answered. They walked, they hitchhiked, they rode buses, trains and airplanes. They obviously were waiting for the "call" and "listening" for [their] name(s).

And when they arrived in Washington over one million strong, these black men, "The Wretched of the Earth," "Menace to Society," "The Incorrigible Nemesis to Just and Righteous Living," heard the call of God. There was no division, there was no killing and stealing. There was only divine caring and sharing. There was only one arrest and that was for a vendor who had improper credentials to sell his wares. What a testament to the power of God!! No one but an Almighty God could do that.

What this event says is Black Men have the God-given ability to achieve anything!!

The Creator showed us, in no uncertain terms, that "Greater is He that is in [US] than he that is in the world; God be for us [Nobody Can Be Against Us!!]" Oh you mighty [black men] accomplish what you will!!

Rev. Willie F. Wilson has pastored Union Temple Baptist Church for over 20 years. Drawing upon African heritage and contemporary economics, the 6,450 member church has distinguished itself with an elaborate investment program which has funneled more than $5 million into neighborhood housing, education and health care services. The church operates a home for homeless teenagers, a counseling and rehabilitation program for alcohol and substance abusers, rites of passage programs and other youth programs.

Photo by Third World Press

59

Part 4
Reflections On the Weight/Wait

Photo by Robert Sengstacke

REFLECTIONS ON "THE MARCH"

Mari Evans

Some ideas stand up under repetition; I believe the following concept advanced in an earlier article, does:

> "The oppressed, and we are oppressed, are crisis-oriented. We can summon a great cohesiveness in ties of extreme sadness or joy. Or trouble. For it is then that we understand on an acutely self-conscious level, our national 'family-hood.' We respond to an understood, unstated mandate, and we move from the very edges of nowhere to come together toward one end: To make, according to our various instincts and experiences, the necessary statement....We are a mystical people, moving instinctively when the drums announce danger...

Clearly the drums of Our War have sounded continuously since 1619 and danger so intensified over the past two decades that we have almost overwhelmed the drumming with the sound of our own internal screaming. I suggest that the slave condition of Africans and their descendants in North America has been more largely psychological than physical despite a 400-year history of genocide, of physical limitation and brutalization. From the beginning the ongoing struggle has always been a war for the mind of the oppressed. Two forces, diametric, opposed to each other by condition, by intent, and by their very nature-engaged in a classic confrontation. Natural opponents, coexisting within the confine of a bruising nation climate where identifiable dichotomies (the 'have and have not,' the 'can and cannot), provide working definitions for life, love, and most importantly--access.

This warfare has been unceasing for survival is the issue, as Vincent Harding has said that "the struggles for the power to define." The oppressor, determined to maintain and strengthen his power position, his privilege, is intent on heightening in-place controls and instituting new restraints and limitations–economic, life-threatening and socio-psychological--to the extent that even nominal leadership, particularly if charismatic, that arises from within the target group to challenge, is subjected to searing attack. Anything perceived as endorsement by the oppressed of ideas or personalities not approved by the oppressor has traditionally been viewed as inappropriate, the offenders loudly denounced and often economically chastised. And tradition, of course, was clearly an element to be considered by many prospective marchers.

Conversely, however, the oppressed, straining for change, had in countless ways and over four centuries of instances beyond any numbering—engaged in single acts of defiance, skirmishes, launched battles and mini-wars of destruction, flexed its muscles and vented its rage and its frustration in acts both of violence and conciliation. Every avenue had been explored. Every avenue, that is, except the physical amassing of over one million Black men in one place at one point. The place? The site of the national gov-

Photo by Roy Lewis

61

ernment, and the official figure suggest there were approximately a million plus men who physically stepped forward to make the unequivocal, unmistakable statement.

The March was an historic, cataclysmic shaking free of psychological restraints imposed early on and reluctantly but quietly shouldered as a seemingly necessary adjunct to survival and to social-economic prosperity.

White disapproval has always been the Presence watching from the sidelines, surveilling, saying who will not 'from now on': The Presence reluctantly--eventually, placated. "Play the game" has long been considered sound advice for the young." "Branch out, have your own agenda but be careful, watch your back. Be diplomatic."

But on the 16th of October, 1995, with the total array of white power (the media, employers, the agencies of minimal succor, etcetera) loudly aligned--ostensibly against the chosen leadership but actually against the implied socio-political threat of The March itself, over one million Black men left their jobs, their promising tomorrows, their acquisitions, their successes and their failures and in each others' company stepped into private cars and onto chartered busses; they boarded trains, took to the air, and by so doing defined themselves, the nature of their intent and the quality of struggle they were willing to wage.

This coming together, this mind-blowing, political agenda-building March, I would argue, is the first significant act of mass rebellion by African men against white psychological control since the onslaught of slavery four centuries ago; the first mass statement of control recovered and of new direction propogated on a national level and that despite the forces of power marshalled against them. Disapproval of such magnitude that many put their jobs, their livelihood, their continued economic survival on the line. They stepped up, bonded and were infused with and resonated to an African spirituality that has already produced challenging initiatives from Mobile to Maine.

On the strength of this new definition of themselves, this new Self-direction, we are all moved to a higher, more focused level of struggle: more inclined to roll up our sleeves, and somewhat less inclined to scream than before–and therefore so much richer.

Vincent Harding should be pleased, and DuBois, Douglas, Garvey, Henry Higland Garnett, Henry McNeil Turner and the rest, those who come down to us nameless, are all probably somewhere giving high fives.

"And to come together
in a comingtogetherness
vibrating with the fires of pure knowing
reeling with power
ringing with the sound above sound above sound

Who
can be born
black
and not exult!

—Mari Evans

Mari Evans, educator, writer, musician and playwright resides in Indianapolis. Formerly Distinguished Writer and Assistant Professor, ASRC, Cornell University, over the past twenty years she has taught at Indiana University, Purdue University, Northwestern University, Washington University, St. Louis, the State University of New York at Albany, the University of Miami at Coral Gables, and at Spelman College, Atlanta. Author of numerous articles, four children's books, several performed theatre pieces, two musicals and four volumes of poetry, including *I Am A Black Woman, Nightstar, and A Dark and Splendid Mass* (1992). She edited the highly acclaimed *Black Woman Writers (1950-1980): A Critical Evaluation.* Her work, familiar to students, has been widely anthologized in over 400 collections and textbooks.

Excerpt from
REQUIEM BEFORE REVIVAL

GWENDOLYN BROOKS

We still need the essential Black statement of defense and definition. Of course, we are happiest when that statement is not dulled by assimilationist urges, secret or overt. However, there is in "the souls of Black Folk"--even when inarticulate and crippled--a yearning toward Black validation.

To be Black is rich, is subtle, is nourishing and a nutrient into the universe. What could be nourishing about aiming against your nature?

I continue my old optimism. In spite of all the disappointment and disillusionment and befuddlement out there, I go on believing that the Weak among us will, finally, perceive the impressiveness of our numbers, perceive the quality and legitimacy of our essence, and take the sufficient, indicated steps toward definition, clarification.

From "Primer for Blacks"
—1979.

In the spirit and fact of the Million-and-a-half Man March, that definition -that clari-fication-came to pass steps toward Revival—

Gwendolyn Brooks

Photo by Robert L. Thornton III

Gwendolyn Brooks is Distinguished Professor of English at Chicago State University, Poet Laureate of Illinois, Pulitzer Prize Winner, recipient of the National Endowment for the Humanities Jefferson Award, and recipient of over seventy honorary doctorates. She is the author of over twenty-one books of poetry, an autobiography and a novel. Ms. Brooks is currently working on her *Collected Poems;* the sequel to her autobiography, *Report From Part Two,* will be published by Third World Press this spring.

Black Monday

Photo by Brian Jackson

by Selwyn Seyfu Hinds

The night before: "Wassup brother?" A grinning, light-skinned kid thrusts a hand towards my midsection. "Mark, Chicago," comes the pithy intro. I blink stupidly as his greeting penetrates the travel fog still clouding my brain. "Mark," he repeats. I hurriedly shift my laptop case and travel bag to the left hand so I can grasp his palm with my right. "Selwyn, Brooklyn," I respond, toothy smile crawling across my face as my defense mechanisms begin to lower. Then, on the marble floor of Washington D.C.'s Union Station, I enthusiastically throw my arms around this black man I've never seen before.

By 9 p.m., Chocolate City's vats are overflowing. A flood of brothers, and quite a few sisters, has been steadily pouring in by train, plane, automobile and foot. Some make their way over to the Convention Center, where a series of speeches and a 1 a.m. breakfast constitute the night's agenda. Others, particularly the younger set, take to the streets. At 11, my cousins and I join the nighttime throng: the fleet of cars whipping back and forth, the brothers outfitted in Brooks Brothers suits parleying with kids clad in low-slung baggy jeans and baseball caps, the gruff bouncers informing pleading patrons that there are no guest lists tonight.

An Acura Integra carrying five women pulls alongside our car. "Excuse me, sisters!" I lean out of the front window, micro-cassette recorder in hand. "I'm a writer doing a story. Would you mind if I asked you a few questions?" The group looks at me as if I'm some bizarre species of pick-up animal. Then the driver smiles and gives an almost imperceptible nod. "Why did you guys decide to come down?" I yell. At that moment, the light changes. As the Acura peals away, giggles erupt from the interior, but her answer comes floating back. "Please, with all these men here?"

Marchday, 9 a.m.: The train from Shady Grove is a Babelian mix. Country-fried drawls, rapid Northeastern tones and measured Midwestern accents are on free-flow this morning—the brothers in my car are certainly a motley lot. But all exhibit the same eager, slightly anxious anticipation: they exchange introductions in quick murmurs, their laughter rings out nervously and loudly. As eyes meet, palms are slapped and nods delivered. The marchgoers have begun to slip into the sense of community that will characterize the entire day.

As we arrive at the Mall, we're greeted by the morning chill and a group of effusive Nation of Islam members. "Good morning brother, thank you for coming!" The bow-tied line bestows an energetic handshake or hug upon everyone that passes within reach. It takes some getting used to. There's an oft overlooked point buried beneath America's pile of race typecasting: no one fears brothers more than brothers themselves. I, for one, have never been among a large group of strange black men without my guard working overtime; usually the feel of unknown brown bodies pressed against my spine sets off a cacophony of fight-or-flight bells.

Letting go of that mindset proves to be the most profound facet of the march. Temporary lovefest or not, the shit feels good. The respect flows in waves: "Excuse me, brother," "How are you, brother?" "Go ahead, brother, you were here first." I find myself wondering if this is what things were like back in the romanticized black past, before my generation sunk into the depths of self-annihilation.

Marchday, 2 p.m.: Tasha stands five feet or so from me, a small woman wrapped in an orange jacket to ward off the afternoon cool. I amble over and introduce myself, breaking her intense meditation on Jesse Jackson's speech. After fixing me with a cool gaze, she responds: "Even though it was originally intended for black men only, I couldn't let this go on without seeing it. I just had to experience it. I'm only 17, and I always wanted to be a part of something that might make changes in our community. I had to come so I could be part of something done during my generation."

She pauses and cocks her ear as Jackson reaches a crescendo. "It's been very inspirational," she says thoughtfully. "I just hope that the men out here now take

something home. I think they should do this every year. It shouldn't end right here."

The afternoon plods forward, the speakers trudge on and off. I amuse myself by standing on my cousin's shoulders and gawking at the sea of black faces. For the most part, the crowd is patient. But by four, legs are tired and the day is getting colder. Folks want to hear the keynote speaker, Minister Farrakhan. Indeed, the final three speakers barely make it through their presentations intact. Finally, the man arrives. Three hours later, I depart, head swimming with numerology, humor, and sociopolitical deconstructions.

On the way home, I reflect upon the familiar litany of complaints about Farrakhan: his bootstrap ideology sounds like a page from the right-wing handbook, he doesn't critique capitalism, and he comes off, all too often, like a raving anti-Semite. True enough. But the complaints strike me as disingenuous—Dole and company, you can't harpoon the NOI for anti-Semitism without accounting for the Christian Coalition, an organization headed by the Jewish-conspiracy-spouting Pat Robertson. Abe Foxman and company, you can't skewer people for trivializing evocations of Hitler and the Holocaust and reserve that right for yourself [as Foxman tries to in a subsequent *New York Times* article when he likened the Fruit of Islam to Hitler's "brownshirts"]. And as for the bootstrap matter, Farrakhan's self-help doctrine hardly resembles hollow right-wing platitudes. The right's practice of telling folks to pull themselves up is coupled with vicious attacks on the structures that lend them a modicum of support, while Farrakhan's is fleshed out by tangible outreach into the meanest streets and souls of besieged black America.

In this way, of this afternoon, Farrakhan has reached me. I ride home lifted by my rekindled sense of communion and spiritual faith.

AfterMarch: In the aftermath, I've been media surfing, amazed at the degree to which folks don't get it. Representative Gary Franks' tap-dancing jigs prior to the march were bad enough. But the degree to which the mainstream focus on Farrakhan has distorted everyone's vision is startling: Newt Gingrich, taking great care not to implicate the participants (after all, the bootstrap thing does seem to mesh with his agenda), carrying on about Farrakhan's "paranoid view" of history while attempting

> **"To me, it's plain that October 16 was just the last gambit in an old contest. Once again America, it's your move."**

to attribute the minister's appeal to "the failure of conventional leadership"; Ray Kerrison's indignant column in the *New York Post* that sought to demonstrate progress by offering Oprah Winfrey and Bill Cosby as examples of upwardly mobile black people flourishing "all over this country"; and A.M. Rosenthal's hysteric outpourings in the *Times* about the march's supposed divisiveness.

Aside from sheer arrogance, there are a couple of underlying assumptions in all this huffin' and puffin' that defeat good sense. First, viewing the march as divisive assumes that American society was "together" in the first place, a view that only the most rose-colored glasses can deliver. Second, as long as folks refuse to acknowledge the destructive and continuing nature of white supremacy—to whites and blacks alike—we ain't going nowhere.

To me, it's plain that October 16 was just the latest gambit in an old contest. Once again, America, it's your move.

Selwyn Hinds is a contributing writer/music editor for *The Source,* a magazine which features articles on rap music and culture. His article was previously published in *The Village Voice.*

Photo by Robert Sengstacke

Photo by Robert L. Thornton III

Photo by Robert L. Thornton III

MY SOUL LOOKS BACK IN WONDER AT HOW WE GOT OVER: REFLECTIONS ON THE MILLION MAN MARCH

Safisha Madhubuti, Ph.D.

Today I was transformed by two spiritual experiences: Mahalia Jackson exhiliratingly singing "My soul looks back in wonder at how we got over" and savoring Tom Feelings' capture of the Middle Passage through his charcoal drawings of African men, women and children during our terror-filled journey to the western world. The question I face daily as a mother of two sons and as a daughter and as a teacher of African-American children and adolescents is what values, beliefs, habits of mind will provide these young people with the tenacity and vision to eke out what Vincent Harding has called liberated zones. These liberated zones are spaces–physical, intellectual, spiritual, artistic, economic–in which Africans in America have the freedom and the sources to develop and implement goods, services, ideas, and forms of social organization that sustain life for our people, now and into the future. As I watched the Million Man March on television, my heart and my mind said this event was the metaphor for the sustenance of such liberated zones.

That Saturday before the March, my husband, Haki Madhubuti, and my two sons, Bomani Garvey and Akili Malcolm, left for Washington, D.C. Because Haki had responsibilities to speak on the podium, I had deliberately indoctrinated my sons with explicit instructions for their safety. I was torn between positive anticipation of a million men, women and children on the Washington Mall and fear of meager numbers. In either case, I did not want my sons separated in a crowd of thousands of strangers. They were never to leave one another's side and stay with the family friend who had made his personal pledge to me to look out for my boys.

The morning of the March, I went to Fairgate High School (pseudonym). I am involved in a research project at that school, working with the faculty to transform the English Language Arts curriculum to reflect and build on the cultural strengths that its African American student population brings. Despite the call by organizers of the March for a day of absence, I felt a moral obligation to be with my students on this fortuitous day. Fairgate High School, like

Illustration Murry DePillars

68

so many high schools in our urban communities, has a force of uniformed policemen and women as well as security guards who patrol the halls and doors of the school daily. Two of my freshmen students are on parole. The vast majority of the freshman class, in fact, the student body, have reading scores well below national norms. More important, the students start the school year, on the whole, so distanced from a desire to learn in school that it is not uncommon to walk the halls, looking into classrooms where teachers talk and students have their heads on desks. Every day I walk the hall, I hear "f...k" and other forms of derogatory language that the mothers and fathers of these young people, I hope, would shudder to hear so openly in school. Every day I hear from administrators or teachers another horror story. I do not share these conversations to criticize the faculty of this school, but rather to highlight how daunting the challenge we as a community, as parents, as educators face. This generation of young people must consider what it means "to get over" in the sense that the spiritual communicates; what it means to get over is much more complex than ever before. Is getting over making money from selling drugs; is getting over thinking you've found love by having a baby when you're still growing up yourself; is getting over hoop dreams that take you as far from the Black community as you can get; is getting over working for, producing for businesses that do not invest jobs and resources into African America communities? One of my freshman students argued vehemently with me one day that becoming a manager for McDonald's was a gateway for management anywhere. Is this vision of getting over what sustained us as a people through the Middle Passage, through the African Holocaust of Enslavement, through Jim Crow, through generations of lynching, through the evils of de jure segregation, through generations of urban and rural poverty? I think not!

I began video taping the March at 6 a.m. in order to have some footage to share with those students who did come to class that morning. Five of the twenty-four students enrolled in my freshman class showed up. As this small group of young people looked at the monitor and saw an ocean of Black men, young and old, women and children flooding the gates of the nations' capital, their eyes shown bright with amazement and pride. There were no words to encapsulate what the students and I shared in those moments.

I returned home after my class and continued taping throughout the day.

The alliance of Nationalists, Pan Africanists, Black democrats, Muslims, Christians, Black Jews, Black men, Black women, Black children, gang leaders and politicians who adorned the podium were the metaphor for community building that is so desperately needed. While I remained skeptical, tears still shed as gang leaders asked for forgiveness and pledged to work for unity and peace. I believed that the energy of those people present, if institutuionalized in neighborhoods across the country, had the power and promise of enforcing that call for peace. The culminating moment for me came when Minister Farrakhan called for the singing of "To God Be the Glory" and cameras captured Black men, most of whom did not know one another, men of multiple generations and political persuasions who hugged, who touched some inner sensibility in one another that brought tears to them and to us. These tears we Black men, women and children shared in those moments were cauterizing, healing, uplifting. They represented how we got over in the sense that spiritual captures. Those tears were shared waters we traversed, a common pain and a common pride, a shared sense of purpose, the sense of being one people–certainly with many differences–but joined by a shared mission. It is this sense of shared mission that took us through the days of share cropping, instilling in our children the necessity of learning to read, write and count; that took us through the days of the civil rights movement to build schools as liberated zones in back hills of the rural, impoverished south. How each of us who was transformed and transposed by the experience of the

Photo by Third World Press

69

Million Man March translated that sense of Black Union into practice will indeed determine the future of the generation of my children and those young people of the Fairgate High schools and elementary schools across this nation. However that practice manifests itself, I am absolutely clear that this spirit is what embodied Harriet Tubman as she risked her life 19 times carrying out guerrilla warfare against the African Holocaust of Enslavement, is what embodied Ida B. Wells as she carried her baby on her back traversing this country in the fight against lynching, is what embodied Septima Clark and Ella Baker as they taught and politically organized in the trenches of the south.

Anecdotal as they may be, I take hope in what I have seen since the March. I stand in stores where Black men announce that they were there, where Black men publicly commit to finding organizations to serve as home bases for work with young people. This I have seen from men I do not know, from men in public places, stores, gas stations, bus corners. This kind of public spirit I have not personally seen since the days of the Black Power Movement of the late '60s and '70s and the Civil Rights Movement of the '60s. Time will surely tell whether this spirit is a short-term high or a sustainable building block for community development.

I can say with awesome pride that I am thankful my sons were there, that my daughter Laini Nzinga, although not physically at the March, shared the spirit with her college comrades, and that I witnessed this monumental moment of definition. The event was unabashedly and mindfully Black, a liberated zone of promise, and a launching pad for our future development and sustenance.

Safisha Madhubuti is Director of The Institute of Positive Education, an African-centered educational institution in Chicago, Illinois and is associate professor in the School of Education and Social Policy at Northwestern University.

The Epiphany

Calvin R. Atkins

Dawn creeps over kindred souls, revealing kings waiting and anticipating being among a million. To study these spirits is to study the development of humanity. From the Nile, Euphrates, Congo, or the Mississippi these souls have seen the opulence of civilization, and experienced the bitterness of enslavement. What makes them so strong? The same force that gave the world life, music, knowledge. The same force that gave the world Steven Biko, Nelson Mandela, and Kwame Nkrumah. The same force that gave the world Nat, Denmark, Gabriel, Frederick, Toussaint, Booker, DuBois, Marcus, Elijah, Malcolm, and Martin. The same force that gave the world Hapshsetsut, Nzinga, Nandi, Harriet, Ida, Mary, Elaine, Sojourner, Zora, and Rosa. The same God that gave the world you. The same God that gave the world me. The same God.

The sun has fully risen and exposes what the darkness concealed; so has the African. The scene of one million Black men descending on the capitol illuminates the plight of a peoples sojourn in a foreign land. The African is the scapegoat for America's domestic problems. The image of our people, our men, are falsely conjured up to absolve someone's crime or fill someone's political agenda. Exhausted with the status of a reprobate, the African sounded the drums. The beat we universally understood; put away our "Willie Lynch" divisions and organize. Empower. The rhythm, melodic and attractive to the spirit, called for unity without the dogmatism of uniformity.

The sun moves, casting shadows in places previously unseen, so are the Africans. From all walks of life we gathered on the capitol. We greeted each other with hugs, shakes, and peace signs. No one was discourteous, disrespectful, or any other "disses" many Black men mortally guard against. The air was filled with the aroma of atonement, the scent of reconciliation. It was not uncommon to see teary eyed men moved by the spirit, moved by the brotherhood. We laughed. We talked. We shared ideas about life, family, and our communities. Each speaker reminded us of our obligation and responsibility as Black men to God and our people.

The sun sets and leaves one location to radiate in another, so too are the Africans. The day is coming to a close, and the keynote speaker is addressing the crowd. We reflect on the previous guides and their insight on the issues that concerned us all. Even though we were optimistic, we are all too aware of the actuality of our situation. Bullet proof glass to protect our leaders, S.W.A.T. teams on every rooftop, helicopters circling the throng, state police officers positioned in five minute increments on the highways, were constant reminders of our reality in America. When the Park District recorded 400,000 instead of a million, it only revealed the fact that this system still sees us as 3/5 man. After the final prayer, we brought closure to that majestic day. A day that the earth-quaked with spiritual resolution, and the aftershocks continue to be felt around the planet. Determined to be the vanguards for community uplifting; affirming our responsibility as fathers, sons, and husbands; accepting the task to be the catalyst for moral transformation of the country; Black men boarded the buses for home. Nightfall darkens the world, so too will the Africans. Hotep

Calvin Atkins is a senior attending Chicago State University. The twenty-four year old Business major is a very active member of the CSU community. He is a member of the campus chapter of the NAACP, the Student Government Association, and Concerned Students of Chicago State University. Mr. Atkins helped to organize fund-raisers so that CSU could send three buses to the march. He was also instrumental in forming the Concerned Students of Chicago State University in order to implement the march's goals.

REFLECTIONS ON AN OCTOBER'S MARCH

Cranston Knight

Whose feet are these that step, one foot in front of the next? Feet that once moved in random direction now march with determined cadence. These feet, some tender, some cracked, sun-baked and blistered: step lightly, others pound, some land with grace, others land uncoordinated. Whose feet are these that walk into the eye of the Nation? They step to the tune of a blues harmonica, up from Mississippi counties, small towns that border the delta mud. Dusty fields from Arkansas and Louisiana, and from the Carolinas: Geeche feet. Feet that walk the streets of Harlem, Watts, Newark, Detroit, and Chicago. Poor feet, class feet, saffron, ebony and bronze feet surround the reflecting pool in Washington D.C. Now joined together these feet march in tempo, certainty, steadfastness, stir red with fervor. Yet, they know instinctively, and from past history, that without touching, they will melt in the pavement, ravaged by forces that loathe their blackness.

Whose hands are these? Hands that reach above and beyond, touching the air currents that carry notes from the Continental Congress. Hands excluded, millions of parted fingers excluded from participating in the glory of democratic principals. Today these once excluded hands are raised in solidarity: Freedom. Hands that have the commonality of slaves, freemen and peons. Hands that have felt segregation, and fought back in the civil rights movement. Hands that have seen incarcerations; shot away, hidden away from sunlight. Hands that know shared blackness, hands that know, as only these hands could, what race can do to hands that dream. "Strange Fruit," so, sang by Billie Holiday, tormented by a lynching she witnessed once as she traveled through the South. Some of these hands have felt her song, they know the price of dreaming: Hands can be cut off, burned, twisted.

Whose ears are these? A million pair once listened to a thousand words that traveled down their auditory canal and called for the abandonment of tyranny in the young Republic. "What is it that gentlemen wish?" Patrick Henry stated before the Virginia Convention of 1775. "What would they have? Is life so dear, or peace so sweet, as to be purchased at the price of chains and slavery? Forbid it almighty God! I know not what course others may take; but as for me, give me liberty or give me death!" These words flowed across the green grass of Lexington and Concord, as did those of Thomas Jefferson. "All men are created equal...they are endowed by their Creator with certain

Photo by Robert L. Thornton III

inalienable rights...among these are life, liberty and the pursuit of happiness."

The philosophical foundation of the Republic has never been dampened, despite the racial intolerance that permeates the Union. Racism has often overridden the words of the Constitution. And yet, it is the word "Liberty" that sings and swirls into the ear drums of a million men who march on the land that their forefathers once tiled. Two hundred years after it was written, these words "endowed by their Creator with certain inalienable rights," poured into the auris of Black Men.

The words were sweet to the taste buds: freedom. Swept upon the euphoria of bodies from the past, spirits, apparitions (King marched this way, and Caney marched this way, and a thousand other unknown names marched this way), their pallets savored the tonality of inalienable rights, the right to be Black in America; march and not be killed or jailed for assembling. To have the right to be seen and heard in America, (Black, heard and seen in America?) this is an inalienable right! Then each man in the crowd of crowds lifted the weight of oppression and clasped hands in brotherhood.

Whose feet are these that stop on the Capitol's lawn? Whose hands are these that feel the cool air? Whose ears are these that hear a two hundred year call? Black Men on the move, marching despite, "Strange Fruit," marching against forces that loathe their Blackness, marching to liberate their souls. They are now filled with the Africanization of the Republic: Amri ina Mungu (commanding is of God).

The Nation of Patrick Henry and Thomas Jefferson, of Lexington and Concord, was shaken, for it had excluded the very men that were now marching. Those men who had not been written about in the very document that would give them the right to march, those who were exiled in their own national of birth: they were marching. The country would ask in both inquisitiveness and fear, "Who are these apparitions that speak to us before the noon sunrise?" The men did not answer back; the country could not comprehend that these men did not come to speak to them, or with them. They had not come from the Carolinas, or Louisiana, Arkansas or Harlem to dialogue with the Nation. They had come for reasons known only to themselves.

On a day, a Fall color would blanket the Capital and a million men of black hue, hearing a distant voice, feeling distant words,would close ranks to affirm themselves as leaders of their people, and to declare their inalienable rights.

Cranston Knight is a professor at Loyola University in Chicago. He holds a Master of Arts degree in East Asian and American History from Northeastern Illinois University. Mr. Knight is the author of *Freedom Song* and the editor of *Tour of Duty,* an anthology of short stories and poetry by Vietnam veterans. His forthcoming book from Third World Press, *In The Garden of the Beast,* is a collection of poetry which charts the lives of an African American soldier, his Vietnamese lover and their child.

THE MARCH IS ON

Steve Cobb

The March is on
The mighty march is on
Let's organize and work together

The March is on
The mighty march is on
working hand in hand with all my brothers

We're a nation inside of a nation
We've come together as mass confirmation
That regardless of denomination
We hear redemption's call

As the love God has provided
The ancestral spirits have guided
Us from all that has kept us divided
Into a spiritual bond
Black men are standing tall

The March is on
The mighty march is on
Let's organize and work together

The March is on
We came here to atone
It's time to pull our house together

As we reconcile ourselves with our history
As we shoulder our responsibilities
For our children, women and our families
Rebuild their faith in us

As we march for this transformation
Through the capital of this violent nation
It's clear that we are owed reparations
Yet we understand our future's in our hands

The March is on
The mighty march is on
Let's organize and work together

The March is on
And now we're millions strong
With our sisters, daughters, wives and mothers

Like the lioness protects her cubs in the pride
Through you the black woman our families survive
You've been the backbone, our refuge when our options were few
Your struggle and sacrifices have brought us all through

Photo by Roy Lewis

Steve Cobb is a musician, composer and producer. Along with his wife, vocalist and musician Chavunduka, Mr. Cobb released the highly acclaimed *Seven Principles* cassette and CD in 1993. *The March Is On* are lyrics from music of the same name; the song was released in October 16th, in observance of MMM/DOA. The tape is available from COBBALA Records, P.O. Box 4353, Chicago, Illinois 60680.

A TIME OF POSSIBILITY:
Continuing the Historical Legacy

Tiamoyo Karenga

The year 1995 initiated many substantive developments in the continuing historical legacy and struggle of African American people. One of the most definitive markers was the Million Man March/Day of Absence (MMM/DOA) on October 16 in Washington, D.C. Thirty years had passed since the definitive struggle marker of the numerous revolts across the U.S. which demonstrated our resistance to the oppressive character of the society. Therefore, this massive march was not only important to us, as a people, but to the country as a whole, as a major demonstration of resistance given the lull in the movement for radical social change.

The MMM/DOA, as a joint project set forth in its Mission Statement, was also important from a Kawaida standpoint because it: (1) put a "priority need" and focus on men without "denying or minimizing the equal rights, role and responsibility of Black women...in our struggle"; (2) continued the historical legacy of mutual support of Black men and women in love, life and struggle; (3) demonstrated the value and validity of the process of building a Black united front through the Kawaida principle of operational unity; and (4) put forward as a positive mirror the possibility and resultant effect of cooperative massive organization and mobilization.

To first see the MMM/DOA as an emphasis on the "priority need" of men to come forward and stand up after constantly being asked to by Black women seems only logical and necessary. For the MMM/DOA in no way denied or minimized our equal rights, our role, our responsibility as Black women in the struggle for our people. It appears that, as some women have said, they were coming forward against the March because they were being asked to do so behind the scenes. This argument was made for the most part by academic-based and professional women out of touch

with the majority sentiment of both Black women and Black people on this issue. For so many more Black women, publicly as well as privately, also said that they were happy to see Black men stand up and commit themselves before the community, nation and entire world to a better life for themselves, their families and their own people.

One of the most negative responses to the MMM/DOA was the intentional misinformation by the media and others to pose the Black man and Black woman against each other because of this March. We will fail to see the importance of the outcome of this March if we do not realize that, yes, initially Minister Louis Farrakhan stated that he wanted women to stay at home, but it was through active historical engagement of our organization Us, both its women and men, as well as others, that we changed this focus early enough to participate fully in the process. We must stop the negative generalizations against one another, as male and female, that only dichotomize and polarize us and confront

Photo by Robert A. Sengstacke

the fact of the oppression of all of us by the dominant society. For only in this way can we move to end our oppression and build the love, life and community we're always seeking.

Secondly, we continue our historical legacy of mutual support in working together in process and function to insure that the project goes forward and succeeds. Our foremothers and forefathers, such as Anna Julia Cooper, Maria Stewart, Frederick Douglass, Marcus Garvey, among so many, taught us the indispensability of mutual support in building our lives and waging our struggle. Here it would be good to remember Anna Julia Cooper's stress on the complementary of men and women in all things good and beautiful. She says that "there is a feminine as well as masculine side to truth, that these are related not as inferior or superior, not as better and worse, not as weaker or stronger, but as complements—complements in one necessary and symmetric whole." This represents the best of our tradition of mutual respect and support. And we continue this legacy through organizing the March and continuing work coming out of the MMM/DOA. Thirdly, the value and validity of the process itself in building a Black united front to carry out the MMM/DOA has also shown that only through this process can we as a people confront those obstacles effectively before us and demonstrate the possibilities that can be shaped and made to come into fruition. It was the coming together of many different and diverse groups and persons under the umbrella of "operational unity," developed initially in 1966 by Dr. Maulana Karenga during the Black Power Conferences, that caused this massive response to a need for Black men to stand up and assume a new and expanded responsibility in the community and in the struggle for liberation.

Finally, the MMM/DOA put forward the positive mirror of possibility and resultant effect of cooperative massive organization and mobilization. There is no doubt, real or imagined, that the MMM/DOA was the largest in the history of the U.S., that one of the most severely demeaned and discredited segments of society, Black men, had come together in their diversity to put forward their statement on the international stage and that the majority of Black people, themselves, benefited and appreciated it from wherever they were. Likewise, Black women must be credited for assuming leadership in mobilizing and organizing still millions more in the boycotts and teach-ins across the country on the Day of Absence in this joint project. We must now struggle to retain the awesomeness and the renewed and expanded sense of responsibility, the self-respect and possibility that this joint project created and transform it into ongoing active engagement in our communities. This was a major event in our lives and history, and we should not let it pass by us to be remembered only by a few newspaper clippings, videotapes, souvenirs and photos rather than ongoing transformative social action. It was an honor to have been part of this effort and simultaneously it created a greater obligation to continue the legacy.

Tiamoyo Karenga is a lecturer at the Kawaida Institute of Pan-African Studies, Los Angeles; a Seba (moral teacher) in the ancient Egyptian tradition; a long-time activist and member of the executive circle of the Organization Us, and a graduate student in anthropology and Black Studies, CSU Long Beach. She is currently co-writing with Maulana Karenga a book on the moral texts of ancient Egyptian women.

ONE MILLION MEN

Walter Gholson

In *Face at the Bottom of the Well*, Derrick Bell uses a quote by Julius Lester to set up the introduction to one of the book's social fiction stories, "The Afro-Lantic Awakening": "The idea of a Black Nation (in America) seems so far-fetched as to be ludicrous, but if you entertained it for a minute, even as an impossible idea, it should give you a feeling of wholeness and belonging you've never had and can never have as long as Blacks have to live in a country where they are despised."

"The Afro-Lantic Awakening" is a short tale about the appearance of a newly developed island off the coast of South Carolina, a mass of land that can only be inhabited by the Americans of African descent. The U.S. Government's first few attempts to invade this new land mass with an American force proved futile and the crew members barely escaped. They reported having difficulty breathing and losing consciousness. This is not the case for the African Americans. "After a courteous first few steps the crew discovered that they didn't need their space suits nor the special breathing equipment." The Black American party reported feeling "exhilarated and euphoric unlike the drug or alcohol induced sensation to escape." They described feeling a heightened sense of self-esteem, of feeling liberated when they were asked to explain the reluctance to return though ordered to do so and why they spent several days exploring this new land that only Black Americans could live on.

Like many of the million plus Black men who attended the march and rally in Washington D.C., I experienced this heightened sense of self-esteem. I felt liberated for the first time since my birth though I had no idea what was going to happen and it really didn't matter because the prospect of assembling one million Black men on the Washington Mall in downtown Washington, D.C., on a Monday morning had no precedent. Nothing like this had ever been proposed before and no group had ever estimated attracting an attendance of one million people during all of the thirteen years I lived in the "chocolate city."

I remember demonstrations by the Hippies, the Yippies, the Moonies, pro and anti-abortion advocates, Vietnam vets, the Shriners, the KKK and the second attempt to March on Washington, but none of these efforts come close to equaling the numbers of people, the discipline of the participants or the unique purpose of the Million Man March.

As I walked towards the train station at Metro Center to wait for some of the brothers I had contacted to get off the subway, I was struck by the obvious absence of the usual number of White people walking around downtown D.C. on a typical Monday morning. In their absence were massive groups of Black men getting off the metro trans coming in from outside of the city. They had been replaced by bus loads of Black people coming into the city from all

Photo by Brian Jackson

parts of the nation. The usual Monday morning crowds had been usurped by car and van pools of dark skinned people from all over the United States moving in the same direction.

As we walked towards the site of the rally, we were joined at every corner by more brothers heading towards the Washington Mall. We were caught up in the pre-dawn spirit of the day that began with the morning call to worship and prayer, to the sound of African drummers, to the sight of a million Black men walking towards the capitol building, coming from every direction as the Monday morning sun began to shine on the mall named for a slave owner who became the first president of this country.

This day we were under the grace and the aura of peace, good will and mutual respect. This theme covered the entire march and rally. There were no reports of disorder, no black-on-black crimes happened. No one required the services of the thousands of government police that were assigned to this event. None of the brothers were intoxicated; there were no dead beat dads, thugs, players, dope dealers, hustlers, pimps in the house. There were no chronically unemployed ex-convicts on probation for life there. All those media image props seemed to vanish when the light on the CNN camera came on at the break of dawn on October 16, 1995.

And just like the first crew to walk on the land mass in Bell's "Afro-Lantic Awakening," we who dared to experience the liberating feeling of security, unity, purpose and love that is often not available in many parts of America, on that day, discovered that we didn't need the specialized attitudes that protected us from being seen as weak in the hood. Most of us Black males found out that we are not as bad off as the mass media has portrayed us.

On this sunny Monday morning, there were no images of gangsters to be found, no child molesters or rapists showed up, no hijackers of cars with little White boys in the back seat came to the Million Man March. No one showed up to sell drugs, alcohol or women on street corners. No users of the infamous N word came by the rally. No gang signs were flashed, and no one represented anything but life and respect for the day designed to move us toward a more perfect union. No one entering the twenty-two blocks designated as the march site could escape the overwhelming feeling of purpose that permeated the collective. In the years to come those who participated will be able to say that they were there and that because of their activity, they changed their direction. These men will be able to say, to all who will listen, that on that day in October, they vowed to cease their unrighteousness.

Those who were there on this day will be able to say that they committed themselves to continue or begin to create positive changes in themselves, to seek enlightenment and to continue the unfinished task of building a national infrastructure that will be able to support us all in the event of a national crisis like the failure of the American economy.

One of the characters in the comic strip Pogo by Walt Kelly says, "I have seen the enemy and they is us." I have also seen the enemy and among them were some of us. Certainly, many of those who condemned the Million Man March wanted to diminish support for the march. Many of them used rationales that ranged from intellectual arrogance to a blatant fear of Black American unity.

The Black Christian Right said they could not preach about Jesus on Sunday morning and then follow minister Louis Farrakhan and the Nation of Islam on Monday. Many of the well-paid brothers said that they didn't want to talk about the march over lunch, that they didn't want to give people the impression that they might be anti-white or anti-Semitic, or that they were Muslims or nationalists. They said that since they had always been responsible parents and good tax-paying citizens, they didn't have anything to atone for, nor anyone with whom to reconcile. And so on that morning in October when the call for Black Men to assemble was sounded, it was not heard by those brothers. And I can forgive their being short-sighted because I know that one of the principle reasons for their not attending is the fact that they knew that if they supported such a demonstration for freedom, justice, equality, and economic independence by Black men, they would be permanently labeled as enemies of the state of White American supremacy.

While I do understand that many of the brothers who really wanted to attend the march couldn't, I will never understand those for whom finance was not a problem . They are obviously suffering from the long-term effects of a brain that has been thoroughly washed clean of its original material. This brainwashing can be the explanation for any belief that we should not come together in love, peace and harmony to take care of some pressing family business.. We all know the startling statistics and the increasing number of victims and casualties from the undeclared war on the Black community.

So on that day the world should have known that we no longer needed to explain our behavior to the network news hounds or the electronic spin doctors. It was clear that we came to heal old wounds, settle disputes, and begin the work of cultivating something that we could take back with us. We came to get something we could plant in our towns and cities, in our churches and mosques, in our hoods and barrios, and we came in numbers too vast for our collective oppressors to count accurately.

Walter Gholson is a poet, artist and coordinator of the African-American Father & Son Program at Chicago State University. He also serves as Acting Director of the Office of Student Activities at Chicago State. Mr. Gholson was the 1994 winner of the Open Poetry Reading Award, sponsored by the Gwendolyn Brooks Center for Black Literature and Creative Writing.

Part 5
The Critical Eye

Photo by Robert Sengstacke

BEYOND THE MILLION MAN MARCH

Dr. Conrad W. Worrill

The Million Man March called by Minister Louis Farrakhan and the Nation of Islam on December 14, 1994 and held on October 16, 1995 was a thunderous success.

More than a million Black men from all walks of life and from all geographic locations in the United States, and parts of the western hemisphere, descended upon the United States Capitol, Washington, D.C., in an unprecedented historic march and rally that has profoundly impacted on the whole world.

Minister Louis Farrakhan and all the laborers in the Nation of Islam, who virtually suspended many of their projects inside the Nation of Islam, over the last ten months, deserve all praise for their dedication and commitment to making this march the most successful Black Movement march in the history of the United States.

The same praise can be rendered to Dr. Benjamin Chavis and the members of the African American Leadership Summit, the members of the National Black United Front (NBUF), the members of the All African Peoples Revolutionary Party, and particularly Bob Brown, the members of the US Organization and Dr. Maulana Karenga, and a host of scholars and activists such as Ron Daniels, Dr. Charshee McIntryre, Dr. Cornel West, Bob Law, and Haki Madhubuti who endorsed the march without hesitation and began mobilizing from its inception.

Most importantly, the Black masses of men who responded to Minister Farrakhan's call for the Million Man March are due the real praise. The unsung heroes are brothers in more than 400 cities throughout the United States in churches, block clubs, fraternities, professional organizations, community organizations, mosques, colleges and universities, high schools, government agencies, factories, corporations, banks, hospitals, Black newspapers, television and radio stations and military personnel who, through their families and extended families, were the foundation of why this march made history.

In this regard, the masses of Black women deserve all praise also for the work they did, across the country, in making the march a success. It was indeed inspiring to observe, all over the country, Black men and women working cooperatively in pursuing all the mobilizing that is necessary to achieve the objective of helping to mobilize a million Black men to participate in the October 16, 1995 Million Man March.

Everywhere that I have travelled and everyone that I have spoken with, since the march, is still focused on this

Photo by Third World Press

80

tremendous impact. The more people discuss their experiences in participating in the march, the more it becomes obvious that the spirit of the Million Man March will live in the hearts and minds of African people for eternity.

Now that we have showered ourselves with praise, it is time to take the spirit of our Holy Day, Day of Atonement, Reconciliation and Responsibility and Day of Absence and begin the process of taking advantage of the great momentum that has engulfed the African world community. We are obligated to take the spirit of the Million Man March and organize around concrete issues, projects and programs that are in the best interest of the African community in America and throughout the world. In other words, what is the next step beyond the march?

As Chairman of the National Black United Front (NBUF), and as a national Million Man March organizer, through the National Million Man March Organizing Committee, I offer the following suggestions for our continued organizing beyond the march.

First, it is imperative that we keep the coalitional aspect of the march alive at both the local and national levels. That is, the Local Organizing Committees that were established in more than 400 cities should remain intact as a vehicle that now begins addressing the variety of issues that impact on local African-American communities throughout the United States.

Secondly, the National Million Man March Organizing Committee should re-direct its energies into helping to build the leadership collective of the National African American Leadership Summit. In this connection, we will continue to expand the work of the National Black United Front (NBUF).

As I have indicated in previous articles, we must not forget that we are still struggling for the acquisition of Black Power and the Mission Statement of the march (which is the official march document) gives us some direction for our continued quest for Black Power and independence.

Again, credit must be given to Dr. Maulana Karenga for not only assembling the material, but actually writing the Mission Statement.

The Mission Statement was published by Sankore Press, Third World Press, and the FCN Publishing Company that had the collective input of Dr. Benjamin Chavis, Ron Daniels, Minister Louis Farrakhan, Dr. Maulana Karenga, Mawina Kouyate, Bob Law, Haki

Photo by Third World Press

Madhubuti, Leonard Muhammad, Dr. Imari Obadele, Rev. Frank Reid, Rev. Willie Wilson, myself and a host of other movement scholars, activists and organizers.

In the Mission Statement, we said "The Million Man March and Day of Absence can only have lasting value if we continue to work and struggle beyond this day. Thus, our challenge is to take the spirit of this day, the process of mobilization and the possibilities of organization and turn them into on-going structures and practices directed toward our liberation and flourishing as a people."

We offered some of the following ideas for continued organizing beyond the march:

- the follow-up development of an expanded Black political agenda and the holding of a Black Political Convention to forge this agenda for progressive political change;
- a massive and ongoing voter registration of Black people as independents; using our vote to insist and insure that candidates address the Black agenda; and creating and sustaining a progressive independent political movement;
- the on-going struggle for reparations in the fullest sense, that is to say, public admission, apology and recognition of the Holocaust of African Enslavement and appropriate compensation by the government; and support of the Coyers Reparations Bill on the Holocaust;
- the continuing struggle against police abuse, government suppression, violations of civil and human rights and the industrialization of prison-

ers; and in support for the freedom of all political prisoners, prisoners' rights and their efforts to transform themselves into worthy members of the community;

- continuing and expanding our support for African Centered independent schools through joining their boards, enrolling our children, being concerned and active parents, donating time, services and monies to them and working in various other ways to insure that they provide the highest level of culturally-rooted education;
- strengthening and supporting organizations and institutions of the Black community concerned with the uplifting and liberation of our people by joining as families and persons, volunteering service, giving donations and providing and insisting on the best leadership possible.

Beyond the Million Man March we are compelled to implement these ideas and many, many more. We now have the power of our spirit to accomplish all that we collectively decide must be done if we get organized and continue to cooperate with each other.

We owe it to our ancestors and those yet to be born to use this moment in history to heighten our struggle for the liberation of African people!

Dr. Conrad Walter Worrill received his Ph. D. from the University of Wisconsin. His field of study is political history, social theory and curriculum and instruction. He is presently chairman and professor of the Department of Inner City Studies Education, Northeastern Illinois University.

Dr. Worrill is National Chairman of the National Black United Front (NBUF) and in this capacity, through its National Plan of Action, has become a leading advocate and organizer of a World African Centered Educational Thrust. Specifically NBUF, under Dr. Worrill's leadership has been working tirelessly the last ten years to change the American public school curriculum to more accurately reflect the contributions of Africa and African people in America in all subjects.

Dr. Worrill writes a syndicated weekly column "Worrill's World" that appears in most African American newspapers across the country. These writings are currently being prepared to be published in book form titled, *African Centered Essays, Critiques and Commentaries*.

Finally, Dr. Worrill is a guest on many radio and television talk shows across the country and is constantly requested to lecture throughout America. Dr. Worrill is a weekly host of WVON's On Target Talk Show in Chicago.

Photo by Third World Press

THE MEANING OF THE MILLION MAN MARCH AND DAY OF ABSENCE

Ron Daniels

No matter what the number count of participants in the Million Man March (MMM) and Day of Absence (DOA), or problems with organization and logistics, no matter what the imperfections in terms of programmatic focus, the MMM/DOA is a defining moment for Black America in this decade. The State of Emergency afflicting the masses of Black poor and working people in Black America and the blatant Republican led drive to turn back the clock on the "gains" of the civil rights revolt of the '60s created a fertile climate for the dramatic call to action by the leader of the Nation of Islam, Minister Louis Farrakhan.

As Africans in America face the dawning of a new century it is clear that we are in the throes of the greatest crisis since the Post Reconstruction period in the 19th century. The re-emergence of raw naked racism and a massive "white backlash" against the "progress" of Black people has set the stage for political demagogues to run for public office on anti-Black, anti-people of color platforms like the Republican Contract on America. Gone is the "sympathetic" government of the '60s and '70s. Gone are the "liberal" politicians who once stood up for civil rights, affirmative action, and social programs to relieve the plight of the poor.

The crisis we face as Africans in America, however, is not simply external, it is also internal. The blatant neglect of the government has shredded the fabric of life in urban inner-city ghettos across this country. The massive unemployment, underemployment, educational inequity and poverty are major contributing factors to the drug traffic, the crime, violence and fratricide that is ripping apart many urban inner-city neighborhoods in Black America. Worse yet, there has been a dramatic erosion in the time tested moral and ethical values which our forebears forged to hold us together as a community in spite of our oppressive conditions. White supremacy has exacted an awesome toll on the sons and daughters of Africa in America.

Minister Louis Farrakhan more than any other leader in this period has captured the imagination of Black America precisely because of his steadfast denunciation of racism and white supremacy and his persistent call for moral and spiritual renewal, self reliance and self determination. Though Minister Farrahkan has remarkable appeal across classes and constituencies within the Black America, his

Photo by Robert L. Thornton III

appeal among the poor and disadvantaged is unrivaled. Hence, the enormous response to the MMM/DOA among people who have not been attracted to or participated in any mass action in their lifetime. When Farrakhan made the call for the MMM/DOA, the masses responded.

The MMM/DOA also emerged at a time when significant strides are being made to build operational unity and a united front in Black America. The call for unity among all elements of Black leadership issued by Kwesi Mfume during his tenure as Chairman of the Congressional Black Caucus, and the subsequent convening of Black Leadership Summit by Dr. Benjamin F. Chavis as Executive Director of the NAACP, were applauded by Black America as much needed initiatives designed to pull the Black Nation together in a time of grave crisis. The Summit process as it unfolded also afforded an opportunity for Minister Farrakhan to interface with a broad range of leaders from whom he had been isolated. The inclusion and leaderships of nationalist and Pan-Africanist in the Summit process has also strengthened the drive for operational unity and set the stage for a diverse spectrum of organizations, constituencies and leaders to join forces to build the MMM as an operational unity project.

All of these factors set the stage for the MMM/DOA. Tapping into the agony and aspirations of the Black masses and forging coalition among Christians, Muslims, nationalists and pan-africanists, civil rights organizations, community based organizations, civic and fraternal societies, and business and professional organizations to mobilize millions of Black people to participate in the MMM/DOA is a monumental achievement which cannot be minimized. The MMM/DOA expressed the anger and outrage of Black people about the conditions within our community thereby placing the concerns of Black America center stage before America and the world.

Obviously, anyone who can issue a call for a MMM/DOA and get massive response becomes a leader to be reckoned with within Black America. Minister Farrakhan, therefore, emerges as the pre-eminent African American leader in this period. How he handles this role will be crucial to the overall outcome of the MMM/DOA. It is vitally important that he use his enormous influence to push for operational unity and to continue to build the National African American Leadership Summit as a united front, exemplifying collective leadership in Black America. What Black America needs is not a "leader" but a "leadership," connected to the masses of Black people.

The National African American Leadership Summit (NAALS) has the potential to become that leadership. The challenge is for NAALS to move decisively to assume responsibility for advancing the social, economic and political agenda which was outlined in the official Mission Statement of the Million Man March and Day of Absence and articulated by Minister Farrakhan and various speakers on October 16: adopting the 25,000 Black children who are now orphans to provide wholesome families for them within our community; the registering of millions of Black voters to create an independent third force in American politics; the convening of a National Black Political Convention to develop a Black Agenda which reflects the interests and aspirations of Black people; the creation of an African American Development Fund to mobilize millions of dollars for business and economic development; utilizing economic sanctions (boycotts) to compel the demand for reparations.

Beyond the jubilation of the moment, the real lasting legacy of the Million Man March and Day of Absence rests on our willingness and capacity to change our attitudes about ourselves, to change our behavior towards each other and take responsibility for the rescue and restoration of the chance to confront ourselves as well as the U.S. government and corporate America; to be absolutely determined, in the name and memory of our ancestors, to enter the 21st century a people, nation and race on the rise again.

If indeed, the National African American Leadership Summit as a collective leadership body for the Black Nation, can effectively meet that challenge, then the MMM/DOA will not only have been a magnificent mass event, but a turning point in the history of Africans in America. Long live the spirit of the Million Man March. God is great!

Ron Daniels: Veteran Social and Political Activist Ron Daniels, Chairperson of Campaign for a New Tomorrow, served as a member of the Executive Council of the National Organizing Committee for the Million Man March and Day of Absence (MMM/DOA). Along with many other progressive nationalists and activists, Daniels adopted a position of critical support for MMM/DOA. From the outset of his participation in the planning and mobilization process he utilized his nationally syndicated column, Vantage Point, to inform people about the MMM/DOA and offer critical perspectives about its character, direction and program.

AT THE START OF A BLACK TIDAL WAVE: REFLECTIONS ON THE MILLION MAN MARCH

S.E. Anderson

This little essay is dedicated to: Brother Mumia Abu-Jamal-now 14 years on Death Row for being a political activist, Brother Ken Saro Wira- an Ogoni people's leader executed by Nigeria's military junta for fighting Shell Oil's eco-imperialism, Sister Assata Shakur-the Soul of the Black Liberation Movement now in political exile in Cuba, and Sister Tegla Loroupe-winner of the NYC Marathon for the second time in a row...in spite of the racist and sexist odds...in spite of the untimely death of her beloved sister.

What happened in Washington, D.C. on Monday October 16, 1995 was a dual event. One was the Million Man March on and around the Mall (really a gathering...a rally) of one out of five African American men–mainly grassroots working class Brothers–and thousands of Sisters. The other was what was happening on the steps of the Capitol. Up there, it was a play for power by those who have no power but think they do because they misinterpret influence for power. Up there, it was a struggle by some Black men who seek to deliver the masses of

Photo by Kenneth Wright

our folk to either the racist Right of the Gingrinch type or to the racist Right of the Clinton type. Up there, it was a photo opportunity not to be missed by those who are media-created and hunger for the cameras like a sunflower following the sun. Up there, it was much speechifying and drama for TV effect. Numbing talks of the mystic numbers. The metaphysics of metaphysics. Soulsearching speeches divorced from the influence and centrality of those criminals in the Capitol and in control of capital.

But, Brother Jesse Jackson's speech was the exceptional speech and most reflective of why we sacrificed and struggled to come by the millions to Washington on a work day. He made the connection between our misery and the ruling class. He exposed for all to see our deepening economic, political and moral crisis and its connection to captialism's mounting institutional racism, sexism and class bias.

We came because the white dominated empire's social, political, and moral conditions have reached such racist and exploitive heights that we felt—and still feel—it so deeply in our bones...in our souls. Sisters feel it too. Often more so than Brothers. But the normalcy of male chauvinism and man-centered social structures imbedded within us directly contradict the progressive nature of our Black Liberation struggle, forcing Sisters to subservient positions–even though throughout history, they have been some of the fiercest and principled freedom fighters.

We came because we wanted to make a statement to our Black male selves that we pledge to continue the liberation fight in spite of the odds and the daily genocidal onslaught of a degenerating capitalist system. We came because we also recognize the normalizing of moral decay in the dominant U.S. society cutting deep into our relations between ourselves and Black women. We came because our youth--the vast majority of our people--needed to see...experience that Black men of all ages and classes can gather in great numbers and not fight each other, not be chained or handcuffed, not be watching some modern day gladiator game sports, not be singing and dancing, not be on our knees praying.

We came for the other 1 in 5 of us who reside in what Brother Mumia Abu-Jamal rightly calls North America's fastest growing public housing development: prison. This other one million man march includes all of our Brothers (and increasing numbers of Sisters, too!) caught in the truly criminal justice system's pre- and post-prison legal maze of hellish trials, detentions and paroles. And yes, we came to demand a retrial for Brother Mumia and the freeing of our over 150 political prisoners and prisoners of war (even

though, up there on the step of the Capitol, it was mentioned only in passing).

We came because we experience the betrayal and death of the U.S. working class by Black and white liberal "allies." There were thousands of Black trade unionists among us represented. After all, 90% of African Americans are members of the working class: still the driving force of this rapacious economic system. We came because we are very aware of our "superfluous" status with corporate America. Our Black collective consciousness...our Raw Memory recalled that we were central and essential to the building of this empire, but now can be discarded like old rags by the very system we helped give birth to. We came to help organize the unorganized workers and the never-to-be-workers (those who have been permanently forced out of the labor market by automation and corporate flight from U.S. labor).

And that was a powerful statement for us to experience and for the world to see: *more than a million Black men defiantly and proudly standing tall in the face of the Capitol Racism.*

No, it was not about putting Black women in their mythical "natural" place of behind and in the kitchen tending to babies and cooking. That might have been the original organizer's intent. But by August of 1995, the masses of Black men's and women's critical wrath pushed that paternalistic/misogynist urge to the background of the organizing efforts. Hence, this became the first time that Black folk across the country openly and publicly struggled with Black male chauvinism within a broad-based mass organizing effort. In the past, if there was a struggle for Sisters' inclusion and power/leadership sharing, it was done only at the top of the leadership and out of the Black Public Eye. This present debate and critique has become a crude but positive beginning that we progressive thinking, revolutionary thinking African American men and women must openly carry on and help shape a truly egalitarian peoples movement for Liberation. Nobody else is going to do it. The right wing among us who only talk of Black unity and economic development and self-determination is actually about putting Sisters "back in their natural (or God-given or Allah-decreed) place": subservient and behind the Black Man. Their goal, like the white Christian Right, is to deliver the masses of our people passively to the fascist will of the growing Contract On America Right.

No. It was not about Black men's "atonement." The vast majority of Brothers there on the Mall were prepared to call for the government and corporate powers to atone for their past and present atrocities of human and civil rights violations. That atonement thing that the organizers originally called for went over like a lead balloon. The minimization of "atonement" reveals the objective sophisticatedness of Black men understanding that to come to Washington was to make a political statement and not a religious or metaphysical one in front of enemy headquarters. We showed the world and ourselves that there is something fundamentally wrong at the very essence of North America-and it is a killing and emasculating thing.

It was great to be there with one of my sons and see and feel that expansive Black Brotherly Love. And to see Brothers and Sisters who I haven't seen in ages. And to meet new ones. All that was the positive personal thing that each one of the 1.5 million of us there will cherish forever. But that does not liberate us--it only rejuvenates and helps hold back the cynicism and apathy. Those good feelings do not pull us into an organized force fighting racism and capitalism. They don't automatically translate into the elimination of our chauvinistic and misogynist ways. And it doesn't automatically make those who called us together our leaders. True leaders don't organize their life and speeches around how to deliver the masses of African Americans to the ruling class. True leaders are shaped and developed through engaging in the hard work of the daily struggles of our people in our communities and workplaces; not negotiating petty bourgeois consolations or selling soundbite wolf tickets to the white corporate media or making grand statements that have no action linked to them.

Instead, we should look upon the Million Man March--with all of its warts and open sores--as one of the necessary moments (like the 1963 March on Washington or the 1965 Assassination of Brother Malik El-Hajj Shabazz or the 1968 Assassination of Brother Martin Luther King) of Black political crystallization. We now need to help organize and strive for, among a bunch of other things, Millions of Black Men and Women standing tall side-by-side along with our Latino, Asian and Native American allies, like a massive unstoppable Black Tidal Wave, marching on the Capitol to crush racist-capitalist America and seize it for the betterment of Humanity.

S.E. Anderson is a long-time political activist, mathematician, writer, Black Studies educator living and struggling in Harlem. He is a member of the Network of Black Organizers and a senior editor of its Journal: *NOBO* (published by Africa World Press) and the NY Coalition to Free Mumia Abu-Jamal. He is also the author of *The Black Holocaust For Beginners (Writers & Readers) and a co-editor with Tony Medina of In Defense of Mumia:* An *Anthology for Mumia Abu-Jamal* (Writers & Readers).

> *It was great to be there with one of my sons and see and feel that expansive Black Brotherly Love. And to see Brothers and Sisters who I haven't seen in ages. And to meet new ones.*

CLAIMED BY BLACK PEOPLE

Herb Boyd

One of the earliest and most troublesome criticisms of the Million Man March was the exclusion of Black women, but this issue, according to many women who support the march, has been grossly exaggerated.

"Most of the women I know—thinking women—support the march," said Dr. Charshee McIntyre, a retired professor and an advisor to the march. "And many of them support it more so than the men. They are saying 'It's about time for the brothers to come together.'"

McIntyre cited Dr. Barbara Sizemore, the eminent educator and currently Dean at Depaul University in Chicago, as another associate who strongly endorses the march. "She told me that the Nation of Islam is the best group in the country for the development of Black men, for instilling unity and camaraderie, and I agree," McIntyre said. "And as women become more educated you'll notice that they are rising to prominence within the Nation, and that to me is a natural progression."

She does not agree with those who contend the march is sexist. "For those who view the march from a feminist perspective the march might be sexist," McIntyre explained, "but you have to remember that this is a man-oriented march. Nothing is said when women have their conferences and seminars for women doctors, lawyers and other professionals. They even recently convened an all-women's gathering in Beijing, and nothing was said about this. The best way to look at this march is to see it as another opportunity for the oppressed to fight the oppressor."

As a teacher of African and African-American studies and the Humanities, McIntyre often stressed a need to place issues within a historical framework, and she welcomes this occasion for Black men to bond. "Among the sisters bonding occurs all the time," she continued. "We pick up friends from our early years to our nineties. Such is not the case with our men, who are often isolated and left to struggle alone. You see, Black women did not lose the roles they had in Africa, but our brothers did, and anything they do to

Photo by Brian Jackson

improve themselves I support."

These sentiments were echoed by Bob Law, a nationally syndicated broadcaster and a key organizer of the march. "We began talking to Black women at the very inception of the idea," he explained. "A number of Black women—grandmothers, single women, professionals—responded with their opinions, and the majority of them thought it was a good idea; they wanted to see their Black men stand up and challenge the stereotype of being irrational, of being unable to stand for anything. In short, they were in full support of the march and its objectives."

Photo by Robert Sengstacke

Among the notable Black women who did not support the march was Angela Davis, and she was joined by such distinguished leaders and writers as Jewel Jackson McCabe, Michele Wallace, and Marcia Gillespie, all of them contending that the exclusion of women was counterproductive. Veteran activist Charlene Mitchell extended her analysis beyond the women's issue to question the march itself. "Yes, it is time to march, but we must march for something tangible—for jobs with decent wages, for decent housing and quality public education and single payer health care," Mitchell asserted. "We cannot afford the division between African American women and men. If we ever needed each other we certainly do now."

Amiri Baraka, for his own reasons, denounced the march, stating that, "First of all, I wouldn't go to war and leave half the army at home," which, whether he knew it or not, was an ironic commentary on Minister Louis Farrakhan's pre-march military metaphor, "You don't take your woman into the foxhole with you."

Even while these arguments were raging, the coordinators were revising the agenda to include the presence of a significant number of women as speakers at the march. It was widely rumored that Rosa Parks, Dr. Betty Shabazz, Dr. Dorothy Height, Maya Angelou, C. Delores Tucker, and Faye Williams would be among those given time at the podium. And should this occur it will mark a vast improvement over the historic March on Washington in 1963, when the only woman's voice heard resounding across the Mall belonged to Mahalia Jackson.

The expected appearance of such an array of prominent women can be in part attributed to the efforts of Chicago community activist Conrad Worrill, Maulana Ron Karenga, Haki Madhubuti, and Ron Daniels, among others. Daniels, best remembered for his role in the Gary convention of 1972 and now head of the Center for Constitutional Rights

in Manhattan, was particularly vocal, insisting the men forge a partnership with women that would put aside patriarchy. "As some Black women have correctly pointed out...the Million Man March should not convey the impression that the crisis in the Black community is simply a crisis of the Black male. The suppression of Black women outside and inside the Black community is also a historical fact," he told the march's organizers.

McIntyre believes that there will be more than a million men at the march. "We should not be surprised by this number," she said. "Some two or three million turn out every year to shake their booties on Eastern Parkway in Brooklyn during the West Indian parades, and they have nothing at all to do with political or economic issues."

While the brothers are marching, McIntyre, who wrote the original statement of purpose for the march, will be conducting a workshop related to the event, but a site has not been determined. "I am not even sure what will be the topic of discussion," she said, "although I would like to talk about our traditional roles in Africa, and how sisters and brothers need to have friendships before they have relationships.

"But the most critical piece about this march has not been presented," she observed. "That will occur after the march, and there is a pressing need for local organizations to set up various programs to deal with action in the political, economic and criminal justice arenas. If they don't come back with a new sense of motivation for political action, then what's the point? And we need to do something about getting well-known New York activist/attorney Alton Maddox's license back. A real united front should be the ultimate result of this march."

Herb Boyd: Herb Boyd is an award-winning journalist and co-editor, along with Robert L. Allen, of the recent publication *Brotherman: An Odyssey of Black Men in America-An Anthology.*

THE AMERICAN POSTMODERN MIDDLE PASSAGE

(A PORTRAIT OF THE MILLION MAN MARCH IN BLACK RELIEF)

Bartley L. McSwine

Photo by Roy Lewis

As I walked among the million black men, and women, and the few whites who attended the Million Man March, here and there I could see glimpses of the past revealed in the present lurching toward the future. The one and the many were present. The many in the one and the one in the many were finally standing up for themselves, for their community, and the oppressed throughout the world. I saw Nat Turner at the march and wondered how his existential question to America—Should slaves kill their master?—would ultimately be answered. Next to him I saw Denmark Vessey discussing the question of betrayal with Sojourner Truth and Harriet Tubman as former President Bush's "most qualified man for the job" now sat on the highest court of the land. Diop and Malcolm were standing off to the side and not far from them I could see DuBois and Douglass edging their way up to the front. Banneker, who I saw standing somewhere in the middle of this mass of humanity, had staked out this territory many years before, and all this time it had been waiting there to be claimed. Strong voices of freedom could be heard in the air as speaker after speaker spoke truth to power—sometimes with love.

First be reconciled to your brother, scripture had said, then bring your gifts to the altar. But this warning had not gone unheeded until now. Centuries of strife which had divided us now led us to the altar. Certainly others were present and even welcome on this bright day in October: women, some whites and the Hispanics who picketed in support of The March. But this was a day for black men, a day so long overdue to let the healing begin.

Millions had died in the name of freedom only to be scorned by the freedom they won. One million and counting: the black men who died in the slave rebellions, the Revolutionary War, the Civil War, World War I, World War II, the Vietnamese War, the Civil Rights War, the War against the Panthers, the War against the police, the War against black manhood, black masculinity, black dignity, black pride—the War against black culture, the essence of the black Self.

On this day, we, the sons of Africa, had come to Washington to represent all the survivors of the Atlantic and American middle passage. We had come together in time and space to atone and to respond to a call—the call of the spirit, the call of the ancestors, the call of destiny. We had come to respond to the silent voice which speaks a language only the oppressed can hear—a hushed voice of subversion that speaks of love and freedom and courage, to those who are born and yet remain unborn behind the veil. It is the silent voice that communicates through the song's silent feeling, and the sight and seeing of the unseen. The voice that communicates the message-of-the-heart from the ancestors: the voice that knows the Truth, that knows the spirit, that knows freedom.

The old tribal prophets who walked among the ancestors had foreseen this day and had spoken of it with great fervor. It was a day their drums had foretold many years before their rhythms were silenced and their language forgotten. They had spoken of this day of unity, and healing and atonement as being a day that would strike like lightning before the thunder is heard. It would be a day of rebellion against internal enemies that now were camped around us—a rebellion against the fears that had immobilized us; the disunity that had sapped our strength; the fratricidal sickness that had kept us ill unto death.

This sickness had to be extirpated at its root—from the very minds of those who had come to believe what their oppressors said about them. These minds were the minds of those Negroes who had come to believe their oppressors would save them, the minds of those "Blacks" who believed in their own inferiority, and the minds of Niggers who now called each other by That Name. These were the minds of the sycophantic pimps who preyed on black women, the minds of the dealers who deal drugs to black youth and give AIDS and syphilis to those yet unborn. All this had to be uprooted if we were to save ourselves from this modern (postmodern) middle passage.

The white community that looked on (some in bemused bewilderment, some in half-hearted contempt) had yet another lesson to learn. That it was not off the hook. The sins of the fathers had been visited upon this generation and there was no escape—not for black, brown, red, yellow or white. That they (these sins) were imminent in every aspect of American life holding all as wrathful hostages in their enlaced iron grip. The sons and daughters of slaves and slave-holders alike, the Nahuatal people now illegal aliens in their own land, the descendants of the Asian concentration camps, the indigenous peoples reserved/preserved on reservations, the poor whites made nameless and faceless by a system they stand under and do not under-stand, the whites who are ignorant of their African ancestry and the legacy of Africa in Europe—all are a part of this modern (post-modern) trail-of-tears. The sins of the fathers had tracked them down in the suburbs and in the corporate board rooms and in the legislatures and in the White Houses of the world. There could be no escape.

Confronted with this "New Deal", the "real" Americans now had to face not only the remembrances of its dark past but the dark present now standing on its capitol grounds. The million plus men that stood on the

Photo by Third World Press

capitol and along with the thousands now warehoused behind bars were visible testimony to the failure of democracy and the triumph of Capitalistic market values. What would become of a country who gains the whole world only to lose its own soul? Should the government now put the Army and the Air Force, the Navy and the Marines on alert? What should be done to solve this problem, to placate this mass, to face this "new" emergency situation? Who and what would have the courage to face what these million black men stood for?

The President left town for Texas. The U.S. Senate and the U.S. Congress closed down and Senators and Congressmen scurried for cover. Downtown businessmen could be seen hurrying across deserted streets, darting in and out of buildings. A furtive look here and there told the whole story. Black and white policemen and women were trying to act as if nothing unusual was going on. And yet here in the heart of the nation's capital that had proclaimed itself to be the leader of the free world, a black cloud had descended and business could not go on as usual.

They came from all over the nation. In cars they came. On buses they came. On airplanes they came. On foot they came. Young and old. Middle class and poor. Businessmen and college students. Teachers and professors. Doctors and lawyers. Janitors and chefs. Something had changed in the black community. Something had galvanized the wretched of the earth. And Sartre's voice could still be heard echoing across time.

They will see you, perhaps, but they will go on talking among themselves, without even lowering their voices. This indifference strikes home: their fathers, shadowy creatures, your creatures, were but dead souls; you it was who allowed them glimpses of light, to you only did they dare speak, and you did not bother to reply to such zombies. Their sons ignore you; a fire warms them and sheds light around them, and you have not lit it. Now, at a respectful distance, it is you who will feel furtive, nightbound, and perished with cold. Turn and turn about; in these shadows from whence a new dawn will break, it is you who are the zombies.

Dr. Bartley McSwine is an associate professor of education at Chicago State University where he teaches courses in the history and philosophy of education and educational issues in the black community. He teaches, lectures and conducts workshops across the country on Afrocentric and multicultural education and is currently at work on a book-length treatment of his experiences with the Million Man March.

A TIME TO
END PRIVILEGE

Thandabantu Iversen

Photo by Brian Jackson

It has been six days since the Million Man March, and I am still trying to sort out what it all really means. In particular, I am wondering what I can say to my little nephew, Wingrove, who at five years old is already acutely aware of things he does not yet understand, and understands things of which we assume he is not aware. How, amidst all the confusion and tendentious "spinning," can I distill some seminal seed to plant in a fertile furrow of his mind?

The raspy hum of the computer becomes more obvious as I momentarily lose focus on the feelings and concerns evoked by my personal experience of an event so deeply moving that I find myself choking with emotion each time I attempt to define its impact. The coffee is not helping...Perhaps it will help if I begin to identify the things

that I do not want to tell my nephew. I am a bit clearer about them.

This event certainly did help to free African-Americans from the vicious and systematic "race" oppression we experience every minute we live--and die--in this "land of the free." In fact, the aftermath reveals a certain formidable resilience of racism, which enables many Americans to make assumptions about the Million Man March which have so little to do with African-Americans and so much to do with the continued (and extremely dangerous) denial of whiteness. Equally troubling and equally dangerous--is the fact that the Million Man March has undoubtedly reinforced the notion that race oppression is more important than gender oppression in the daily lives of Black people in North

America. The political and organizational mobilization for the demonstration obviously generated intense pain, anger, and debate amongst African-Americans about the current state of gender relation. Yet that debate--so necessary for our healing and liberation--has been shunted aside as a distraction too divisive to consider, and much too painful to engage. So now, as Blacks beam with unabashed pride amid the incessant din of detractions by certain white (and certain Negroes who feel obliged), we can easily ignore the male privilege that allows us to forget that the March would probably not have happened had it not been for the many Black women who worked to bring it off. And it is just as likely that many of us will minimize the intense feelings of rejection being expressed by women all around us--maybe even beside us--who know what they hurt and their need for validation of their voices and their lives will be silenced, again, as will the screams and whimpers of those women and children being abused by men intoxicated by unexpected whiffs of their own validation.

It will also escape many of us that homophobia and class have been little affected by the Million Man March. Like sexism, these forms of oppression have been de-emphasized as too trivial to merit our anxieties about the future, and the present, of the nation within the nation. Yet the suffering (and death) caused by these multiple-and-interacting oppressions threaten the new shoots of hope and resolve, just as deeply-rooted weeds always threaten to choke the life from new plants.

There is something wrong with this piece, something too one-sided, too preachy. Perhaps if I talk with Sulaiman we can straighten out the kinks...I feel a bit unbrotherly calling him so early this Sunday morning, but he is gracious as usual, and I am relieved. He wants to hear what I have written, and as I read to him I am choking with emotion, my eyes brimming with tears. Something is right here, yet something is still wrong...As soon as Sulaiman begins to speak I know: I am leaving out what is most positive about the Million Man March, the tide of concern, the waves of deep desire for change, the willingness to become different, better, new. This is what is happening between Sulaiman and me at this moment: two Black males reaching out to one another, less afraid than before, less constrained by fears of what will be thought (even by ourselves) about our touching each other's heart, engaging each other's mind. This is a mere option of the remarkable outpouring of an entire people's feeling that justice must come in season and that we must take the risks to bring it forth. I multiply all we share by one million. This is why I called Sulaiman, a "friend of mind." I sit with all my brother has given, all we are sharing, and I realize that we men must keep wrestling with the demons of privilege--including that "good guy" demon that makes me want to preach to other men, believing that just because I have decided to change, I am already changed. There is so much more work to do, on myself, on the institutions I inhabit...

Which brings me back to my nephew Winnie. Perhaps I should simply tell him that the Million Man March is a message, much like the message my sister or brother-in-law send when they call Winnie to dinner. The message tells us that it is time to come in, time to clean up, time to be real with family, time to make a home. In short, the message is that it is time to stop playing...time to end all forms of privilege.

Thandabantu Iversen is an East Coast writer and activist.

COUNTDOWN, THE FINAL CALL, THE AFTERMATH AND BEYOND

E. Ethelbert Miller

"Every Man Prays in His Own Language."

--Duke Ellington

Part I: Countdown

"So, do you intend to march in October?" It seems as if every week someone asks this question to an African-American man. The Million Man March being organized by Louis Farrakhan, Benjamin Chavis and others on October 16th has all the makings of being a historical occasion. Just the idea or sight of a million African-American men gathering in front of the American monuments in Washington will be an image the media will either embrace and hype or attempt to downplay and ignore. The success of the march has the definite possibility of enhancing the political power of minister Louis Farrakhan and the Nation of Islam. One can almost predict the type of discussions which will take place on radio and television talk shows after the march is over. "What does Louis Farrakhan want?" will be one question asked. Benjamin Chavis might benefit by having another civil rights organization take a look at his resume, while Cornel West will probably try to place an intellectual spin on what it all means.

The October march is being coordinated at a time when the Republican Party and its ideology is shaping the debate regarding such issues as welfare reform, the role of government, affirmative action and the many concerns that relate to the well being of the family. The liberal response to this ideological assualt has been weak in terms of a coherent and theoretical rebuttal and at times almost seems to borrow the rhetoric of the Right.

For the last several weeks, I've been talking with friends who are activists involved in a number of issues and have found that what is needed from our "progressive" community is a response to such developments as the "Million Man March." What does it mean to have African-

Photo by Roy Lewis

95

American men coming together for what is being described as "A day of Atonement?" What are the politics of the organizers?

There has already been considerable discussion about the role of women and the march. Several African-American women leaders have applied their make-up and have excused themselves from the need to participate in a manner which might distract "the brothers" from taking care of serious business. One can read what one wants into this. Anyway, another absent group from the discussion has been Black gay men. This might be a result of Farrakhan's involvement, but it overlooks the serious need to address the issue of homophobia, and the large number of Black gay men who are dying from AIDS. Whether one agrees or disagrees with the gay lifestyle, one should not ignore the concerns and needs of these men.

Much of the preparation for the March has been filled with religious rhetoric. This could almost pass as an ad campaign for the Christian Right. Within the African-American community, the focus on family values, how to respond to crime, law and order has grown. So has the number of Black Conservatives and Republicans. Even leaders or groups we define as radical within the African-American community are only radical when the issue is race. Ask for their views on other issues and topics and they show their "true" colors.

The African-American community in many ways has become a conservative community. Calling for a Day of Atonement further supports this claim. The focus on spiritual development is an outgrowth of self-help principals and beliefs which have also been embraced by many African-American leaders. It is easy to be distracted from the struggle of fighting to improve social conditions if one is staring at one's navel or chanting. Still, the moral objective of a movement must not be ignored. It is important however to have a progressive agenda which builds a foundation for coalitions with other groups in our society. So while talking about African-American men, someone like Benjamin Chavis must once again talk about environmental racism and justice. Jesse Jackson and other participants must talk about workers and the labor movement and the need to find employment for African-American men. The push for increasing voter registration must be linked to local and state elections and not simply the Presidential election of next year. We must talk about rural problems and land lost in the South while searching of resolutions across the urban landscape.

It must not be forgotten that African-American men and women have marched before. We even went through a period when people believed marching served no purpose. Yet, here we are at the end of the century still troubled by the state of the "souls" of Black folk...

Part II: The Final Call?

I flew back from Nashville in order to attend the March. My plan was to take only my son Nyere. However, my daughter Jasmine Simone insisted she was going. Only 13, she has her mother's personality. I was very happy to observe my daughter's concern. She found the decision for women to stay home unacceptable. In many ways it went against the beliefs I have held and supported most of my life. My wife's decision to stay home was not political. She dislikes crowds. The last large event we attended together might have been the Jackson Victory Tour at RFK stadium several years ago.

I called my friend James Early and we decided to make the trip to the Mall together. James was bringing his son and Howard Dodson was visiting from New York . . .so we had a nice entourage. Leaving my house around ten o'clock in the morning we stood waiting on 16th Street near Malcolm X Park for the downtown bus. The streets were filled with brothers walking in small groups, everyone who passed us spoke or nodded. It has been a long time since you could feel so much energy in the air. I recall the day after the Mt. Pleasant riot in Washington, and how neighbors began to talk to each other. Trying to pull together as a community. That took place in the late 1980s. Now, here was a day beginning with so much positive energy.

Unable to wait for the bus, the six of us hailed a cab and traveled downtown. We were surprised to find the traffic moving without any problems. When we arrived at the Mall, the number of men already there was breathtaking. People were already eating fish sandwiches, vendors selling shirts and buttons, and members of the Nation of Islam standing around like soldiers on leave. It was late morning and people were still amazed at how many people were already on the Mall and how many were still arriving. It was not a time for listening to opening speeches but instead, the acknowledgement of inner strength which develops when one feels connected to something much greater than oneself. My daughter conveyed to me the type of excitement a child demonstrates when an event or occurrence knocks them off their feet. I knew how important this March was for African-American men, but here was my daughter being a witness to members of her race standing tall. What memories will she have of this day, years from now?

Walking 'round on the Mall, with James, Howard and our children, I found myself stopping every few minutes and talking with old friends from in town and out of town.

Everyone was so happy with what was taking place...it was obvious history was being made.

But how do we interpret history? I knew before the day ended that much attention would be given to the number of people who attended. Would one million men show up? If so, what does it mean? Is this the final call?

Part III: The Aftermath

I've been clipping articles about the March from different papers and magazines. Much of the commentary is disappointing. There is no real analysis . . .too much discussion of how long Farrakhan spoke. There is the unnecessary comparison to King's speech of 1963. One can see the pie dripping from the faces of Negro leaders and reporters. Everyone wants to know what will happen next.

It is ironic that an African-American leadership summit is held on the campus of Howard in November, 1995. Other than reading about the plans for this summit in the *Washington Post*, I have difficulty obtaining information. The morning of the first day, as students head to class, members of the Nation of Islam begin to appear. By coincidence someone decides to hold the Education Workshop next door to the African-American Resource Center. People arrive, asking questions, wondering what's going on. I ask to see someone's registration folder; it contains a schedule. I feel I finally know what's going on.

I have been a witness to this before. Small groups sitting in rooms trying to solve the problems of the race. This type of activity will make you believe in ghosts. I spend the day talking to "people of the summit" and observe there is still excitement from the October March. This is good but what does it mean?

Part IV: Beyond...

The worst thing that can happen is for folks to attempt to have another March in 1996. More attention must be given to grassroots organizing. If African-American men were to return to the Mall the symbolism would be gone. What is needed are small steps and major leaps.

The day after the October March, my son and I started picking up the garbage in front of our house. It is not our job, but our responsibility. I give my daughter money each morning for a newspaper. We discuss the news...and this too is a small beginning. I watch her giving a few coins to a homeless man, and I am reminded that this too is "brotherhood."

E. Ethelbert Miller is a poet and the Director of the African-American Resource Center at Howard University. He is also the author of *First Light: New and Selected Poems*. Mr. Miller has been at the forefront of the poetry scene in the Washington, D.C. area for several years.

HISTORIC EVENT

Cornel West

The Million Man March was an historic event—called by Minister Louis Farrakhan, claimed by Black people of every sort and remembered by people around the globe as an expression of black men's humanity an decency. Never before has such black love flowed so freely and abundantly for so many in the eyes of the world. and never before have we needed such respect for each other than we do now.

When Minister Louis Farrakhan presented his vision of a Million Man March at the first African American Leadership Summit called by Dr. Rev. Benjamin Chavis in June 1994, I was intrigued. I like the idea of putting black people in motion in the form of a massive demonstration. I knew that Minister Louis Farrakhan had held numerous gatherings of Black men throughout the country to highlight the issues of dignity, respect and responsibility. I saw this march as a kind of culmination of these noteworthy series of gatherings.

My support for the march was fourfold. First, we had to make black suffering center stage for the country and world. If only we could jump-start a critical dialogue on the legacy of white supremacy among Americans of all colors, including the President, Congress, corporate and bank elites. Second, we had to send a sign of hope and a sense of possibility to Black America. The growing despair in chocolate cities and towns had to be countered by a perception that we were on the move, in motion, capable of seizing the time and shaping the direction for our future. If only we could display a Black united front of committed black men—a symbol of Black and Islam, the humanity of gays and lesbians, and the fundamental role of corporate power in America. Needless to say, Minister Louis Farrakhan was brilliant, gracious and open—as was his wife, Khadijah. My wife and

pushed the King legacy with integrity, but also with a respect for the Black Nationalist Tradition.

Since this substantive meeting I have been trashed by many (some former friends and acquaintances) and eschewed by others. And in the eyes of some in the Jewish world, I've met and collaborated with the new Hitler. This is sheer nonsense—and part of the problem. When black people sit and talk with their white adversaries, they are praised. When Martin Luther King preached that he loved such white supremacists as Bull Connor, the white media showered him with approval and admiration. When Black people trash and denounce other Black leaders—demonized by the white media—they also are praised. But when Black people who disagree in public decide to meet in private—all of us are trashed and denounced. When Martin Luther King preached that he loved Elijah Muhammad—and met with him in private—the white media denounced him. The double standards and differential treatment—the core of white supremacy—are evident.

My support of the march and dialogue with Minister Louis Farrakhan is based on neither blood nor race. As a radical democrat and, most importantly, Christian, my sup-

Photo by Richard Muhammed

port and dialogue are based on spiritual, moral and political grounds. Spiritual, because I view each an every one of us as human beings made in the image of God capable of growth, development and maturity. Hence, I give up on no one of us—we are all in process, in need of one another. Morally, because though I believe patriarchal, homophobic and anti-Jewish sentiments are wretched sins, we all must be pushed to minimize the evils in all of us. None of us are pure and pristine,free of sin or evil. Yet we grow, develop and mature owing to loving criticism, not hateful castigation. Politically, I am convinced that white supremacy is the major dam holding back the progressive energies in the American body politic. If we can target white supremacy, then the other crucial issues of poverty, maldistribution of wealth, corporate power, patriarchy, homophobia an ecological abuse will be brought into the daylight. Why so? Because race matters so much in American society.

In retrospect, our support of the march was wise. The hard work of unsung heroes like Ron Daniels, Rev. Wendell Anthony, Conrad Worrill, Haki Madhubuti and others warrants our attention and admiration. The contribution of BET's Robert Johnson for a free hour to publicize the march made a difference. Minister Louis Farrakhan and Benjamin Chavis' leadership was indispensable. And the beautiful Black men and women who made the march the march deserve our accolades. Long live the loving and dignified spirit of the Million Man March!

Cornel West is an activist, writer and scholar of national renown. He is the author of numerous publications about the tenuous relationships between the races, including the seminal work *Race Matters*. Dr. West teaches in the Department of Religion, at Harvard University.

The Day of Absence: Its Value and Benefit to Our Struggle

Subira Sekhmet Kifano

In the midst of rising racism in this country, the dismantling of hard-won gains, the deterioration of urban communities and the fragile voice of social justice weakening, we posed a significant challenge to this process and to ourselves with the idea and implementation of the Million Man March and Day of Absence. Both components of this joint project provided an opportunity for Black men as well as Black women to take a leadership position in and make an essential contribution to a structure that would advance the image and interests of African people in America and force the opposition to retreat. With other nationalist groups throughout the nation, the Organization Us played a fundamental role in amplifying the project's success. Our contribution included our serving on the national organizing committee, co-planning and co-convening the event, writing the mission statement and speaking at the March. Our women's formation, The Senut Society, supported the principle and practice of the March, contributed, along with the men in the organization, to framing the mission statement and expanded the impact of the March. We accomplished this by mobilizing and organizing people, and raising money to send Black men to the March. We also sent a representative to the March, wrote a women's position paper on the project, and sponsored, as well as coordinated, a series of Day of Absence activities at our headquarters in Los Angeles and other chapters throughout the country on October 16.

It is with this in mind that I would like to discuss the values and benefits of the Million Man March and Day of Absence, giving special attention to the women-directed Day of Absence. The women, in partnership with men of the Organization Us, self-consciously chose to participate in the Million Man March and Day of Absence in order to see the values and benefits of this joint project in several ways. The first value and benefit is that the project reintroduced and rein-

forced the important principle and process of operational unity on the local and national level before, during and after the joint project. Secondly, it reinforced the principle and practice of women and men taking leadership positions—with women being in the leadership of the Day of Absence, without exclusion of men, while men were in the leadership of the Million Man March without exclusion of women. Thirdly, it offered the opportunity for women to organize a Day of Absence in over 318 cities, touching, mobilizing and organizing millions upon millions of African people, which would lay the foundation on the local level for the projects introduced in the mission statement to be implemented after October 16.

The first value and benefit is that the project reintroduced and reinforced the important principle and process of operational unity on the local and national level before, during and after the joint project. The concept of operational unity was advanced by our Organization Us in 1966 in the process of building the Black Power Conferences. It was

Photo by Third World Press

put forth to stress principles which teach recognition and respect for the various persons and varying ideas in the structure while building on common ground. This remains a central principle of our political work on the local, national and international level. Even though our organization disagreed with some of the ideas initially advanced by the leadership of the March, we understood and were committed to the common goal of Black men in particular, and the Black community in general, confronting the crisis in our communities throughout the nation and posing solutions to it. This process gave us an opportunity to challenge, question and eventually expand the goals of the project at the National Organizing Committee meetings.

Prior to our participation on the National Organizing Committee and from the moment the announcement of the March was made, we raised several concerns regarding the goals and process of the March. The major concerns rested in five areas: ideology, structure, organization, communication and resources. Discussions ensued in inclusive community meetings, at our annual Summer Institute on Leadership and Social Change as well as small focus groups within and outside of our organization. Eventually what developed was the support of the principles and practice of the Million Man March and Day of Absence after several lengthy discussions around our concerns.

During our dialogues, we raised our concerns about the ideological stance that women should not go to the March but stay home. We opposed this position not because we objected to Black men coming together to reinforce, support and strengthen each other, for we understood that there was a need in this instance for a priority be given to men. As the mission statement says, some of the most severe criticism against the African American community has been made against Black men; our men in particular must be in the forefront of challenging, responding to and correcting these areas of criticisms. Moreover, since we know and understand that freedom is indivisible, we realize that none of us are free until **all** of us are free. We urged successfully that while the March focus primarily on Black men, Black women's issues and concerns would not be excluded.

Parenthetically, neither out-of-touch leaders nor disgruntled gratuitous attacks, whether in white or Black face, could reverse Black men's decision to atone, reconcile and take responsibility for their lives and the lives of their families and communities. Those observing the naysayers' unjustified attacks wondered why these people would oppose a project with the potential to help shape and create a better life for African men, women and children. Whose and what interests do the naysayers really represent? What is important to note is that this work and representation of Black women at the Million Man March, and more importantly at the Day of Absence, was not obtained by sitting on the side complaining, but rather through constant dialogue and struggle around issues which have the potential to separate or unify African women and men. With this expanded perspective, our next task was to make the women-focused and directed component of the March, the Day of Absence, an equally successful event.

This commitment to the principle of operational unity was also replicated in our work on the local level, where there was disagreement on how women should participate in the March as well as the Day of Absence and when this activity should be held. We resolved this conflict by respecting the diversity of positions within our group and called on those who chose prayer and mediation as essential ways of observing to do this and those of us who chose to have teach-ins and mobilization efforts to do that. The importance here is that each person's position was respected.

The second value and benefit of the joint project was that it reinforced the principle and practice of both women and men taking leadership positions—with women being in the leadership of the Day of Absence without exclusion of men, while men were in the leadership of the Million Man March without exclusion of women. Therefore, the women of US met with other women's groups and individuals to organize a Day of Absence activity in Los Angeles. We agreed and were comfortable with the male-focused Million Man March activity because we understand that in certain situations there is a need to give added attention to female or male issues and challenges. Consequently, we have had and continue to have female-focused activities on the international, national and local level that did not exclude men but rather expected and requested their support. On a number of occasions we held women's conferences and forums, where the focus was on women and the majority of the participants were women. Some men may have come and joined in the dialogue, but they understood the priority and focus of women's issues. In fact, before the October 16th project, we discussed the importance of African American women's participation in the Fourth Annual UN Women's Conference in Beijing, China. Our discussions lead to a forum where we raised money to send a representative. No one challenged this. We also sponsor a Rites of Passage program for young girls; no one challenges our rights to do this because they understand our need to instruct our girls on what it means to be both African and woman. So too is it with the March; there remains a need for Black men to stand up and take responsibility if they have not done so in the past and assume more if they have.

As we moved toward the Day of Absence, we built a local Black United Front (BUF) of women and men which stressed the need of working collectively, in partnership to create a better world in which we want to live. Furthermore, the Day of Absence was a culmination of a long process of clarifying and expanding the mission, mobilizing and organizing large groups of African American men and women and holding discussions around the fate of Black people, as we self-consciously and collectively construct it.

One of the pivotal exercises of our local project was the dissemination of correct information about the mission of the Million Man March and Day of Absence, especially given the negative media and public thrashing and trashing of Black men by some mistaken Black women. Unlike these women, we saw our work and participation in this process as continuing the historic legacy of women like Mary McLeod Bethune, Ida B. Wells Barnett and Mary Church Terrell, who never let the dominant society dictate and direct the quality of Black male/female relations or allow themselves to be misdirected and/or manipulated by the dominant society against our own image and interests. They, on the contrary, reserved the right for us to have gender-focused activities, established key women's organizations, organized women to work on behalf of the community with their men, participated in the major organizations of the times and issued manifestos on behalf of Black men, women and children.

The third value and benefit of the Million Man March and Day of Absence is that it offered the opportunity for women to sponsor a Day of Absence in over 318 cities that would eventually lay the foundation on the local level for the projects introduced in the mission statement to be implemented after October 16. As an example of what occurred in these 318 cities across the nation, our Los Angeles organizing committee met weekly and outlined several tasks which would be instrumental in making the Day of Absence successful. We then established several committees to carry out the tasks. For example, to disseminate information to the community we had a media committee which developed press releases, PSA announcements, flyers and other literature and arranged speaking engagements on local radio programs. We also had a "Say It Loud" Committee that rode through the community with a bullhorn, educating and encouraging the community to strike, stay away from work, school and entertainment venues, grocery stores and shopping malls. We had a Speaker's Bureau which arranged presentations to other community organizations, a Program Committee to design the Day of Absence program, a Voter's Registration Drive to register people and encourage them to vote for the interests of African people and a Fundraising Committee to underwrite the cost for these projects. In fact, one of our first events was a fund-raiser that was held at a local park where

we raised several thousands of dollars to help send Black men who were financially unable to go to Washington, D.C. We invited local political officials and community representatives to speak to the mission statement. We sponsored cultural events and vendors donated a portion of their profits to the cause.

By the time the Day of Absence arrived, we had initiated debates, dialogues and forums across the city and brought a large group to our Center for an informative and inspirational exchange of ideas around foster care, economic ventures, parenting, male/female relations, politics, voter registration, and a host of other topics. The quality, depth and breadth of the presentations gave those in attendance a deeper understanding of ourselves, society and the world, as well as the opportunity to join existing organizations to realize our goals. The Day of Absence also offered an opportunity for Los Angeles women and men and women and men across the nation, representing millions upon millions of African people, to contribute to the national project of creating a better and more beautiful life.

As a result of our collective efforts, we were able to strengthen our resolve to continue to struggle for a better world. We are all better for that; even organizations which initially boycotted the project benefited from it because the call to action encouraged all to join existing organizations and participate in activities which will advance the image and interests of African people in the social, economic and political arenas. The Day of Absence and the Million Man March, components of one joint project, was an historic event which not only brought together more than a million African men at the seat of government but also mobilized and organized unknown millions in the cities across the country. With this magnificent beginning we are reaffirmed in our knowledge that the monumental task of the liberation of African people is possible and certain, if we stay together, love each other and work and struggle together to achieve it.

Subira Sekhmet Kifano is cultural advisor for the Language Development Program for African American Students (LDPAAS), Los Angeles Unified School District; director of the Mary McLeod Bethune Institute; co-vice chair, The Organization Us; Chair, Western Region, International Black Women's Congress; member, LOC Million Man March/Day of Absence; and Ph.D. student in education at Claremont Graduate School.

Part 6
We Are Partners/Lovers/Family

Photo by Robert Sengstacke

A
WOMANIST LOOKS AT
THE MILLION MAN MARCH

Geneva Smitherman

Womanist: referring to an African American woman who is rooted in the Black community and committed to the development of herself and the entire community.

I saw all that crowd, and I thought, uh-oh. But I never heard so many "Scuse me's" and "Sorry, Brothaman's" in my life. —Kofi, my 15-year-old nephew from Detroit, who attended the March with his father.

The Million Man March—and make no mistake about it, at least a million Black men were there—on October 16, 1995, in the Nation's capitol, marked the culmination of Minister Louis Farrakhan's "Stop the Killing" lecture campaign, which he embarked on several years ago. Controversy surrounding Farrakhan notwithstanding, everyone agrees that the condition of Black males is at an unprecedented low. The indices are undeniable. One in three Black males in the age group 20-29 is under the criminal justice system. There are 72 Black male homicide victims per 100,000, compared to 9.3 homicides per 100,000 for white males. In terms of work, 11.1% of Black males are unemployed, compared to 4.9% of white males. For at least the past seven years, in the age group 16-19, the Black male unemployment rate has been over 50%; it hit 59.3% in 1993. For those fortunate enough to be holding down a job, there is still an inequity in wages: the median salary for Black men is $23,020, compared to $31,090 for white men. And in a nation rapidly deindustrializing, 30.7% of Black males' jobs are in the category of industrial labor.

For me as the mother of a son, a Womanist, and an educator, the Million Man March brought back memories of the King ("Black English") Federal court case: of the eleven children remaining in the case—several had moved

Photo by Roy Lewis

away—by the time it finally came to trial in July of 1979, nine were boys. The King case involved a group of African American women, all single parents living in a housing project, who had sued the Ann Arbor, Michigan School District for failing to provide equal educational opportunities for their children. I served as an expert witness and advocate for these Sisters who had been frustrated for years as their children, of normal and above average intelligence, were labelled "learning disabled," tracked, and trapped in remedial classes. They were not taught and were not expected to learn. The ruling in our favor essentially mandated the School District to educate the children and teach them to read, rather than throwing them upon the ash heap of special education merely because of their language (and cultural) differences. As a much-too-young parent during my son's elementary schooling, I had almost let this same thing happen to him because his school had deemed him "hyperactive" and in need of medication and special classes. Only the intervention of an older Sister that I used to baby-sit for saved him. I remember her words well: "Well, I ain't got no whole lotta education, but ain't nothing wrong with that boy—it just don't sound right to me." Compared to Black females, and white males and females, Black males are disproportionately placed in special education and other kinds of slow track classes in the educational systems of this nation. Still today. Yeah, we needed that March—and anything else that will highlight what is happening to our boys and our men.

There were two marches, the one in D. C. and the "march" at home. Black folk on the homefront used the day to gather in churches, community centers, and around television sets and discuss the Black condition, critique the speakers, and debate African American issues. All over African America, block clubs, community organizations, and individuals who don't belong to any organization came out to participate in local marches and to hear speeches about the crises facing African Americans and ways of addressing these problems. Any forward thinking Black person had to love it. For that one day we were all focused on the same thing. What if we did that all year long, over the long haul, on other issues? That's movement.

Yet some Blacks, such as 1960's activist and writer, Amiri Baraka, took issue with the March because it did not include women. Baraka remarked that if he were going to war, he wouldn't leave half the army at home. In fact, only half the army has been fighting the war over the past two decades! With so many Black men dead or injured from street violence, in jail, on drugs, or unemployed, it is Black women who have been raising the children, battling school boards for adequate education for Black youth, providing financial support for the Black elderly, sustaining the churches, and doing most of the work in the NAACP, the Urban League, PUSH, and other Black institutions. Props to Brother Farrakhan for sounding the clarion call to wake up the other half of the Black army.

A group of Black women intellectuals, notable among them 1960's activist, Angela Davis, called a press conference to denounce the March on the grounds of sexism. To be sure, the request for women to remain home may have seemed to resonate with patriarchal prescriptions of old. However, women were not urged to stay at home for the sake of staying at home. Rather, the charge to women was to use this time to revisit Black issues and Black historical traditions. Further, women, and men who would not be journeying to D.C., were urged to implement a work stoppage and an economic boycott of places of business on the day of the March.

Black women must be wary of the seductive feminist trap. White males hold the power in this society, not Black males. (Does it need saying? It seems so obvious.) Black males—as well as all members of the UNworking class—are victims of the machinations of a capitalist monopoly and a technology-gone-wild system which has been set up and continues to be run by white males. To launch an attack against the first mass-based, sorely needed, long overdue, positive effort by Black men on the grounds of sexism is to engage in a misguided, retrogressive brand of feminism. With the ratio of Black men to women being 33 to 100, I would think my Sisters are weary of bearing the burden of the Black family and the Black struggle alone. The fact of the matter is we can't do it alone. Sisters have been climbing up the rough side of the mountain, and, yes, we have produced some successes here and there. But the crisis of Black youth sharply demonstrates what happens when only half the army is doing battle. And unless we do something quick, this will be the plight of the next generation of African Americans in the 21st century.

This is not to argue that Black men don't display sexist attitudes. Of course. Such attitudes are in the very fiber of American society; they have infected us all—including women. However, the practice of patriarchy, the subordination of women, and men, requires power, on a grand scale, and control over the nation's institutions. Sorry, but the Brothers ain't there.

Sadly, many Black intellectual women, like those at the anti-March press conference, seem out of touch with mainstream Black women in our communities. Lacking the privileged station of the "D" women (i.e., Ph.D., M.D., J.D., etc.), our less fortunate Sisters do not have the luxury of debating the possible sexism of the Million Man

March. They know that their/our men need healing, inspiration, uplift, and a Farrakhanesque talk about responsibility, respecting women, caring for children, standing up, and stopping the killing. I'm sure these feelings were on the minds of Black Women Behind the March, a Los Angeles group organized to raise money to send Brothers to the March. According to a report in *Newsweek*, one Sister said, "I think the March will last us a while. I really think the Brothers got the message this time." Another talked about the telephone call from her husband the night of the March: "He...began telling me how much he loved me and how much he wanted to make what we had work. He hadn't said that to me in years...I haven't heard him this happy in a long time...I don't know how long this will last, but I'm going to ride it as long as I can."

About the numbers. 400,000? One million? 670,000? Two million? Minister Farrakhan attacked the National Park Service's count of 400,000 as a racist effort to write the hundreds of thousands of Black men at the March out of history. He threatened to sue. A reanalysis of the Park Service's photographs by Boston University's Center for Remote Sensing produced an estimate of between 670,000 and 1.04 million men. A *Detroit Free Press* headline four days after the March stated: "New estimate: 870,000." All of the men I've talked to who attended the March estimated the attendance figure as "easily a million."

Contrary to Black journalist Carl Rowan's dismissive comment that this is a "stupid debate," the numbers are crucial because they provide political leadership with a gauge of the people's will. The expression of public opinion, via support of a march in the nation's capital, provides the potential for shaping public policy. In the case of African American men, marginalized in so many ways, their political will is unknown since many do not vote and few write letters to their Congresspersons. But over a million showed up for the March. Farrakhan had his hand on something.

I have said little about Minister Louis Farrakhan, the "messenger" as the media hyped his role. That is because in the final analysis, the Million Man March was not his. Yes, he called it. And yes, given the current leadership vacuum, he is the only one a million men would have journeyed to Washington for.

Quiet as it's kept, Farrakhan is respected by millions of African Americans, on all socio-economic levels, for his courage in standing up to an oppressive system and his penchant for calling white folk out. Truly "unbought and unbossed," he often says the things that many Blacks feel but don't have the freedom to express. According to a poll reported in *Time*, 59% of Blacks believe Farrakhan is a good role model for Black youth and that he speaks the truth. (Since the March, some Black folk have started saying things like: "Now, I tell you what the problem is with her son, even though it's gon hurt, cause I'm like Farrakhan, uhma tell the truth.")

When Farrakhan sent out the call to the Black universe, the March took on a life of its own. Men—and yes, women—battlescarred, weary, and hungry for creative answers and new thought vibed with the call. And gradually "Farrakhan's March" became Black people's March—a defining moment in our history calling all Black men to task. In an article in *The New York Times*, a Brother from Maryland, speaking from the Update Barber Salon, summed it up this way: "The March is a line. This is where we cut the madness off."

Now, a little more than two weeks after the March, one looks for signs of the March's impact. To be sure, in the long run, we have to come to grips with the profound economic and structural problems plaguing African Americans. Jobs are few and decreasing rapidly, even for those with a four-year college degree. Wealth continues to be concentrated in a small white male segment of the population. And the Republicans' "Contract with America" only increases America's economic injustices. The systemic problems of inequality, which hurt African Americans more than any other group, will have to be dealt with.

In the short run, though, the focus has to be on those areas in African America that we ourselves can do something about—right now. In his talk at the March, Farrakhan outlined an eight-point agenda for Black men which included some things that could be put into place as soon as they returned home, such as setting aside their individualism and joining organizations working for Black uplift.

Signs of renewed social commitment are emerging. *Newsweek* described Thomas J. Miller of Atlanta who came home, turned over management of his company to his wife, and volunteered to work full-time at the Southern Christian Leadership Conference to help in that organization's community work. In Los Angeles, former members of the Crips and Bloods, Charles Rachal and Leon Gulette, renewed their pledge to work with gangbangers to get them to lay down their weapons. (My nephew Kofi couldn't believe his eyes when he saw rival gang members hugging each other at the March.)

In the city I know best, the "Big D," as we Detroiters call it, the after-effects of the March are being displayed everywhere. The new Big Brothers-Big Sisters mentoring center is now getting daily phone calls from Black men.

Associate Pastor Mangedwa Nyathi, of Detroit's Hartford Memorial Baptist Church, said that for the first time, 150 men attended their recent men's group, which focuses on problems of the elderly and economic development. The "East Side Chapter-Million Man March" has been established to work on problems of blight, crime, and other ills plaguing Detroit's east side neighborhoods. A Detroit Public Schools-based organization has been formed to recruit Black male mentors for every Detroit Public School. One hundred fifty men, including a State Representative and members of the New Marcus Garvey Movement, marched on Detroit's west side to protest a crack house that has been operating there for the past two years.

The big pay-off for my city was the reduced arson rate for the Halloween period, a long-standing problem for Detroiters. This year, with over 30,000 volunteers (compared to about 3,000 in 1994), the number of fires for the three-day period was 158, compared to 354 last year. While the Mayor (who attended and spoke at the March) did significantly more to mobilize the community this year, credit and praise must be given to the people themselves, especially Black men inspired by the March, who turned out in such large numbers. One of the first-time volunteers, Brother J.J. Webster, a 42-year-old cook who attended the March, put it this way: "...there's a new spirit of determination by Black men in the city."

As a Womanist, I am encouraged by these signs of the Brothers' involvement in our struggle to be free. In the absence of a movement that would provide a space to focus our pain, to analyze it, and devise ways to stop it, our men (and a few of my Sisters too) seemed to have resigned themselves to powerlessness, given up on the ability to make our communities work, and retreated from responsibility to and for Black youth. The Million Man March was a symbolic reminder to Brothers of middle class persuasion not to forget the ones they have left behind. It was an admonition to Brothers of "thug life" persuasion to abandon the streets and reclaim their legacy of strength, pride and brotherhood. And it was rejuvenation for all of the faithful who have stayed on the battlefield of the Struggle: the posse is on the way, yall just keep on keepin on.

Dr. Geneva Smitherman is University Distinguished Professor at Michigan State University in East Lansing, Michigan. In 1990 she established "My Brother's Keeper," a Black male mentoring program for elementary and middle school students in Detroit. "My Brother's Keeper" is presently operating at Detroit's Malcolm X Academy, an African-Centered, predominantly male public elementary school. Educating Black Males, which Dr. Smitherman co-authored with Dr. Clifford Watson, founder and Principal of Malcolm X Academy, will be released by Third World Press next month.

THE MILLION MAN MARCH: FROM PATRIARCHY TO PARTNERSHIP

Ron Daniels

What follows is a selection of three of the articles which Ron Daniels wrote as a part of his series on the MMM/DOA. "The Million Man March: From Patriarchy to Partnership," was an attempt to address one of the most controversial issues which the organizers were forced to confront, the role of women in the MMM/DOA. "Farrakhan Made the Call - But the March Belongs to Us All" traces the evolving character of the MMM/DOA as a mass action being affected by the voices of key forces external to the planning/mobilizing process and inside the National Organizing Committee of the MMM/DOA. "The Meaning of the Million Man March and Day of Absence," attempts to capture the essence of the conditions which spawned the MMM/DOA, its potential impact and the challenges ahead.

From the moment that Minister Louis Farrakhan called for a Million Man March criticism erupted from some African American women challenging the motive and objectives of the March. This criticism was fueled by the initial declaration that the men should march and the women should take off work and stay at home to teach the children on October 16th. The rationale was that Black women have suffered enough, that they have been forced to the forefront of leadership in the Black community because of the abdication of responsibility by Black men. Therefore, the March will be an opportunity for Black men to stand up, assume responsibility and take their rightful place as head of the household.

While some Black women agree with this assessment and requisite prescription for corrective action, other Black women take offense at the assumption that a patriarchal model of the Black family and the role of Black women in community life should be fostered and perpetuated by the Million Man March. From the beginning there has been the potential that the role of women in the Million Man March, or lack thereof, could become a divisive issue detracting from the importance of this event as a major

mass action. Hence, the March leadership has grappled with the issue of whether the March would promote patriarchy or partnership.

There are legitimate reasons for organizing an all male march (or an all female march for that matter). There is no question that within a patriarchy system of White supremacy, much of the effort to subdue the African community has been directed at breaking the Black male. The chronically

Photo by Third World Press

108

high incarceration rates of Black men and persistent depression levels of unemployment and underemployment are indicators of the historical attack on the Black male. This brutalization and criminalization of the Black male has contributed to the crises of drug trafficking, crime, violence and fratricide which now plague the Black community. Consequently, many Black men are unable or unwilling to shoulder their responsibility for sharing in the leadership of the family, community institutions and the Black Freedom Struggle.

A Million Man March as a mass action which seeks to address these circumstances is on the mark. Minister Farrakhan is calling on Black men to atone for the failure to assume responsibility in the family and the community and the neglect and abuse of Black women by Black men that has hampered our ability to develop as a wholesome people. Another objective of the March is to challenge Black men to end the deadly violence/fratricide that is killing many urban inner city communities within the Black Nation. Equally important, the March will focus on the root causes of the crisis afflicting the Black Nation--racism, cultural aggression and poverty within a capitalist system of White supremacy. The March will make demands on Black men and women, the U.S. government and corporate America to transform the oppressed condition of the Black Nation.

As some Black women have correctly pointed out, however, the Million Man March should not convey the impression that the crisis in the Black community is simply a crisis of the Black male. The suppression of Black women outside and inside the Black community is also a historical fact of life. Contrary to the image of the Black woman in leadership, for much of our history, the Black church, major Black institutions, the civil rights organizations and the Black Freedom Struggle have largely been led by Black men. The reality was, and to a great degree still is, that Black women do the trench work and Black men do the leading.

Black women are also bearing the brunt of the present assault on the Black community. More and more Black women comprise the statistics of the prison/jail industrial complex as desperate conditions drive Black women to commit economic "crimes" to subsist. The growing feminization of poverty in the Black community is also well documented: a phenomenon which is related to workplace inequality and the dramatic increase in single female headed households.

A Million Man March which seeks to address the crisis of the Black Nation must take the issues and concerns of the entire Black community, women and men, into account and be structured and programmed accordingly. A number of Black women have been making this point, and to their credit the March organizers have been listening and responding. A Black Women's Task Force has been organized to ensure that Black women's issues will be part of the platform of the March and will be articulated at the March at all levels. The evolving view is that Black women must play a substantial leadership role in the events that take place in various cities across the country on the day of the March.

It now appears that Black women will be asked to organize mass events at churches, mosques and community centers on October 16; events where women and men who are unable to attend the March will be able to engage in a number of meaningful activities e.g., prayer/meditation for atonement, voter registration, securing commitments to adopt Black children, articulation of local issue agendas etc.

As a supporter of the Million Man March, I am confident that this mass action is moving from patriarchy to partnership. Therefore, rather than wreck the March with criticism from outside, I recommend that women and men who support the principle of partnership should continue to press their case. There is every evidence that Dr. Benjamin F. Chavis and the March organizers are listening and responding. October 16, 1995 will be a historic day in the life and times of Africans in America if we collectively work and struggle to shape the Million Man March into an event that mirrors the interests and aspirations of the entire Black Nation.

Ron Daniels: Veteran Social and Political Activist Ron Daniels, Chairperson of Campaign for a New Tomorrow, served as a member of the Executive Council of the National Organizing Committee for the Million Man March and Day of Absence (MMM/DOA). Along with many other progressive nationalists and activists, Daniels adopted a position of critical support for MMM/DOA. From the outset of his participation in the planning and mobilization process he utilized his nationally syndicated column, Vantage Point, to inform people about the MMM/DOA and offer critical perspectives about its character, direction and program.

A MILLION IS JUST A BEGINNING

Kalamu Ya Salaam

Photo by Roy Lewis

I didn't go. I stayed home with Black women and our daughters. I watched the worldwide media event of the moment on C-Span. A friend who had been in South Africa called a few weeks after the march. I could hear the glow in his voice as he told me how impressive the Million Man March looked on cable broadcast. Nonetheless, as impressive as the march was, I harbor no regrets about not going.

I didn't go mainly because I disagreed with the exclusion (& diminishing) of women both explicit and inherent in the call. Unsurprisingly, the vast majority of Black women decided to support this effort, choosing to embrace the potential & ignore the problems. As always, anything that would help get us together, Black women are for, and they are willing to work out the problems later. Perhaps this capitulation to the march's chauvinism will help people understand how the virulent sexism of the Black Power movement was broadly accepted by both women and men.

Black women who did openly criticize and/or oppose the march were an obvious and ostracized minority. Without a doubt their minority status on this issue will make it harder for them to speak up, be heard, and be included on future issues.

This exclusion of women is symptomatic of a general assault on progressive struggle under the guise of "(back to basics) Blackness". But regardless of historic moment, I am both wary & weary of marching backward in the name of Blackness. Marching backward because of some patriarchal need to put men in the lead — when the truth of all our movements is that men (from Cinque and Nat Turner, right on thru Malcolm, King & elected officials) have been the majority of our leaders.

I am unwilling to pretend that there is even one iota of salvation in this genuflecting to a patriarchal, genitally based struggle. Had women been encouraged to come out in support of Black men, the march would easily have tripled in size and probably raised real issues of healthcare, childcare, battering and rape (the leading violence in our community), environmental concerns and other issues which aren't usually on men's minds when we talk about the problems of "the community".

Moreover, this was the first march I ever witnessed when the marchers kept saying the leaders didn't matter — what kind of self-doubt is this? The leaders don't matter? Since when?

The two key leaders of the march were Rev. Chavis and Minister Farrakhan. Rev. Ben Chavis has been, at best, inadequate as an administrator, questionable as a moral authority and extremely suspect in his dealings with women. Minister Farrakhan's penchant for demagogic language does little to help us understand the source and complexity of our problems as a people. The fact that they continue to struggle is admirable but their failings can not be ignored.

The major problem facing our community today is capitalism. The bottom line of drugs, politics, sports, and entertainment is making big bucks. We are the victims of rampant commercialism and cultural commodification. Everything is for sale. Everything—and when everything is for sale, nothing is sacred. Farrakhan spent hours on numerology, free masonry and trying to convince White supremacists that this country needs a more perfect union, surely such an eagerly anticipated and lengthy speech could have included a succinct critique of capitalism.

What solutions were proposed? Really none. Registering 8 million Black voters was mentioned, but strategies for creating a political party were specifically ignored. Why register people to vote and offer no direction? All that does is validate the political status quo and further entrench career politicians who have, over the last decade, presided over the disintegration of the Black community. So we get a million men together and talk about a "pregnant nine". Or make scattershot recommendations such as adopt a prisoner, adopt a foster child, join an existing organization. Clearly, other than moving toward a more perfect union, there was no vision of the future provided precisely because there was no hard analysis of our current realities and very little understanding of our history.

On one level the Million Man March was a manifestation of both our pain and our impotence, of our inability to separate and the undesirability of integrating. At its most successful, the Million Man March was a spiritual moment that held great meaning for those who participated. Unfortunately, the march also was a resurrection of traditional religion, an elevation of religious doctrine rather than politics and/or economics as the way forward.

Regardless of the specific deity, we have focused on religion in the patriarchal sense. Whether called Jehovah, Christ or Allah, their home is in the sky and between their loins is the jewel of patriarchy: the penis. I know this reads as insanity to those who reveled in the success of the March, but the success of the March was simply one of numbers, not of progressive movement—and yes, I am defining patriarchal religion as non-progressive.

I can not bring myself to pretend that I accept Muslim metaphysics, or that I am lead by some sky god, nor will I co-sign or accept religious hegemony by showing up in response to an A-Tonal call that women can't hear.

I know we all want something to happen. Want another movement like the '60s to bubble up from us and overwhelm the ugliness of this nihilistic present. However, if there is to be such a movement, it will not be a media creation. The next movement will not be a jihad intent on forcing submission to Christian or Islamic religious doctrines, both of which historically were used to justify our enslavement. Moreover, we certainly can not have a real movement if the leaders exclude the female majority of our people. Above all, a movement of liberation won't be as a result of metaphysical, non-critical thinking.

Kalamu ya Salaam is a professional editor/writer, producer and arts administrator. He is a senior partner in the public relations firm Bright Moments, located in New Orleans. He is also the literary coordinator for the Contemporary Arts Center, also in New Orleans, and literary consultant to the National Black Arts Festival, out of Atlanta. Salaam is the editor of *WORD UP-Black Poetry of the '80's From the Deep South* (1990). His book *What is Life?* was published by Third World Press in 1993.

FARRAKHAN MADE THE CALL - BUT THE MARCH BELONGS TO US ALL

Ron Daniels

This slogan advanced by the All African Women's Revolutionary Union of the All African People's Revolutionary Party (founded by Kwame Ture aka Stokely Carmichael), captures the essence of the evolution of the Million Man March (MMM) and Day of Absence (DOA). A vision in the mind of Minister Louis Farrakhan which was initially promoted by the Nation of Islam has been embraced by millions of Africans in America and thus has emerged as an evolving mass action of major proportions.

Minister Farrakhan and the Nation of Islam clearly remain the principal guiding force and institutional anchor for the MMM (which is appropriate given the call). But, to his credit, Minister Farrakhan has consistently pressed to have the March become more than just a Nation of Islam event. In that regard, the National African American Leadership Summit (NAALS), under the leadership of Dr. Benjamin F. Chavis, has played an instrumental role in building the MMM. Indeed, the meetings of NAALS have been a critical sounding board where various proposals on the character of the March and criticisms/recommendations have been heard.

In addition, key leaders from the Nationalist and Pan-Africanist community, most notably Dr. Conrad Worrill, Chairman of the National Black United Front, have played important roles in planning the March from its inception. Bob Law, Haki Madhubuti, Dr. Maulana Karenga, and Imari Obadele are also at the center of the planning/organizing process, and Bob Brown of the All African People's Revolutionary Party is the Director of Logistics for the March. Adding to the ecumenical character of the MMM, prominent African Centered and progressive Christian ministers are actively involved in the mobilization for October 16, e.g., Rev. Frank Reid, Baltimore, Rev. Willie Wilson and Arch-Bishop George Augustus Stallings, Washington, D.C., Rev. Calvin O. Butts and Rev. Johnny Youngblood, New York, Rev. Wendell Anthony, Detroit and Rev. Al Sampson, Chicago.

It is understandable that an event of this magnitude would evoke strong debate about its character and direction. The role of women, concerns about "Atonement" focus, and questions about the "political" direction and follow-up have been among the issues most hotly debated and discussed across the country. Though it is not likely that the ultimate shape and form of the MMM will satisfy everyone, the March has been significantly impacted and changed as a result of the discussion/debate, criticisms within the community and the input/recommendations from various leaders and constituencies.

Photo Courtesy of Senator Carol Mosely-Braun

What began as a male march with women staying at home with the kids has evolved into an event with a two prong programmatic focus: the Million Man March and the Day of Absence which is being organized and led by women. Those who are unable to go to Washington D.C., for the March are being urged to take off work on October 16th to engage in various action as defined by the women's leadership within the Local Organizing Committee across the country. Black people are also requested not to spend any money on the Day of Absence as a concerted demonstration of Black consumer power in this country. High school and college students are also being encouraged to play major roles in the Day of Absence. The Day of Absence is envisioned as a major exercise of Black Power led by Black women. In another change, four women will speak at the MMM to address Black women's issues and to articulate the holistic nature of our struggle in terms of the participation and leadership of women and men. Dr. Charshee McIntryre, C. Delores Tucker, Dorothy Height and Rosa Parks are among the women who have endorsed the MMM/DOA thus far.

Though the MMM was always conceived as having a three fold emphasis, Atonement/Reconciliation, Demands on Government and Demands on Corporate America, for a period of time Atonement was projected as the dominant emphasis. Around the country there was substantial criticism of the implication that we as African people are responsible for our plight. Responding to this criticism, in recent weeks there has been much more projection of the other areas of emphasis. Though the complete set of internal and external social/economic/political goals have not been finalized, the following ideas are under active consideration: A challenge to register at least a million Black voters leading into and following the MMM/DOA; a drive to adopt the 25,000 African children who are now in orphanages; a public policy/political agenda which includes the demand for reparations, the release of all political prisoners, the repeal of the Omnibus Crime Bill and a Domestic Marshall plan; and, the targeting of a major U.S. corporation of economic sanctions (a selective buying campaign/boycott). The National African American Leadership Summit is viewed as the principal vehicle to spearhead and monitor the follow-up to the MMM/DOA.

With a few weeks left, the MMM/DOA is still not sufficiently clear on gender equity issues and political direction for many social and political activists. Though I share these concerns, my own view is that even with its flaws, the MMM/DOA has evolved and is still evolving into an event which will be one of the most significant mass actions of this decade. Therefore, the MMM/DOA deserves the critical support for the broadest range of forces possible. One thing is quite clear, on the street corners, in the barber shops, pool halls and bars, the MMM/DOA has more support than any mass action in recent memory; at the grass-roots there seems to be an understanding that, "Farrakhan made the call - but the March belongs to us all."

Ron Daniels: Veteran Social and Political Activist Ron Daniels, Chairperson of Campaign for a New Tomorrow, served as a member of the Executive Council of the National Organizing Committee for the Million Man March and Day of Absence (MMM/DOA). Along with many other progressive nationalists and activists, Daniels adopted a position of critical support for MMM/DOA. From the outset of his participation in the planning and mobilization process he utilized his nationally syndicated column, Vantage Point, to inform people about the MMM/DOA and offer critical perspectives about its character, direction and program.

WHY FOCUS ON THE MEN?

Charshee McIntyre, Ph.D

Many people asked me "Why would I support an all-male march?" Quite frankly, l couldn't understand the question. My readings of the social conditions within the African American community clearly identify young Black males as the population targeted for extinction.

Media imagery profiles Black women as long suffering "mommas" and/or dominant females who with males of the power elite have and/or do conspire to emasculate Black men and, as a consequence, create youthful Black criminals, the prime population for prisons. These matriarchal, conspiratorial female, and emasculated male myths confuse and divide the African American community, such that instead of analyzing the white supremacists' exploitative system, we turn against one another.

The men believe the women cause the males' problems because we don't give unconditional support to our brothers all the time. The women accuse the males of being patriarchal, disregarding the males' general economic and socially inferior status in this society.

We live in a society guided by interpretations of maleness and femaleness which reinforce these myths. The Judeo-Christian holy books identify the Most High as a male deity and the "mother of all humanity" as the chief sinner. Every entity blames another being - Adam points to Eve, who points to the snake. We first must ponder how Adam and Eve in their state of ultimate innocence could conceive of wrongdoing - since they knew only rightness. We also must question why an all powerful, all present, all seeing, all knowing Male Deity allowed any of these mishaps to occur.

Despite unanswerable questions, the prevailing explanation of this society remains that somebody else is basically responsible for whatever happens to us and always on an individual level despite the claim that the Male Deity has punished all humanity, one by one, for what the original couple did. These ideas give us a world in which personal responsibility is dis-connected from the collective good.

The slavemasters and oppressive class preached this doctrine of collective sin but individual punishment. This approach allows white supremacists to indoctrinate each individual into believing that one by one we save ourselves from this collective damnation. African Americans have come to see our struggle individualistically. We recognize our collective identity as the root cause but often do not understand that a collective response must be the root solution. This brings us to the Million Man March.

Why focus on the men? Many African American women face the inordinate responsibility of holding themselves together, finding help to make things better for their offspring, and directly confronting the social agencies and shifting social policies. They recognize the need for a collective response but do not have time to mobilize, unify, and organize the wider African American community.

Many brothers willingly would contribute in myriad ways but need a means by which to enter the collective process. During the Million Man March, they pledged to commit individually to the process of building an organic

Photo by Third World Press

114

community, to develop using the ancient African moral authority MA'AT - *truth, justice, propriety, harmony, righteousness, balance, reciprocity,* and *order* and couple it with the seven principles of the *Nguzo Saba - unity, self-determination, collective work and responsibility, cooperative economics, purpose, creativity,* and *faith.*

I believe that this process had to begin with the most endangered segment of our society, that brothers needed to stand up for themselves in order to stand up for the rest of us, that brothers needed to experience the victory of their Africanness.

A congressman in New York stated on the radio that the great warrior Geronimo was crazy to fight the United States cavalry because the overwhelming forces of the oppressor meant that the Native peoples eventually had to lose. His kind of criticism comes from a mindset that does not understand the difference between perceiving oneself as a victim or as a victor. In the Native tradition, we believe in Malcolm and Martin's idea that "If you have nothing you willingly will die for, you have nothing you truly will live for."

The solution this government has set forth for African Americans is not as clearcut as their extermination of the indigenous people here or the Jews by Hitler. Rather, the genius of the contemporary plot was set when this new nation created the modern American penitentiary system in 1790. At that time, the disproportionate imprisonment of African American males began. For over 200 years, the United States' criminal justice system buttressed by the racist laws and social and political policies have insured this overincarceration of our men.

Before the Million Man March, many of us believed that imprisonment reflected the level of crime in our communities. Now, we see the prison population for what it is–means by which middle and working class communities buoy up their deflated economies by investing in the proliferation of prisons in their cities and counties. Prison building has become one of the best growth industries in America. And as we know, the disparity between Whites' and Blacks' punishments for similar infractions serves up African and Latin American youth quite rapidly to the prison system.

Some three years ago, we were appalled that more young Black men were in prison than Blacks in college. Today, this nation has incarcerated nearly a million of our youth and by the year 2000 will be warehousing two million plus. Collectively, we cannot allow this government to continue the **denial** of their historic and systemic destruction of our people. We must respond to each and every attack. But, we must respond as a nation, not one by one for affirmative action but collectively in demand for reparation; not one by one for government hand-outs but through mobilization and political pressure; not one by one by choice of purchases but collectively through disciplined economic strategies. We won't buy from people who do not return our investments. Yes, we began with the focus on the men to raise our collective consciousness but the struggle requires us all.

Minister Farrakhan, Rev. Dr. Benjamin Chavis, and the organizers of the Million Man March focused on the theme of **atonement, reconciliation,** and **responsibility**. **Atonement** is the key word above and beyond the idea of recognizing the things we must improve about ourselves individually so that we can become **at one** with our own minds and spirits. **Atonement** also encompasses the notion of the collective union. **At one ment** - being **at one** with ourselves, the Most High, and our people. That goal in and of itself is so lofty it should require no explanation.

Atonement represents the first step toward **reconciliation**. For if we have not come together with all the forces which make up our beings, individually and collectively, how can we possibly **reconcile** anything with anyone. More important, where will we receive the vision of what must be **reconciled**. That vision must be for the collective. It cannot be fueled simply by the hoped for personal salvation of each individual. Each of us may seek salvation, but if we seek it outside the collective, it is an egotistical goal and will not be forthcoming. A people without vision must perish.

Once we accept the idea of collective focus, we move to the ultimate requirement - meeting our **responsibilities**. And, once again, that is to ourselves, to the Most High, and to the collective. **Responsibility** means we must collectively establish and accept our rights, roles, rules, and rituals. If we accept and meet our **responsibilities**, we must mobilize, unify, and organize our communities - locally and globally. With a collective mindset, organized political programs, concentrated educational programs, and disciplined economic strategies coming out of the Million Man March, African Americans will realize that we are a nation within a nation, that we must respond as a nation that understands the attack on any of us is an attack on all of us. One million plus men stood up to say this realization is coming to fruition and the best is on its way! I cannot conceive of any sisters who would not be pleased at this beginning. Unity is the key. One God, One Nation, One love!

Charshee McIntyre is the immediate Past President of the African Heritage Studies Association. She is also associate professor of humanities at SUNY at Old Westbrook. Dr. McIntyre is the author of *Criminalizing A Race: Free Blacks During Slavery.*

THE MILLION MAN MARCH

Courtney Horne

I was not present that glorious day
when a million Blackmen marched to the
nation's capitol from near and far away

They marched with rich and ghetto families.
They all gathered so orderly and hospitably.

I was not present when they appeared
like a great sea; full of fish of a mass variety.
Unique was each kind.
They were harmonious and of one mind.

I was not present when they rededicated themselves
to who they are.
A Black man, a husband, a father,
a brother, a friend and like the wind,
strong and mighty by far.

Peace prevailed that day.
When prominent Black leaders came to say,
stand up Black man,
one for all and all for one.

Protect your children.
Show them you are concerned
Give them love, educate them
and help them learn

No, I was not present that day,
but I write this to proclaim;
the Million Black Men March
will not be in vain.

Courtney Horne is a fourteen year old student in the Detroit
Public School System. She is active in the African Heritage
Cultural Center, where her poem in tribute to the Million Man
March has been received with much fanfare and praise.

A MILLION STRONG, CAN RIGHT ANY WRONG

Laini Mataka

ONCE upon a time, u RULED
words fell out of yr mouth & pyramids jumped into being,
when u cracked yr knuckles, rhythm found a reason to exist.
when u cleared yr throat, musik was born &
when u took yr first step, trees begged to become drums
so they cld follow u around.
the earth bathed in plenty & the blessings were many
til a strange ship pulled into yr inner-most harbors,
carrying a cancer that wld feed off yr very souls
til there was nothing left but the holes yr vitality ustah fill.

caught naked in an undeclared war
u kept dying & dying in an effort to understand what
was happening to u, but
yr enemy knew that the trick to enslaving u
was to do to u what u wld never conceive of doing to anotha.
& trapped in the crux of that knowledge, u opened up yr soul
& swallowed defeat
believing that the reason u lost was becuz u were weaker
& yr enemy was stronger, but u were wrong,
u lost becuz u were human & yr enemy was not.
u lost becuz he tricked u into believing u had to fight
on his terms: raping, looting & pillaging.
u lost becuz u put yr weapons down & tried to adapt to his.
when the epitome of yr every thought & gesture has always
been rooted in yr unconquerable spirituality.
u lost becuz u stopped believing in yrself
& when u found yrself unable to protect yr women & children
when u found yrself stripped & sold like a barrel of rum
u though yr manhood had died/but it didnt,
& when yr woman bore children who looked more like yr enemy
than u/u thought u wld die, but u didnt. & when leather
ate strips of flesh from yr back, u thought it was the end
but it wasnt. becuz inside of u was something greater than
u even realized/something u cldnt lose even if u wanted to.
the invincible might of yr ancestors just kept re-surfacing
to pull u thru the middle passage, it covered yr loins when
u were being examined for sale, it shielded yr mind when u
were put out to stud, it pumped u like adrenalin when u

waited for harriet to fetch u from the grove.
the indomitable strength of yr ancestors gave u WINGS
when bloodhounds were on the chase, & told u/u were a man
when everything else said u were not. & even after pulling
u from the fire, after taking the rope from yr neck, after
giving u the power to teach yrself how to read & enabling
u to make something out of nothing again & again; u
are still not convinced, that VICTORY is just anotha name
for the way u do the things u do
u have crawled, walked & kicked yr way into this century
still ashamed of a dried-up piece of defeat;
a defeat that yr presence here, today, will surely undo
as u kill the shame-filled, broken–down, head-hanging–low
NEGRO in u, by forgiving yrself for all the acts u've
ever committed that kept the race in chains. the day of
ATONEment is here & no one can look at u in any way that
is not compassionate.

this pome invites u to sing along/cuz its a healing song
guaranteed to take u back to where u can FORGIVE YRSELVES
for being descendants of people who sold yr ancestors into
slavery. stop blaming afrikans at home for helping to
enslave u/& try to understand that they sold u to keep from
losing their own loved ones, & that they had no idea
initially, that they were sending u to hell instead of
servitude.

FORGIVE YRSELVES for allowing yr vision to be controlled by
those who enslaved u & stop looking at those who resemble u
as if they were yr enemies.

FORGIVE YRSELVES for ever having been afraid of wite people
in any way, shape or form & understand that they used the
most ostentatiously crippling forms of terrorism to keep u
afraid. just remember that no condition is permanent & that
the intrepid make-up of yr genes, demands that u fill yrself
with luv for yr people/leaving fear with no space to grow.

FORGIVE YRSELVES for letting those who hate u, name & define u
while they maim & kill u, stop wearing the skin they put u in
& step up into the beauty of yr own multi-colored selves.

FORGIVE YRSELVES for being light & thinking that that makes
u better than people who are not & stop being dark and hostile
towards people who happen to be light/all of us are all of us
& if u dont believe me/ask the klan.

FORGIVE YRSELVES for contemptuously calling blks who have money
toms or sell-outs/& if u're one of them, stop looking down on
those who havent been as lucky as u, for if the truth be known
we are all standing on somebody else's shoulders.

FORGIVE YRSELVES for calling otha men faggots for not being
able to live up to yr expectations of manhood, stop calling
women whores for inviting u into their bodies.

FORGIVE YRSELVES for trivializing people who keep talking that
blk stuff & stop denigrating people who are still colored, about
to become black & almost afrikan.

FORGIVE YRSELVES for referring to some blks as "those people"
becuz they dress colorfully & talk loudly, stop looking down
at people who dress ivy league & speak standard english. if
u're willing to listen, both have something to say.

FORGIVE YRSELVES if ever u had a moment of insanity, that caused
u to side with the enemy instead of yr own, stop begging those
outside of the race to luv u & come on home.

FORGIVE YRSELVES for preferring a neighborhood where u can be
the only one/& for othas, stop degrading yrselves til the ones
who can help u the most want to be with u the least.

FORGIVE YRSELVES for letting those who look like u/walk into
life-threatening situations w/out u pulling them up. stop
minding yr own business so well, that yr only concern is u.
u cant help but be yr brotha's keeper, becuz yr brotha is u.

FORGIVE YRSELVES for murdering the Malcolms & the rest/who
willingly laid their lives on the line on our behalf.

FORGIVE YRSELVES and stop giving more credence to what alien
sources say about u than what yr own experts say & write about u.

FORGIVE YRSELVES and stop waiting for the people who hate u to
come to their senses & luv u/more than u lov yr blk self.

FORGIVE YRSELVES and stop stomping on otha people's dreams by
saying "u cant do that" or "they aint never gonna let u do that"
move THEY out of the way, & try to encourage instead of discourage.

FORGIVE YRSELVES and stop complaining about the holes in otha
people's plans to free us/if u can do better, then step up into
greatness/or slide into silence.

FORGIVE YRSELVES and stop being angry about the things yr family
never gave u/be it luv, money or understanding. if the people
u were born into dont support u/then go out & find people who will.

FORGIVE YRSELVES and stop bad-mouthing the memory of ancestors
who did all that they cld so u can be here right now, confirming
& reaffirming yr manhood.

FORGIVE YRSELVES and stop giving wite people more slack than u
give yr own brethren/allowing them to get away with murder
while nailing yr own relatives to the wall for the slightest infraction.

FORGIVE YRSELVES and stop holding onto secrets that tear yr heart
apart, like once u ran & let anotha brotha fall becuz u were
afraid/once u stole from anotha blk person/once u beat a blk woman
once us lusted after a relative/once u forced someone to have sex
once u desired anotha man/once u slept with a wite woman/once u
lied about being somebody's fatha/once u snitched/once u turned
yr back on somebody whose only hope was u/once u killed somebody
killed somebody, killed somebody.

FORGIVE YRSELVES and stop putting poisons in yr bodies; stop
smoking. stop getting drunk. stop eating pork, first. stop
snortin. stop listening to mind-rotting lyrics. stop watching
anti-life images on bigger & bigger screens.

FORGIVE YRSELVES for pimping our culture & find a way to give us
back to ourselves in beauty & light.

FORGIVE YRSELVES and stop arguing with yr woman over who is
oppressed the most, when the foot is evenly distributed over
all of our necks. the issue is how to get from under the foot,
or how to destroy it.

FORGIVE YRSELVES for believing aliens when they insist that the
blk man & woman are having problems. all men & women of all
races & ethnic groups have problems, the most official thing we
need to recognize about ourselves is that if we lost each otha,
WE WILL DIE.

FORGIVE YRSELVES for getting mad at yr woman for making more money
than u/especially since u know that the main reason the system
accepts her is so u will look & feel impotent.

FORGIVE YRSELVES and stop impregnating women whose lives u dont
want to be a part of/& if it happens anyway, stop leaving them
& later blaming them for not doing a thorough job.

FORGIVE YRSELVES and stop denying child–support to the motha becuz
she's found anotha lover. stop calling baby-sitting what u're
doing when u're watching yr own children.

FORGIVE YRSELVES and stop being angry with yr children for being
angry with u for not being in their lives. stop looking evil-eyed
at brothas who take on yr responsibilities.

FORGIVE YRSELVES and stop hiding from yr children becuz u have
no money & give them bits of time & pieces of yr heart instead.

FORGIVE YRSELVES and stop paying women for horizontal dancing.
if u want to help a sistah, do it from the heart, not from the
pointed head, help her to understand that her body is not a
commodity but a temple where u have come to pray.

FORGIVE YRSELVES and stop moving yr clothes from one woman's
house to anotha & anotha & anotha next time u see a woman who
moves u/dont even approach her unless u're in a self-help mode.

FORGIVE YRSELVES and stop going on riki lake, buck-dancin,
talkin stupid & rattling yr chains & shackles for all to see.
and MOST importantly,

FORGIVE YRSELVES and stop begging God to come & get you out of
this mess. u've been equipped since the beginning of time,
with enuff spirituality to see u thru any trial.

this is the day of ATONEment, so forgive yrselves my brothas,
& when u can, turn to us, yr sistahs & FORGIVE us too
for this is the day of ATONEment & all can be forgiven
as long as all is not repeated...tomorrow.

Laini Mataka is a poet, activist and author of *Restoring The Queen,* and other books.

Photo by Richard Muhammad

No Spaces Between Our Men

Reflections of the Author and Excerpts from her Epic Poem
Tribute to Black Men,
I Say A Prayer For You Black Men

Ginger Mance

If I could
I would
heal the wounds
branded into your backs
for 500 years

Even more
would I heal
the invisible wounds
inflicted
upon minds and souls

I would free you
not from unforgotten chains
clasped around ankles and wrists
But chains
upon your spirit
I would unshackle
for I love you.....

On Monday, October 16, 1995, I had the honor of being on the steps of the Capitol during the Million Man March along with members of the press, speakers, ministers, elected officials, and entertainers. I was in Washington because I had written a 50-page epic poem tribute to Black men and the Million Man March entitled, I Say A Prayer For You Black Men. The book, inspired by my reflections on the condition of life in this country for Black men and the march itself, was published by Third World Press and released October 9, 1995– one week before the march.

I observed the march in the capacity of an author and was there to autograph copies of my book and present excerpts of the poem during pre-march festivities and meetings that I was asked to present at. I was honored to receive a number of standing ovations for the poem from audiences made up predominately of Black men and to autograph copies of the book. I was also there because of a strong call from our community for excerpts of my poem to be read during the march. I felt spiritually that it was in order for me to be in Washington during the march. However, in respect for the call to Black men to march and because I fully understood the need for our men to come together at this time in our history, I did not participate on the level that our men were asked to participate. I was in Washington to serve and to share the gift of my poem which was inspired by the Most High Allah God. I also had the honor of volunteering at the national headquarters by answering telephones the day before the march.

During the Honorable Minister Louis Farrakhan's address, I

Photo by Roy Lewis

moved forward to the edge of the Capital steps so that I could experience how it felt to actually witness one million men of African descent standing in unison. As I looked over the crowd of our beautiful Black men, I was spiritually moved to tears. As I gazed out upon this most holy alliance – one of the holiest that has ever occurred since our arrival in this country, I realized that for the first time there were no spaces between our men. For the first time, all forces present that threatened to create spaces between our men were reduced by the spirit and power of love and unity to a level of nonexistence.

I say a prayer for you
a prayer of unity
a prayer of numbers
One million
steppin'
beats and rhythms
Djimbe drums
Force of shekere
serenity of M'bira

flute
saxophone
xylophone
harp

I would dance with you
My father
My brother
My man
My son
You evolved from me
and I you

Men of Africa stood shoulder to shoulder in total unity and harmony—displaying the kind of strength, respect and courtesies that one would expect to find only in the healthiest, most functional families—or in an African village. To witness this power of unity was like witnessing a spiritual revelation. Indeed, the Million Man March was a spiritual revelation. This historic march revealed our strength, our strength in numbers. It revealed the power we have when we come together as one. It revealed that we can come together and that we can rise even above our differences to answer a most central need, a need for unity. As I stood on the edge of the Capitol unable to move, unable even to wipe the tears flowing from my eyes, I reflected upon my earlier experience of moving from the very back of the crowd of men to the steps of the Capitol about 7:00 that morning. My journey through this Nile Valley of Black men was equivalent to about three or four city blocks and the Mall was already filled. As I moved forward and graciously said, "excuse me", our men opened the way for me and extended

a red carpet of respect beyond measure. On two separate occasions, when I arrived at a wall about six feet high, there was a spontaneous call from our men to, "Help the sister!" Help the beautiful sister!" Without hesitation, a number of Black men moved around me, lifted me up and sat me over the six foot wall with the grace and quickness of our own Michael Jordan. These men exhibited a sense of pride as I acknowledged them with the appreciation of a smile warm as a Ghanaian wind and a simple "thank you, my brothers." These men represented my father, my grandfather, my brother, my man, my future husband and perhaps, my son. I felt a closeness that I had not known before, a closeness that was indeed imbued with spirit.

I was honored to witness what I believe was the most significant historical event since our arrival on the shores of this country. Never in our history has one million of the world's most oppressed citizens stood together in unity to remove the remaining remnants of racism that continues of bind our people from the freedom to reach our full potential as human beings. No other group of people in the entire world has been as negatively affected by the evils of racism than Black men. No one has endured this kind of pain and humiliation for the duration of hundreds of years as have Black men. This is why I supported the concept of the march as a Million Man March. It is definitely time for our men to stand up and take control of their lives and the lives of their families. It is important to note; however, that what happens to our men, happens to our women and our children . It is important to note that when the wounded conditions of life for our men are healed, the condition of life for our women and children are automatically improved. And so it is that we were not left out of this march.

They say,
a nation cannot go forth
without its men
that it will perish
I say,
so too will its women
for without you
I am unable to produce
the likeness of ourselves
to bring forth blossoms
that look like you...

With the mere power of unity and numbers, these men removed barriers that stood in my way and opened the path for me to go forward.

As I pondered the meaning of the Million Man March, I realized that the entire historical event was, is and will continue to be about removing barriers, opening paths and clearing the way for our people to truly experience the kind of freedom that permits us to go forward and reach our highest potential in life. That in reaching our potential, we might contribute in a positive way to our families, community, nation and the world. This march was not about hating others. Rather, it was about loving self. It was not about excluding others. Rather, it is about including self.

We must pay whatever price it cost
to buy ourselves back
from the evil
that stole us
from ourselves
that continues
to steal us
from ourselves
today
Buy ourselves back
from this new age slavery...
Buy ourselves back
into the bosoms of mothers
The strong hand of fathers
The whole
That once raised us

The Million Man March is about unity, about numbers, about power. It is about exercising that power to effect positive change in the quality of life for our people on multidimensional levels: spiritually, mentally, physically, psychologically, educationally, economically and politically. It is about freedom. Freedom of the highest order. Freedom to determine one's own destiny - to open one's own path - to open the path for others and in doing so to rise like the lotus blossom of Ancient Egypt up from the grit, grim, rock, and concrete of a foreign land and return to the rich fertile earth of our own history, our own culture, our own selves. It is about realizing the great value that extends far beyond ourselves when we lift ourselves up. For when we lift ourselves up, we lift up our families, our neighbors, our community and ultimately, our world. This march was about atonement, becoming "at one" with ourselves, with our people. About self correction, growth, becoming whole on a million individual levels that we may become whole collectively in such a way that we can never be divided again.

I am Aset (Isis)
My wings outstretched
I receive you
I, Aset
collect your parts
scattered around the world
put you together again

From the four corners of the earth
I call you...

As I witnessed this monumental event, our history unfolding before my eyes, I thought about how much I love Black men. I thought about how much, as I looked out upon them, I wished my arms were long enough, wide enough to take all of these beautiful, strong Black men into my embrace, look each one singularly in the eyes and say: "I love you. I need you. I need you in my life and in the lives of my beautiful sisters and look forward to the day when we will march yet again, this time together, two million strong, hand in hand.

March on
March on
Two million feet
creating anthems
two million feet
conducting symphonies
I believe
I believe
will wash skies
birth new sons
for my tomorrow

I say a prayer
for you
I say a prayer
for you
I say a prayer
for myself
for Us

Black men...

Excerpts printed by permission of the author from her new book, *I Say A Prayer For You Black Men,* by Ginger Mance

Ginger Mance is a poet, an attorney and a community activist. Ms. Mance's poetry has been featured extensively in several private and public readings. She presented her poetry in Cairo, Egypt during the Association For the Study of Classical African Civilizations' Conference in 1987. Her poetry has appeared in *Say The River Turns: The Impact of Gwendolyn Brooks,* published by Third World Press, *The Chicago Defender,* and numerous other journals. Ms. Mance is the author of a collection of poetry titled *An Ancient Fire Burns,* and a book-length poem, written in tribute to the MMM/DOA, called *I Say A Prayer for You Black Men.*

The Million Man March and Day of Absence

Chimbuko Tembo

The Day of Absence as a parallel activity to the Million Man March in Washington was a project of sisterhood, community service and social action. In Los Angeles, it was a collective project organized by sisters from various community organizations: the Organization Us, the Nation of Islam, the Brotherhood Crusade, Mothers in Action, the UNIA, the Senut Society (Us), Mothers Rock, the New African American Vanguard Movement, as well as many individuals. Many of us were meeting for the first time. From our first meeting it was obvious to all in attendance that we came from very different political and religious backgrounds, with different ideas and conceptions about how women should participate in the March, about what it meant to be in "support" of the March and about what it meant to "atone."

We organized around the principle of operational unity advanced by our Organization Us in 1966, that is unity in diversity, unity without uniformity. What held us together as "Women in Support of the Million Man March" and "Women Organized for the Day of Absence" was this principle of operational unity, the respect we had for one another as African women, our sense of the historical importance of the project and our desire to see Black men stand up, make and keep commitments to be better persons, build stronger families and struggle to bring into being a just society and better world.

From the inception of the call for the March, the women and men of Us, along with other women and men across the country carried on discussions about the meaning of the March, the form it should take and how it fit in our struggle to build family and community and end our oppression as a people.

From these discussions, our women's group , the Senut Society (Us), wrote a position paper (see document section), which reaffirmed the principles of mutual respect, equality, complementary and shared responsibility in male/female relations. As we said in our position paper, we were concerned that the March and the activities and discussions surrounding it represented the best of our tradition as a people in struggle. Therefore, along with other women and men across the country, we worked hard to expand the original conception of the March so that: a) the priority focus on men in no way suggested the exclusion or lack of concern for women; b) that women at all times were viewed and treated as equals and partners; and c) that a joint project be created in which this equality and cooperative partnership were expressed.

From the extensive exchange at the local level and in national meetings, we of Us and other women and men with similar concerns expanded the idea of the Day of Absence (DOA) so that it became an essential part of the overall project of standing up and assuming a new and expanded responsibility by Black men in particular and the Black community in general. We especially stressed the need for

Photo by Robert Sengstacke

a moral vision of society and Black male-female relations that upholds equal rights, roles and responsibilities of Black women and men in the life and struggle of our people.

As women of the Organization Us, we made a significant input into the formulation of the mission statement, written by Dr. Maulana Karenga, on behalf of the National Executive Committee of the MMM/DOA. This statement summarized the best of our thoughts as a people concerned about the state of the world in which we live and the impact of this on the quality of our lives.

The Senut Society (Us) wanted to mobilize, organize and direct in positive ways the collective energies of our people which had become ignited around the idea of a Million Man March. Therefore, in critical dialogue with our sisters, we expanded the Day of Absence so that it became a day for community teach-ins, service and social action. Borrowing from the mission statement and its expanded conception of atonement, we argued for the need of a collective assessment in terms of our personal involvement in community institutions and organizations and our commitment to struggle.

We organized the DOA to serve the needs of our community and to raise political consciousness on several levels. As an educational structure, we engaged the community in dialogue about the purpose and goals of the MMM/DOA; the value and possibility of collective struggle; the power and significance of staying away from work, school, places of entertainment and a 100% consumer boycott, as well as the formation of an independent Black party. We went to the people, to housing projects, high schools, restaurants, beauty shops, the airport, etc., to distribute information and to engage in community dialogue.

We organized two community teach-ins, both held at the African American Cultural Center (Us). The first was organized prior to the MMM/DOA, in order to discuss the larger meaning of the March and Day of Absence and to present the Mission Statement for a critical understanding of the issues, purpose, goals and continuing projects. The second teach-in was held on the Day of Absence and involved the participation of a number of community institutions and organizations: health care institutions, parent advocacy groups, adoption agencies, school board members, senior citizens groups, teachers organizations, etc., which engaged the community in discussions concerning the challenges we face, the services they provide as well as to solicit volunteers and suggestions for improvement. Though organized by the assembling of women in the community, the Day of Absence teach-ins were attended by the entire community—women, men and children who did not attend the March in Washington but wanted to build a joint project with the March; to strengthen themselves, their families and community; to come together and to be with others to share their concerns and aspirations; to be a part of this historical moment in history; and to share in the new sense of possibilities. Also in attendance were young

women from the Senut Society's Rites of Passage program, ages 10-16, who not only participated in the teach-in, but also in the boycotts and in follow-up assignments around the MMM/DOA.

In all our activities, we were concerned about both our sisterhood with other women and our partnership with men. In our philosophy of Kawaida, "the measure and meaning of everything is determined by the quality of relations it creates and sustains." So, we worked to build a joint project in which sisterhood was strengthened and expanded and our partnership in love and struggle with our men was reaffirmed and reinforced. In each case, principles of equality and mutual respect, mutual support and ongoing cooperation were stressed as indispensable. Through principled relations and cooperative work, we were able to set an example for future small and massive projects. But we also honored the best of our tradition, which teaches that "whatever good we do, we must do together as men and women." Our task then, as our Senut Society (Us) position paper states, is "to build an empowered community, a just society and a better world together as mutually respectful and mutually supportive partners. We take up this task fully aware that our very future depends on it."

Chimbuko Tembo is chair of the Senut Society (Us); a Seba (moral teacher) in the ancient Egyptian tradition; a lecturer in Black Studies; a member of the executive circle of the Organization Us; a member of the Los Angeles Local Organization Committee, MMM/DOA; and publisher of the University of Sankore Press.

Photo by Richard Muhammad

Part 7
Media, Media, Media

Photos by James Wethers

THE MESSAGE AND THE MESSENGER

George E. Curry

The Detractors of the Million Man March all seemed to be reading from the same tired script. "You can't separate the message from the messenger," was the refrain. Of course, that carefully crafted mantra was designed to separate Minister Louis Farrakhan, the controversial leader of the Nation of Islam, from the African-American community.

But instead of discouraging African-American men from attending the Oct. 16 gathering in the nation's capital, attacks on Farrakhan had the opposite consequence. Every time Farrakhan was vilified, it seemed, thousands more decided to head for Washington, D.C. In the end, at least 1 million Black men participated.

Ironically, many Whites—and some Black conservatives—who urged Blacks to shun the Million Man March because the message supposedly couldn't be separated from the messenger, failed to understand what the message was in the first place. To borrow a phrase from the women's movements they just didn't get it. The message they associated with Farrakhan was one of hate, especially his broad-brush harangues against Jews and the Nation of Islam's Black supremacy teachings. By contrast, African-Americans were attracted to his appeals to racial pride, accepting personal and family responsibility, and economic empowerment. And that's the message marchers from around the country were unable—or unwilling—to separate from the messenger.

I found it odd that some critics who opposed the march on the grounds that it would produce disunity among Black males and females made the round of talk shows to voice their displeasure, as though doing so would help the cause of unity. And many of those same critics had recently returned from the United Nations' Conference on Women in Beijing—with no objections from Black men—yet they saw something wrong with an all-male gathering.

A handful of Black conservatives were equally hypocritical. After calling for Black men to accept more personal responsibility, when a march was called to do just that, they, too, showed up on television, saying why they would not be in attendance. Not that they were missed. This is not to suggest that all opponents of the march were not well-intended—some were—but this was an important first step that was successful even without their support.

Something emerged from the Million Man March that is far more important than how critics viewed either the march or Farrakhan. The nation of Islam leader made two significant overtures to traditional civil rights leaders and Black politicians. Unlike the past, when he shunned both Democrats and Republicans, Farrakhan urged African-Americans to register as either Democrats, Republicans or Independents.

He also encouraged African-Americans to return home and join an organization— any organization—working on behalf of Blacks, including the NAACP and the National Urban League, neither of which endorsed the Million Man March. In other words, don't stand on the sidelines criticizing what Black groups are not doing.

Despite all the criticism enveloping Farrakhan, the Million Man March was a stunning success. There was a sense of love and brotherhood that cannot be adequately conveyed to those who chose to stay away. Man after man said, "Pass the love," as they gently pounded one another's fists. They even passed money to total strangers. Now the challenge is to take that love and trust, and spread it among our respective communities.

George E. Curry is the editor-in-chief of *Emerge Magazine*

BUCK PASSING: THE MEDIA, BLACK MEN, O.J. AND THE MILLION MAN MARCH

Ishmael Reed

The Nazi medias' treatment of Jewish Males, especially the Ostjugend, immigrants from Russia, whom the German Jews feared would reinforce Anti-Semitic stereotypes, is very instructive. A scholar writing for *Lillith*, a Jewish feminist publication, says that Jewish women were treated in a chivalrous manner up until the Holocaust, but that Jewish men bore the brunt of a right wing government and media's hostility. Just as black men are labeled "underclass" by the American political establishment and media, Jewish men were Nazi Germany's underclass. Jewish women were critical of sexism in Germany's Jewish community. In fact, the history and ill-fated alliance between Jewish and Aryan feminists might be a lesson to black women who have joined Brownmiller feminists like Tammy Bruce, the bane of O.J. Simpson, in an effort to single out black males as symbols of the cruel attitudes that men hold toward women. After Hitler cemented his control of the German government, these Jewish women were abandoned by their Aryan feminist allies.

White feminists, whom bell hooks accuses of using black feminist celebrities as "caretakers of the soul," which was how the Hollywood Mammies related to the frail southern belles, will usually explain their clinging to the black feminist ikon of the moment by relating unhappy experiences they've had with men, many of them white men. Black men have been designated by the culture as the sacrificial lambs for male evil. Men from other ethnic groups whose treatment of women is, in some cases, worse than that accorded black women by black men, join the attack on black men as a way of covering their own record of abuse against women; they pass the buck to black men which is what feminist Andrea Dworkin suggested when she said that the image of the black male rapist is pushed by white men who wish to cover their own participation in this crime. (Murder of black women by their husbands and boyfriends has declined by 40% since 1976 and murder of black men by black women and that of black women by black men is about the same percentage, due to black women's tendency to retaliate. The murder of white women by white men hasn't declined.)

In the case of Ms. Bruce, who has decided that Simpson should "leave the culture and the country" and who revealed his agent's private number to dangerous cranks, it was her father. She is permitted to shrilly offer misleading data about black female/male relationships on CNBC, because CNBC is run by Roger Ailes, one of the architects of George Bush's Willie Horton campaign.

The white male commentariat and media salesmen

Photo by Roy Lewis

aided the prosecution by evidence distortion and demonizing the defense team, in the O.J. Simpson case, in which Simpson was used to chastise all black men. These media salesmen hypocritically posed as feminists, and the bourgeois feminists, who depend upon white men for employment, like the women at Ms. Magazine, one of the centers of black male bashing, let them get away with it. Geraldo Rivera, whom Kurt Vonnegut called "the vilest" human he'd ever known, because of his abuse of Vonnegut's daughter, Edie, posed as a supporter of women against domestic abuse, and is a confidant of the Brown family. He still leads the chorus of those who believed in Simpson's guilt, even before the trial was underway.

After the verdict was rendered, Rivera's rhetoric got hotter as he referred to Simpson as a "punk," when it was Geraldo, in his autobiography, appropriately entitled, *Exposing Myself*, who admitted to have homoerotic desires for Rudy Nuyerev and Mick Jagger. Another feminist, who scolded Simpson for his male chauvinist attitudes, was Larry King. According to Spy Magazine, Larry King was accused by a woman employee of sexual harrassment. Feminist Richard Thornburgh, former Attorney General of the United States, was another television commentator who believed in Simpson's guilt before the defense began its case. Mr. Thornburgh was one of those justice department officials who set up Marion Barry with women, an act for which he was accused of "pandering" by *Times* columnist, William Safire, who said of the prosecution in the Barry case that "never has the United States stooped so low." Other feminists who lined up against Simpson were the head of the Nicole Simpson Foundation, set up to aide battered women. He was a convicted batterer. And Bob Guccione, who contributed to the foundation, he is the publisher of Penthouse, which occasionally will exhibit a nude woman in chains. He was accused by one woman of holding her as a sex slave. His son, Guccione Jr., who is brought in from time to time to convict Michael Jackson, in television's ongoing lynching of the superstar, has been accused of sexual harassment by women also. The white male commentariat's response to the M.M.M. was also hypocritical. Since the march was billed as an atonement for black men, these white men behaved as though white men had nothing to atone for, engaging in a phony effluvia of congratulations to black men for finally getting themselves together. Though the majority of black women have been very supportive of black men, Nicholas Von Hoffman traced the origin of the Million Man March to criticism of black men by a handful of highly publicized black commercial feminists, and cleverly used these women to represent all black women. Though over 90% of black youth are not involved in the criminal justice system, Mr. Hoffman, writing in the *New York Observer* characterized the pre-March black youth as "Mr. Mofo" (Mr. Motherfucker) who" pissed in front of Smith College women shopping on their lunch

hours...African American women had obviously had it with Mofo and the bloods a long time ago...they were no longer sticking by their man...The recent Million Man March is a clue that one more great change is underway."

Black women, who have been enlisted to chastise Simpson, Michael Jackson, Mike Tyson, and the Million Man March by white men who run *The New York Times, The Village Voice, The New Yorker,* and National Public Radio, should ask themselves, why we never get any stories about the abuses of women who share the ethnic backgrounds of the white male publishers and broadcast producers who invite them on to do their black male bashing commentaries? Latino, Irish-American, Italian and Jewish American feminists claim that the abuses the women and their groups suffer are being covered up by a conspiracy of silence, which is the way most ethnic groups in this country deal with their pathologies, and the media assists in the cover-up by pointing to black men as the main culprits for crime, drugs and violence, when studies show that such activities cut across racial and class lines. Are these women aiding in the cover-up? Do the white men who own National Public Radio (though it has a black figurehead) use black feminists to criticize Simpson, Tyson, Thomas and the M.M.M. as a way of deflecting from their own male chauvinism?

A few weeks after a white feminist brought a suit against NPR for promoting men over women, the white men at NPR did a story about sexism in Africa. That's how the white male-owned media like NPR and CNN, which lent the L.A. District Attorney its investigation team, and is now rooting for crazy Fred Goldman's personal vendetta against Simpson, deal with sexism. It all takes place in the inner city or in Africa.

The blaming of black men for sexism and the silence about that of men in other groups is not the only place where white pathology is excused. A report of skyrocketing heroin abuse among the white middle and upper classes was barely noticed by the *New York Times* which regularly features front page stories about black male pathological behavior.

As long as right wing white males control the media, the media will be used as a weapon against black men. They will be aided by some aging Ku Klux feminists and some younger feminists, black and white, who are simply naive, like Kristal Brent Zook, who blasted O.J., Mike Tyson and the Million Man March in the *New York Times* magazine section, a publication whose record of vilification against blacks is so bad that CEMOTAP (Committee to Eliminate Media Offensive to African People) demonstrated against the *Times* after they ran a photo of a black woman with a baby strapped to her back about to fellate a white john. Her article, whether she knew it, was part of an ongoing vindictive attack on black men by the editors of the magazine, neo-conservative ideologues, who believe that black male behavior is at the root of all social pathologies. They regularly run what amount to emotional rants by black feminists against black men. Even the two black male intellectuals whom they profiled within the last two years are those who are into prominence by an uncritical devotion to feminism, blasting Africentrics and blaming black people for the country's anti-semitism. These people are little more than hired mouths. If a black editor ran a magazine, like the *New York Times* magazine, or *New York* magazine, or *The New Republic*, which was as vicious against Jews as these magazines are against blacks, the ADL and the JDL would be all over him.

An example of the lack of black media power is that magazines which often engage in Nazi styled rhetoric against blacks like the *New Republic*, whose editor, Martin Perez, recently said that black women are culturally deficient, and the *Atlantic Monthly*, where *The Bell Curve* was first published, exercise power over who is and who isn't a black intellectual. FAIR (*For Accuracy In Reporting*) tried to get some of those journalists who condemned Louis Farrakhan's wild Anti-Semitic rhetoric to condemn Perez for his Nazi views about black women. None of them, including Tina Brown of *The New Yorker*, and *Vanity Fair*, would do so.

Joseph Goebbels ran a newspaper called *Der Angriff* which scapegoated Jews and idealized the German population which was portrayed as hard-working and devoted to family values. The same kind of disparity exists in the coverage of black males in this country. In fact, I have compared Nazi stereotypes about Jewish men and those promoted in the American media about black men and have found perfect matches.

Robert Lypsite, a *New York Times* sports writer bonded with those black women who demonstrated against Mike Tyson's Harlem Homecoming. For the last few years, he has been touting an unpublished dissertation by a Mormon scholar which blames black athletes for the rapes committed against women in sports. Even Lypsite said that the book might be considered racist. Lypsite even called for a boycott of the network that carries Tyson's fights. A few weeks ago, barely noticed by the white male owned and operated media, was the arrest of Tommy Morrison, former WBO Heavyweight Champion, a white fighter who owns one of the most devastating punches in boxing. Ask Razor Ruddick and George Foreman, two of this victims. Tommy Morrison was arrested for punching one woman and biting another and there wasn't a peep from the black-male obsessed feminist movement, nor was there a call for a boycott of his fights by black feminist, Robert Lypsite.

A number of women have accused Senator Packwood of sexual wrong doing, but when his colleagues announced that his case would be aired behind closed doors, none of the pandemonium occurred that ensued when a similar decision was made during the Clarence Thomas vs Anita Hill episode. There was no marching up the steps of the capitol, which is what happened when feminist kamikaze and their cannon fodder, Anita Hill, denied Clarence Thomas his right to due process. Of all black feminists, Anita Hill has become one of the most usable, even permitting herself to be used by Gil Garcetti, the unscrupulous prosecutor in the Simpson case. Her being a guest of the prosecution during the trial was part of a blatant effort to influence the nine black women on the jury. It didn't work. In fact, the difference in attitudes between the black women on the jury and that of the black feminists who were summoned by the *New Yorker* to convict Simpson, without citing a scintilla of evidence, and to denounce the Million Man March, merely shows once again how out of touch the hand-picked Talented Tenthers are with the feelings of ordinary black Americans. Michele Wallace said as much in her *Village Voice* piece covering the meeting held by some of the march's critics, at Columbia University, on the evening of the March. "The results, not surprisingly, were disappointing," she wrote.

The Talented Tenthers, whose ideology is feminism, also run the risk of being associated with right wing racist prosecutors and police, and of supporting women regardless of whether they are lying, apparently believing, with Anita Hill, that the woman must always be believed. There is enough evidence to suggest that Marion Barry, Mike Tyson and O.J. Simpson were set up by malicious prosecutors and by the kind of degenerate police who are ever present in the black ghettos. A *New Yorker* magazine article, which included the views of 13 black intellectuals, also showed the Talented Tenther's cavalier disregard of abuses in the criminal justice system. It doesn't matter to them that the police lied in the Simpson case or violated his fourth amendment rights. It doesn't matter that a woman policeperson who worked with Mark Furhman reported that Furhman abused her and humiliated her. (It didn't matter whether Furhman beat up Jews and belonged to the Nazi party, either). The black feminists and white feminists have not uttered a word about Furhman's testimony that the and other officers used a Mexican American woman as a human shield during an exchange of gunfire with a Mexican American gang, giving credence once more to the charge that bourgeois feminists don't give a hoot about poor women. The feminists in the *New Yorker* who dissed Simpson and the Million Man March—some linked the individual to the event—convicted both the individual and the March simply because men were involved. They think that they know more than forensics experts Henry Lee, and Michael Baden, microbiologist John Gerdes, and other scientific experts brought in by the defense to make mincemeat of the prosecution's case. Cyril Wecht, one of the country's top forensic pathologists, said that the paucity of blood pointed to Simpson's innocence.

Some of these commercial feminists are hypocrites, too.

They were opposed to the March that called for male attendance, yet some of the women attend conferences which, if not excluding men, certainly give the impression that men are not welcomed. (Kristol Zook admitted this in her *Black Feminist Manifesto, Sort Of.* When is Jack Rosenthal going to publish a Jewish Feminist Manifesto that would document the abuses against Jewish women by Jewish men, a history of abuse and gender conflict that is contributing to the extinction of Jewish America?) In fact, there were more women in attendance at the Million Man March than at the typical feminist conference, attended by those feminists whom the *New York Times* and the *New Yorker* used to denounce the March. (The anti-Simpson, anti-March slant of Henry Louis Gate's *New Yorker* article was predictable. Simpson hater and Denise Brown companion, Roseanne Barr is a power behind the *New Yorker* these days. *New Yorker* editor, Tina Brown, even flies to Los Angeles to discuss the direction of the magazine with this comedian, prompting some *New Yorker* staffers to resign in protest. Both the *New Yorker*, and *Vanity Fair*, Tina Brown publications, favored the prosecution's side in the Simpson case. Jeffery Toobin, who was the media's authority on the attitudes of black people about the case, wrote a series of kiss-behind articles in favor of the prosecution in the *New Yorker* and the deranged and sleazy Dominick Dunne did the hatchet jobs on Simpson and Johnny Cochran for *Vanity Fair*. Barr is another one of these sick wounded women who wants to make a black man pay for whatever problems they've had with men.

Feminist scholars like the ones the *New York Times* brought on to its front page to denounce the Million Man March even endorse conferences which exclude heterosexual women. Before denouncing the MMM some of them attended an all-woman's conference in China where they held a lynch mob "trial" of Simpson, way over there.

These Bourgeois feminists' idea of oppression is being hassled about first class seats on a plane. Though some of them are sincere in their criticism of black male chauvinism, others are obviously in it for the money, and brag about their huge publishers' advances—their earnings from dissing black men—on network television.

Unlike the grievances of black mothers who must face drastic welfare cuts, who can't afford to buy food, and the millions of working poor black men and women, those of the college educated academic black feminists seem trivial. The young feminist, Kristal Brent Zook, who denounced the Million Man March, O.J., Tyson, Mel Reynolds, Clarence Thomas, Tupac Shakur, etc., on behalf of the right wing white males who run the *Times* magazine section, said that her idea of abuse was a Guatemalan immigrant touching her private parts and a white man luring her into lifting her dress for a photo opportunity, which must strike the generation of black women, who were mauled by southern cops during the Civil Rights movement, as a little silly.

Previously, another black feminist, in the pages of the same magazine, traced her oppression to a remark that her father made to her about an immodest bathing suit she wore on the beach one day. Her black male bashing book which promises to make her wealthy will be published soon.

While O.J. Simpson's lawyers and consultants exposed a racist criminal justice system before the world, in which the prosecution, for example, withheld exculpatory evidence, defended the testimony of lying witnesses, investigated and harassed the defense's scientific experts, planted prosecution agents like the Brooklyn born Gloria Allred, CNN's official basher of black men, as an objective media expert (for CBS, whose minority hiring record is so bad it's called Caucasian Broadcasting Co.) and brought in experts who were prone to examiner bias, The Million Man March challenged the media's lies and stereotypes about African American males. One day in Washington did more to challenge a racist, segregated media than all of the reports, studies, boycotts conducted by media critics over the last twenty five years. The problem was that members of other groups took this Day of Atonement to mean that black men were the only ones to have something to atone for. (The other problem was that the most prominent speaker has a history of making bizarre comments about Jews and bigoted statements about other groups. Maybe he doesn't realize that Anti-semitism in this country is only tolerated when it issues from the mouths of powerful white men like Pat Robertson, George Bush, Pat Buchanan, Richard Nixon, former Secretary of State, James Baker, and Billy Graham, the world's second most powerful religious leader, who once said that the Jews were satanic and owned the media). White men could use some atonement and so could black and white women. Women perpetrate more violence against children than men, yet black and white feminists seldom discuss this form of domestic violence, or women committing psychological oppression as well as physical oppression against men. Black men are 55 percent of the male victims murdered by women.

One black feminist appeared on C-Span, which runs what amounts to a propaganda hate bulletin board against blacks every morning, to denounce the March as being controlled by patriarchal and nationalistic black men, yet her refusal to refer to any social pathologies perpetrated by women makes her a nationalist for women. She is a rich leader of the feminist nation with a full endorsement from the patron of black feminists, Gloria Steinem, another one of these feminists who have denounced Clarence Thomas and O.J., yet said she's embarrassed when a man of her own ethnic background is ensnared in a scandal. Ms. Steinem is president of the feminist nation. (Ms. Steinem has never clarified her ties to the C.I.A. and when a Random House book contained some information about these tips, Ms. Steinem intervened and had the offending passages removed. If I were a member of the secret government, I couldn't think of a better way to paralyze the country's most progressive and militant community than to start a fight between black men and women). Nationalists are those who believe that their side is of higher moral superiority than the enemy. For the feminists who are making money and gaining publicity for denouncing O.J., Clarence Thomas, Mike Tyson, and the MMM, the enemy is black men.

The emancipation of black men has been abandoned. The communications with black men have been cut off, which is what happens when you're on a war footing with the enemy. Talks break down and hostility begins. Their books are seldom used in college courses anymore. A variety of viewpoints from black men are ignored by the white male run media who prefer athletes and criminals, and other dopey people and use black and white feminists to blame all of the social evils of the society on black men, while theirs go unchecked. (Why doesn't Steven Spielberg do a movie about patriarchal abuses that occur in Jewish homes against Jewish women?)

Politicians like Newt Gingrich (a hypocrite who preaches family values, but whose sexual escapades were exposed by *Vanity Fair*) are permitted to run wild with unrebutted Nazi rhetoric against black men and poor black women. All of the anecdotes about moral depravity contained in his "inaugural speech, " delivered when the Republicans captured Congress, as well as the speech celebrating the 100 days of Republican rule, and his most recent comments about the grisly Illinois murders, involving white victims and black perpetrators, allegedly, have to do with black people, when I could provide Gingrich with ten instances of white pathology for every black case that he can cite. While a variety of viewpoints from whites are presented by the media, the only black opinion maker on the media's Rolodex seems to be Clarence Page, whom Bryant Gumbel referred to as less strident. Other establishment approved black commentators felt compelled to denounce the O.J. verdict as well as the MMM.

The black male, whose creative genius has made billions for others and who is only applauded by right wingers like Ben Wattenberg when he goes to war, has been shunt-ed off to the margins of the American discourse. The Million Man March showed that no matter how much his enemies seek to silence him, the black man will not shut up.

There are other steps that can be taken to counter the heavy propaganda treatment by the enemies of black men who control the media. Black members of Congress should be urged to support the restoration of the Fairness Doctrine, which requires the media to voice opposite points of view on controversial issues. The corporate supporters of anti-black propaganda centers like the Heritage Foundation, and The American Enterprise Institute, and the Manhattan Institute should be exposed and their products boycotted. A new black think tank, which would do for blacks what the Anti-Defamation league does of Jews, that is, oppose every slur and distortion against blacks that occurs in the media, should be established.

Finally, there should be an all out Montgomery styled Bus Boycott against the media until they hire more black journalists, not just collaborators, but those with independence, who present a variety of viewpoints from the black community and provide a balanced picture of black people in the media. When I took the floor at the Unity 94 convention to denounce Ted Turner of CNN as the American Goebbels for his network's daily slander against black Americans--slanders that reach 90 countries–and to ask panelist Jesse Jackson whether a boycott of the networks was in order, he said that it was a good idea. It's still a good idea. Given the shaky financial status of the American media, a sustained boycott against newspapers alone in major cities would bring these propaganda agencies to their knees.

Ishmael Reed is best known as a satirical novelist, as well as an essayist, poet and editor/publisher. His poetry in particular has made him a major force within the African American literary community. His works of long fiction include *The Freelance Pallbearers* (1967); *Yellow Back Radio Broke-Down* (1969); *Mumbo Jumbo* (1972); *The Terrible Twos* (1982); *The Terrible Threes* (1989). Reed currently resides in Berkeley, California, where he is a professor at UC Berkeley, and one of the founders of the Yardbird Publishing Company.

THE TRUTH, THE MEDIA AND THE MILLION MAN MARCH

Richard Muhammad

Over 1,500 journalists--cameras flashing, tape recorders clicking and video cameras rolling--were on hand to cover the Million Man March on Washington. But in a society that mouths the value of a free press and the exchange of information and ideas, media coverage before and after the march exposed the gap between a free press and truth.

Missing from the coverage was objective, balanced analysis, respect for the event and its significance, and present was an obsession with negative images of march convenor Minister Louis Farrakhan that the media created in the first place.

Min. Farrakhan, for the majority of white America, emerged on the national scene in 1984 during Rev. Jesse Jackson's presidential campaign. After a spirited defense of the civil rights leader, who was barraged with attacks following his Hymietown remark, Min. Farrakhan was branded an anti-Semite, a racist, and a hate teacher.

Despite his explanations and the truth, the media mischaracterizations have continued. Therefore when Min. Farrakhan envisions a massive demonstration that captures the mind, heart and soul of Black America, an explanation becomes necessary, not because Min. Farrakhan is controversial but because the media has created an image that it cannot simply walk away from .

For the media, "the Farrakhan issue" had to be raised with Black leaders, organizations and ordinary Black people in order to perpetuate a myth that serves the media's appetite for controversy, articulate a position that does not offend America's ruling class and cater to those adamantly opposed to the leader of the Nation of Islam.

The preoccupation with seeking out and elevating critics of the march was more evidence that controversy and condemnation, no truth seeking, was sought by reporters.

Republican Gary Franks, who represents a nearly all-white, relatively affluent, congressional district was elevated to the status of a credible Black leader, who opposed the march. In reality, Mr. Franks was a politician whose district faces little of the crisis in inner cities and Black America, who could not afford to endorse the march.

So while Mr. Franks was viewed as a "legitimate," Dr. Dorothy Height, a civil rights stalwart and president of the National Council of Negro Women, was given little credence as she defended the march against charges of sexism.

The National African American Leadership (NAALS), a coalition of leaders and groups spawned by Rev. Ben Chavis when he was NAACP executive director, was also ignored by the media. NAALS endorsed and embraced the march with member groups providing expertise and support.

Since NAALS and its meetings were given token coverage, journalists were not in position to see the groundswell of support of the march that was growing.

Its bias would not allow the media, white-owned media, to really grasp the march or its significance. Trapped by its own lies and unwillingness to admit that the Nation of

Photo by Richard Muhammad

Islam, as a movement, is interwoven into the fabric of Black culture, the media view was skewed from the outset.

By contrast, the Black press, Black owned-media, never functioned under the popular "mainstream" misconception and was free to explore the reason and appeal of the march. Weekly Black newspapers, radio and television stations, *Emerge* magazine and, in particular, Black Entertainment Television, recognized the significance of the march early and provided the proper debate, discussion and ultimate support that helped make it successful.

Early "mainstream media" coverage was slanted to make the projections of Million Man March Executive Director Chavis, who predicted over one million men, look overblown and foolish. Newspapers reported that roughly 1 in every 11 Black men in America would have to show up for the march to reach one million. March-sanctioned travel agencies have booked few people, major Black religious denominations had not endorsed the march and traditional groups were lukewarm about he march, said the media. All the "evidence" present was designed to lead to the conclusion that the march would be a flop.

The media's lack of respect for the march wa shown in it's preoccupation with the "legitimization" of Min. Farrakhan, instead of the birth of a new movement.

With the 1980's Reagan Revolution and 1994 Republican sweep of Congress, the debate was not centered solely on the personality of those who led the country's right-ward shift. The media acknowledge personalities that helped make these events happen but deeper attention was paid to grasping the message the American public was sending and in determining where the country was headed.

The same debate should have occurred about the march, the historic collaborative effort needed to pull it off, the healing of wounds within the Black community, the desire for a unified approach to common problems and a budding united Black front.

White America typically wants to diminish any Black leader to a personal agenda. Remember, "What does Jesse want?"...the media mantra during Rev. Jackson's 1988 presidential run. Here was a Black man who registered more Democratic voters than anyone in history, enjoyed a lifetime of activism, captured some 7 million votes, and articulated a political agenda and vision. Despite all that, the media wanted to limit its focus to what does an individual crave, not what does this man's appeal represent.

The same is true of the Million Man March, in that, the media speaks of the legitimization of Min. Farrakhan. Min. Farrakhan, standing on the solid foundation laid by the Honorable Elijah Muhammad, the Nation of Islam's patriarch, occupies a place within Black America that cannot be denied and was legitimate before the march.

With some 40 years of personal service and the 60 year old legacy of the Nation of Islam, "the Minister" speaks not only to the hurt of the underclass but to the pain of the middle-class. And by grooming men and women for leadership, building institutions, standing on principles and independent of the white power structure, Min. Farrakhan is loved, respected and trusted.

His humility, candor and ability to speak straight words, along with the Nation of Islam's proven ability to solve problems, have made him a champion for Black people.

It is his vision and spiritual grounding that makes him able to challenge anything he deems harmful to Blacks either inside or outside the community. His place in the march was not for personal reasons but dictated by the place he occupies in the heart of Black people by the grace of God.

If early white-media coverage was non-existent, late media coverage was designed to scare away those who might be caught up in its momentum. Two days before the march, the media covered a "story" falsely alleging that Min. Farrakhan in an interview accused Jews, Palestinians and Asians as bloodsuckers.

Amid the hoopla, O.J. Simpson Attorney Johnnie Cochran and Gen. Colin Powell were among those the media spotlight and lies helped to keep away. Yet the day of the march the same news service, in a brief article, reported Min. Farrakhan's comments in a fuller context. The story showed that Min. Farrakhan did not attack the ethnic groups but talked about the destruction of communities by those who refuse to reinvest where they do business. His remarks were critical of Blacks who did the same thing.

On the other hand, Min. Farrakhan's speech was derided as numerology and wasted opportunity by media pundits and professionals instead of analyzed for its lucid message of a divine purpose for Black suffering. America's sinking moral state, the disease of white supremacy, the blessing of unity and the need for atonement and divine mercy.

Largely missed were the beauty of Islamic and Christian prayers at dawn and a traditional African libation to consecrate the event. A major statement against child sexual abuse and a call for an end to domestic violence went largely ignored by America's free press.

For those uncomfortable with talk of conspiracy, media coverage betrayed a common mindset that is rooted in America's ideology of white supremacy. That ideology promotes an arrogance and hostility that ignores, marginalizes and makes it nearly impossible to appreciate Black movements and Black leaders, which makes independent Black information sources critical for our survival.

Richard Muhammad is Managing Editor of the Nation of Islam's *Final Call* newspaper. As the newspaper's former East Coast Correspondent, he worked in Washington, D.C., before his promotion took him to Chicago. Mr. Muhammad covered march developments from the time it was announced until the day it ended.

'We, Too, Are Black Men and Women'

Amidst The Many Stories, Area Reporters Speak On The March

Alvin Peabody

All of them were credentialed as media representatives to the Million Man March, which drew a record number of the African Americans to the nation's capital on October 16.

But for most African American reporters and photographers, they too, were Black men and women, who were somehow affected by what they witnessed across the Capitol several weeks ago.

Radio reporter and columnist George Wilson saw it this way: "For me, the most defining moment was when I saw thousands of Black men hold hands and took a pledge to do better for themselves. The look in their faces was real, and it showed sincerity and unity."

"The thing that inspired me the most was walking through all those people and just seeing them in a festive mood," said James Wright, a reporter for the Washington Afro American newspaper. "At one point, John Thompson, the famous basketball coach at Georgetown University, was able to walk through that crowd without anyone mobbing him. It was simply an exciting feeling to be out there, especially as a Black man."

Dazine Kent, a staff photographer for the Washington Informer, recalled the help she received from a group of men from Arkansas, who lifted her up in the air when she told them that she couldn't get through "to do my work."

"It was so crowded, I couldn't move and I couldn't take a picture," she said. "I didn't ask for help, but when these men saw that I was a photographer, the next thing I knew was that I was in the air, being passed on to the front."

Ernest White, a talk show host at WDCU-FM, also spoke of his feelings when he looked back over his shoulders and saw a "sea of Black hands passing dollar bills across that mall in blind faith. That said to me that there's a level of trust within the Black man. It's really encouraging to know that when called upon, Black men are going to respond."

Another photographer, Roy Lewis, has been covering marches across the United States for the past 30 years. Yet, the Million Man March has left an impression that he said he will never forget. "When I stood up on the Capitol and got that wide angled picture, it was fascinating. I think I was blessed to have been in a position to not only be able to photograph that picture, but to see a site so wonderful as

Photo by Richard Muhammad

that," Lewis said.

"My most defining moment was when I stood up in the midst of all those people and held hands with my son and a son of a friend," said William Reed, executive director of the National Newspaper Publishers Association. "Let me tell you that I didn't go to the march as a reporter. I went as a Black man and it was a very good feeling."

For columnist Askia Muhammad, the march provided a "musical quality" that will never be forgotten. He particularly remembers the moment when Stevie Wonder took the stage to address the Million Man March.

"When he got up to speak, a hush came over the crowd, and then people started to clap," Muhammad said. "Soon after, that clapping turned into a musical wave, starting at the back and then got closer and closer to the front. It was just wonderful."

The "musical quality" also involves Rosa Parks, who, according to Muhammad, brought back memories of a record by the Neville Brothers' entitled, "Thank You, Sister Rosa:" You are the spark, you started our revolution...Thank you, Sister Rosa."

Then you had Nation of Islam leader Louis Farrakhan, an accomplished musician himself. "I thought about the calypso music he's fond of," Muhammad said. "Everything fell right into place, just awesome, just like a big musical symphony."

While there were many stories reported about the Million Man March, these are the personal moments experienced by our Black reporters and photographers. "Oh, yes, we were there as Black men and women first, then reporters and photographers afterwards," said George Wilson. "It was a great day for all of us."

Alvin Peabody has served as news editor for *The Washington Informen,* for almost five years. *The Informen* is a weekly newspaper whose primary audience is the African American community of the Washington, D.C. metropolitan area. Formerly a reporter with the *Miami Times,* Mr. Peabody brings a strong African-centered perspective towards the MMM/DOA. He is originally from Liberia.

Excerpt from The B Network

the critical best is that
brothers better be the best if they are to avoid backwardness
brothers better be the best if they are to conquer beautiful bigness
Comprehend that bad is only *bad* if it's big, Black and better than
boastful braggarts belittling our best and brightest
with bosses seeking inches when miles are better.

brothers need to bop to being Black & bright & above board
the black train of beautiful wisdom that is bending this bind
towards a new & knowledgeable beginning that is
bountiful & bountiful & beautiful
While be-bopin to be
better than the test,
brotherman

better yet write the exam.

        Haki R. Madhubuti

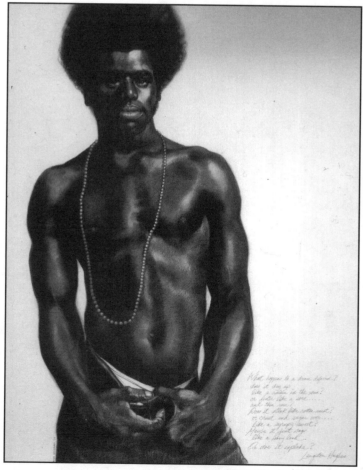

Illustration by Jon Lockard

138

Part 8
Documents

Planning
A
Mission

Editor's Note: This mission statement, written by Maulana Karenga, on behalf of the Executive Council of the MMM/DOA, represents both a process and product of a continuing and current dialog about who we are and what we should be about as a people. It also represents the core moral vision of community and society around which groups and individuals built the operational unity to produce such an impressive joint project of the Million Man March and Day of Absence on October 16. It serves now as a focal point for a continuing discussion across the country in the local organizing committees of the MMM/DOA and other community groups on critical issues facing us as a people and how we should address them.

THE MILLION MAN MARCH/DAY OF ABSENCE MISSION STATEMENT

Preface

This Mission Statement is, on one hand, the product of the ongoing concern and conversation in the African American community about who we are as a people, where we stand and what we are compelled to do in view of our self-understanding and the conditions confronting us. But more specifically, it evolves out of a wide-ranging, vigorous and many-sided discussion that was initiated by the call of Minister Louis Farrakhan last year for a Million Man March in Washington, D.C. Immediately, questions were raised about the priority-focus on men, the call for a day of atonement as a component part of the March proposal, the relevance of the March, its goals, its possible results and a host of related concerns. Moreover, the discussion is focused and expanded by Minister Farrakhan's invitation to a broad spectrum of scholars, activists and religious, political, business and civic leaders in May 1995 to gather and help shape the March in the most inclusive and effective form.

From this meeting, local organizing committees were established in over 318 cities and conversations continued about the meaning, goals and possibilities of the March. Moreover, a National Organizing Committee was established to coordinate the continuously expanding circle of participants. The inclusive and diverse character of the National Organizing Committee and the numerous local organizing committees allowed discussions to draw on a wide-ranging source of knowledge, experience and differing views. Our frequent meetings were marked by lengthy debates over critical issues and a series of fraternal and sororal disagreements as well as agreements. However, by the end of this lengthy process, an impressive agreement on common ground had developed. The Statement thus reflects a document and project shaped in exchange. As more and more people embraced the idea of the March, the idea expanded to reflect new and varied concerns without compromise of principle. And thus, it is out of this inclusive and diverse gathering and process that the context and content of the Mission Statement were developed.

The Statement, then, reflects the common ground in principle and the operational unity in practice forged over a long period of vigorous and expansive exchanges. It represents our consciousness of the critical juncture of history at which we live and the challenges it poses for us, our profound concern for increasing racism, deteriorating social and environmental conditions and the urgent need for a transformative and progressive leadership in such a context. The Statement also reaffirms our commitment to the ongoing struggle for a free and empowered community, a just and good society, a better world and the self-determination, sacrifice and hard work this requires.

Finally, the Mission Statement reaffirms the best values of our social justice tradition which require respect for the dignity and rights of the human person, economic justice, meaningful political participation, shared power, cultural integrity, mutual respect for all peoples and uncompromising resistance to social forces and structures which deny or limit these.

The document is collective in both conception and completion. For all of the members of the Executive Council brought their own summaries and understanding of the exchanges on the local and national level and gave critical input into the shaping of the document. Those members include: Dr.

Benjamin Chavis, Executive Director, NMMM/DOA Organizing Committee; Mr. Ron Daniels, Campaign for a New Tomorrow; Minister Louis Farrakhan, Nation of Islam; Dr. Maulana Karenga, The Organization of Us; Ms. Mawina Kouyate, All African People's Revolutionary Party; Mr. Bob Law, Million Man March Citywide Coordinating Council; Mr. Haki Madhubuti, Third World Press; Mr. Leonard Muhammad, Nation of Islam; Dr. Imari Obadele, Republic of New Africa; Rev. Dr. Frank Reid, Bethel African Methodist Episcopal Church; Rev. Willie Wilson, Union Temple Baptist Church; and Dr. Conrad Worrill, National Black United Front.

We acknowledge with deep appreciation Minister Louis Farrakhan's development of the initial idea of the March and his willingness to share it with us, and invite us all to participate in it and help shape its form and content for the common good of our people. And it is in this spirit of openness and cooperation for the common good that we seek to put forth in this document a vision of possibility that will advance the struggle for an empowered community, a just society, and a better world.

Dr. Maulana Karenga   Executive Council
_____
                                   National Million Man March/Day of Absence
                                   Organizing Committee

I. INTRODUCTION

We, the Black men and women, the organizations and persons, participating in this historic Million Man March and Day of Absence held in Washington, D.C., on October 16, 1995, on the eve of the 21st century, and supported by parallel activities in cities and towns throughout the country:

conscious of the critical juncture of history in which we live and the challenges it poses for us;

concerned about increasing racism and the continuing commitment to white supremacy in this country; deteriorating social conditions, degradation of the environment and the impact of these on our community, the larger society and the world;

committed to the ongoing struggle for a free and empowered community, a just society and a better world;

recognizing that the country and government have made a dangerous and regressive turn to the right and are producing policies with negative impact on people of color, the poor and the vulnerable;

realizing that every man and woman and our community have both the right and responsibility to resist evil and contribute meaningfully to the creation of a just and good society;

reaffirming the best values of our social justice tradition which require respect for the dignity and rights of the human person, economic justice, meaningful political participation, shared power, cultural integrity, mutual respect for all peoples, and uncompromising resistance to social forces and structures which deny or limit these;

declare our commitment to assume a new and expanded responsibility in the struggle to build and sustain a free and empowered community, a just society and a better world. We are aware that we make this commitment in an era in which this is needed as never before and in which we cannot morally choose otherwise.

In doing this, we self-consciously emphasize the **priority need** of Black men to stand up and assume this new and expanded responsibility without denying or minimizing the equal rights, role and responsibility of Black women in the life and struggle of our people.

Our priority call to Black men to stand up and assume this new and expanded sense of responsibility is based on the realization that the strength and resourcefulness of the family and the liberation of the people require it;

that some of the most acute problems facing the Black community within are those posed by Black males who have not stood up; that the caring and responsible father in the home; the responsible and future-focused male youth; security in and of the community; the quality of male/female relations, and the family's capacity to avoid poverty and push the lives of its members forward all depend on Black men's standing up;

that in the context of a real and principled brotherhood, those of us who have stood up, must challenge others to stand also; and that unless and until Black men **stand up**, Black men and women cannot **stand together** and accomplish the awesome tasks before us.

II. THE HISTORICAL SIGNIFICANCE OF THE PROJECT

This Million Man March, forming a joint project with its companion activity, The Day of Absence, speaks to who we are, where we stand and what we are compelled to do in this hour of meeting and posing challenges. Its significance lies in the fact that:

1. It is a timely and necessary statement of challenge both to ourselves and the country in a time of increasing racism, attacks on hard-won gains, and continually deteriorating conditions for the poor and vulnerable and thus an urgent time for transformative and progressive leadership;

2. It is a declaration of the resolve of Black men in particular, and the Black community in general, to mobilize and struggle to maintain hard-won gains, resist evil and wrong wherever we find it and to continue to push our lives and history forward;

3. It is a reaffirmation of our self-understanding as a people that we are our own liberators, that no matter how numerous or sincere our allies are, the greatest burdens to be borne and the most severe sacrifices to be made for liberation are essentially our own;

4. It is an effective way to refocus and expand discussion on critical issues confronting our people, this country and the world and put forth our positions on them;

5. It is both an example and encouragement of operational unity; unity in diversity, unity without uniformity and unity on principle and in practice for the greater good;

6. It is a galvanizing and mobilizing process to raise consciousness, cultivate commitment and lay the ground work for increased positive social, political and economic activity;

7. And finally, it is a necessary continuation of our ancient and living moral tradition of speaking truth to power and seeking power for the vulnerable, justice for the injured, right for the wronged and liberation for the oppressed.

III. THE CHALLENGE TO OURSELVES

1. The Million Man March and Day of Absence are posed first in challenge to ourselves. We understand that the challenge to ourselves is the greatest challenge. For it is only by making demands on ourselves that we can make successful demands on society. In this regard we have raised three basic themes: **Atonement, Reconciliation and Responsibility**. For it is through being at one with the Creator, each other and creation, and reconciling our differences with each other, that we can stand up and together in unity, strength and dignity accept and bear the responsibility heaven and history have placed on us at this critical juncture in the life and struggle of our people.

ATONEMENT

2. For us, atonement in the best spiritual and ethical sense is to recognize wrongs done and make amends, to be self-critical and self-corrective. It means turning inward and assessing the right and the wrong, recognizing shortcomings and committing oneself to correct them.

3. Atonement means being always concerned about standing worthy before the Creator, before others and before the creation, being humble enough to admit mistakes and wrongs and bold enough to correct them.

4. We call then for a Holy Day of Atonement on this October 16, 1995, a day to meditate on and seek right relationships with the Creator, with each other and with nature.

5. We call also for a special remembering of the ancestors on this day and honoring them by a renewed commitment to speak truth, do justice, resist evil and always choose the good, as they taught us through word and deed.

6. To the extent that we have failed to do all we can in the way we can to make ourselves and our community the best of what it means to be African and human, we ask forgiveness from the Creator and each other. And therefore, we dare to atone:

   a. for all our offenses, intentional and unintentional, against the Creator, others and the creation, especially those offenses caused by our accepting the worst and weakest conceptions of ourselves;
   b. for not always following the best teachings of our spiritual and ethical traditions of Islam, Christianity, Judaism (Hebrewism), Maat, Yoruba, Akan, Kawaida and all others; and sacrificing and ignoring the spiritual and ethical in pursuit of material things;
   c. for over-focusing on the personal at the expense of the collective needs of our families and our people;
   d. for collaborating in our own oppression by embracing ideas, institutions and practices which deny our human dignity, limit our freedom and dim or disguise the spark of divinity in all of us;
   e. for failing to contribute in a sustained and meaningful way to the struggle of our people for freedom and justice, and to the building of the moral community in which we all want to live;
   f. for failing to do as much as we can to protect and preserve the environment through practicing and struggling for environmentally friendly patterns of consumption and production;
   g. for any time we have turned a blind eye to injustice, a deaf ear to truth or an uncaring heart away from the suffering and pain around us;
   h. for not resisting as much as we can sexist ideas and practices in society and in our own relations and failing to uphold the principle of equal rights, partnership and responsibility of men and women in life, love and struggle;
   i. for lacking the moral consideration and human sensitivity towards others that we want for ourselves; and
   j. for not always practicing the Seven Principles: unity, self-determination, collective work and responsibility, cooperative economics, purpose, creativity and faith.

7. And thus we commit and recommit ourselves on this day and afterwards to constantly strive to be better persons, live fuller and more meaningful lives, build strong, loving and egalitarian families, and struggle to make our community, society and the world a better place in which to live.

RECONCILIATION
8. We call also for reconciliation which is a companion practice of atonement. For it means, for us, to bring oneself into harmony with the Creator, others and creation.

9. This means we call for all of us to settle disputes, overcome conflicts, put aside grudges and hatreds in our personal and social relationships and in and between our organizations and institutions in the spirit of brotherhood and sisterhood, to reject and oppose communal, family and personal violence, and to strive to build and sustain loving, mutually respectful and reciprocal relations; in a word, to seek the good, find it, embrace it and build on it.

10. Reconciliation also means that we must strive for and achieve a principled and active unity for the common good. This we call **operational unity**, a unity in diversity, a unity without uniformity, a unity on **principle and in practice**.

11. We therefore commit and recommit ourselves to the principle and practice of reconciliation. For it is in and through reconciliation that we can embrace, stand together, organize our community and solve the problems in it, harness its energies for maximum development and struggle to end injustice and create the just and good society.

RESPONSIBILITY

12. Finally, we challenge each Black man in particular, and the Black community in general, to renew and expand our commitment to responsibility in personal conduct, in family relations and in obligations to the community and to the struggle for a just society and a better world. And for us, to be responsible is to willingly and readily assume obligations and duties; to be accountable and dependable.

13. It means to stand up, stand together and stand in practice; to stand up in consciousness and commitment; to stand together in harmony and unity as men, as brothers, as women and sisters, as partners, as family and as community; and to stand in the practice of struggle, dedication, discipline, sacrifice and achievement; always building, doing good, resisting evil and constantly creating and embracing possibilities for fuller and more meaningful lives.

We thus commit and recommit ourselves to take personal and collective responsibility for our lives and the welfare and future of our families and our community. And we commit ourselves to stand up in knowledge and resolve, to stand together in principled and active unity and to stand in moral and liberating practice.

14. In raising the challenge of a new, renewed and expanded assumption of responsibility, we call on those Black men and women with greater means to shoulder greater responsibility; to invest in the community and transform it; and to avoid imitating the established order in its disdain for and blame of the poor and the vulnerable.

15. Our obligation is to remember the ancient moral teaching that we should give food to the hungry, water to the thirsty, clothes to the naked and a boat to the boatless, that we should be a father for the orphan, a mother to the timid, a shelter for the battered, a staff of support for the aged, a companion and comforter of the ill, an aid to the poor, strength for the weak, a raft for the drowning and a ladder for those trapped in the pit of despair. In a word, we must love justice, hate wrongdoing, resist evil and always do the good.

IV. THE CHALLENGE TO THE GOVERNMENT

16. Central to our practice of responsibility is holding responsible those in power who have oppressed and wronged us through various challenges. At the core of the practice of speaking truth to power is the moral challenge to it to be responsible, to cease its abuse, exploitation and oppression, and to observe its basic role as a structure instituted to secure human rights, not to violate them or assist in their violation. And where it has violated its trust, it must be compelled to change.

17. Historically, the U.S. government has participated in one of the greatest holocausts of human history, the Holocaust of African Enslavement. It sanctioned with law and gun the genocidal process that destroyed millions of human lives, human culture, and the human possibility inherent in African life and culture. It has yet to acknowledge this horrific destruction or to take steps to make amends for it.

18. Moreover, even after the Holocaust, racist suppression continued, destroying lives, communities and possibilities. And even now, members of the government are pushing the country in a regressive right-wing direction, reversing hard-won gains, blaming the victims, punishing the vulnerable and pandering to the worst of human emotions;

19. We thus call on the government of the United States to atone for the historical and current wrongs it has committed against African people and other people of color. Especially, do we call on the government of this country to address the morally compelling issue of the Holocaust of African Enslavement. To do this, the government must:

   a. publicly admit its role and the role of the country in the Holocaust;
   b. publicly apologize for it;
   c. publicly recognize its moral meaning to us and humanity through establishing institutions and educational processes which preserve memory of it, teach the lessons and horror of its history and stress the dangers and destructiveness of denying human dignity and human freedom;
   d. pay reparations; and
   e. discontinue any and all practices which continue its effects or threaten its repetition.

20. We call on the government to also atone for its role in criminalizing a whole people; for its policies of destroying, discrediting, disrupting and otherwise neutralizing Black leadership; for spending more money on imprisonment than education, and on weapons of war than social development; for dismantling regulations that restrained corporations in their degradation of the environment; and failing to check a deadly environmental racism that encourages placement of toxic waste in communities of color. And of course, we call for a halt to all of this.

21. Furthermore, we call on the government to stop undoing hard-won gains such as affirmative action, voting rights and districting favorable to maximum Black political participation; to provide universal, full and affordable health care; to provide and support programs for affordable housing; to pass the Conyers Reparations Bill; to repeal the Omnibus Crime Bill; to halt disinvestment in social development and stop penalizing the urban and welfare poor and using them as scapegoats; to adopt an economic bill of rights including a plan to rebuild the wasting cities; to craft and institute policies to preserve and protect the environment; and to halt the privatization of public wealth, space and responsibility.

22. In addition, we call on the government of the U.S. to stop blaming people of color for problems created by ineffective government and corporate greed and irresponsibility; to honor the treaties signed with Native Peoples of the U.S., and to respect their just claims and interests; to increase and expand efforts to eliminate race, class and gender discrimination; and to stop pandering to white fears and white supremacy hatreds and illusions and help create a new vision of human and societal possibilities.

23. We also are compelled to call on the government of this country to craft a sensible and moral foreign policy that provides for equal treatment of African, Caribbean and other Third World refugees and countries; that forgives foreign debt to former colonies; that fosters a just and equitable peace and recognizes the right of self-determination of peoples in the Middle East, in the Caribbean and around the world; that rejects embargoes which penalizes whole peoples; that supports the just and rightful claims and interests of Native Peoples; and that supports all Third World countries in their efforts to achieve and maintain democracy and sustainable economic and social development.

24. Finally, we call on the government and the country to recognize and respond positively to the fact that U.S. society is not a finished white product, but an **unfinished and ongoing multicultural project** and that each people has both the right and responsibility to speak their own special cultural truth and to make their own unique contribution to how this society is reconceived and reconstructed.

V. THE CHALLENGE TO THE CORPORATIONS

25. We begin our challenge to corporations by rejecting the widespread notion among them, that corporations have no social responsibility except to maximize profit within the rules of an open and competitive market, through cutting costs, maximizing benefits and constantly increasing technological efficiency. Our position is that no human conduct is immune from the demands of moral responsibility or exempt from

moral assessment. The weight of corporations in modern life is overwhelming and their commitment to maximizing profit and technological efficiency can and often does lead to tremendous social costs such as deteriorating and dangerous working conditions, massive layoffs, harmful products projected as beneficial, environmental degradation, deindustrialization, corporate relocation, and disinvestment in social structures and development.

26. We thus call on corporations to practice a corporate responsibility that requires and encourages efforts to minimize and eventually eliminate harmful consequences which persons, communities and the environment sustain as a result of productive and consumptive practices.

27. We also call on corporations to respect the dignity and interest of the worker in this country and abroad, to maintain safe and adequate working conditions for workers, provide adequate benefits, prohibit and penalize racial and gender discrimination, halt displacement and dislocation of workers, encourage organization and meaningful participation in decision-making by workers, and halt disinvestment in the social structure, deindustrialization and corporate relocation.

28. Moreover, we call on corporations to reinvest profits back into the communities from which it extracts profits; to increase support for Black charities, contribute more to Black education in public schools and traditional Black universities and colleges, and to Black education in predominantly white colleges and universities; to open facilities to the community for cultural and recreational use; and to contribute to the building of community institutions and other projects to reinvest in the social structure and development of the Black community.

29. In further consideration of profit made from Black consumers, we call on corporate America to provide expanded investment opportunities for Black people; engage in partnership with Black businesses and business persons; increase employment of Black managers and general employees; conduct massive job training among Blacks for work in the 21st century; and aid in the development of programs to halt and reverse urban decay.

30. Finally, we call on corporations to show appropriate care and responsibility for the environment; to minimize and halt pollution, deforestation and depletion of natural resources, and the destruction of plants, animals, birds, fish, reptiles and insects and their natural habitats; and to rebuild wasted and damaged areas and expand the number, size and kinds of areas preserved.

VI. THE DAY OF ABSENCE

31. We call on those who do not come to Washington, especially, Black women, to mobilize and organize the community in support of the Million Man March and its goals. The Day of Absence is a parallel activity to the Million Man March and a component part of one joint and cooperative project: the standing up and assumption of a new and expanded responsibility by the Black man in particular and the Black community in general.

32. Women are in the leadership of the Day of Absence without exclusion of men as men are in the leadership of the Million Man March without exclusion of women. And both activities are equally essential.

33. The Day of Absence is a **sacred day, a holy day**, a day of atonement, reconciliation and responsibility. It thus has activities to reflect this. To observe this sacred day, we call on all Black people to stay away from work, from school, from businesses, and from places of entertainment and sports and to turn inward and focus on the themes of atonement, reconciliation and responsibility in our lives and struggle.
34. We call on those who choose prayer and meditation as essential ways of observation to do this in groups of family and friends at home or in larger groups at mosques, churches, synagogues, temples and other places of worship.

35. Also, we call for teach-ins at homes and in community gatherings on:

    a. the meaning of this day and the juncture of history at which we are as people;

    b. the meaning of the Million Man March, the Day of Atonement, Reconciliation and Responsibility, and the Day of Absence and the goals of this joint project as set forth in the Mission Statement;

    c. the importance and requirements of our struggle for liberation and justice;

    d. the indispensability of spiritual and ethical grounding in our families, our communities and our struggle; and

    e. the glory and burdens of our history as fathers and mothers of human civilization, sons and daughters of the Holocaust of African Enslavement and authors and heirs of the reaffirmation of our Africanness and our recommitment to liberation in the '60s.

36. Furthermore, we call on this day for massive voter registration as an essential act of responsibility for being politically active and morally engaged persons profoundly committed to the improvement of the quality of life in the community and larger society.

37. And finally, we call on all to contribute to the establishment of a Black Economic Development Fund as also an essential act of responsibility for the economic development of the community and to embrace the ancient and excellent teaching that small things given return in abundance and the good we do for others is actually done for ourselves. For it helps build and strengthen the moral community we all want to live in.

VII. CONTINUING PRACTICE AND PROJECTS

38. The Million Man March and Day of Absence can only have lasting value if we continue to work and struggle beyond this day. Thus, our challenge is to take the spirit of this day, the process of mobilization and the possibilities of organization and turn them into ongoing structures and practices directed toward our liberation and flourishing as a people.

39. Central to sustaining and institutionalizing this process is:

    a. the follow-up development of an expanded Black political agenda and the holding of a Black Political Convention to forge this agenda for progressive political change;

    b. a massive and ongoing voter registration of Black people as independents; using our vote to insist and insure that candidates address the Black agenda; and creating and sustaining a progressive independent political movement;

    c. the building and strengthening of Black united fronts and collective leadership structures like the National African American Leadership Summit to practice and benefit from operational unity in our addressing local, national and international issues;

    d. the establishment of a Black Economic Development Fund to enhance economic development, cultivate economic discipline and cooperative practices and achieve economic self-determination;

    e. the reaffirmation and strengthening of family through quality male/female relations based on principles of equality, complementarity, mutual respect and shared responsibility in love, life and struggle; and through loving and responsible parenthood that insists on discipline and achievement, provides spiritual, moral and cultural grounding and through expanding rites of passage programs, mentorships and increasing adoptions;

    f. the ongoing struggle for reparations in the fullest sense, that is to say: public admission, apology and recognition of the Holocaust of African Enslavement and appropriate compensation by the government; and support for the Conyers Reparations Bill on the Holocaust;

    g. the continuing struggle against police abuse, government suppression, violations of civil and human rights and the industrialization of prisons; and in support of the freedom of all political prisoners, prisoners' rights and their efforts to transform themselves into worthy members of the community;

h. the critical task of organizing the community as a solid wall in the struggle against drugs, crime and violence in the community which we see as interrelated and which must be joined with the struggle to reduce and end poverty, increase employment, strengthen fatherhood, motherhood and family, support parents, provide education and prevention programs; and expose and reject those who deal in death for the community.

    None of this denies external sources of drugs nor stops us from demanding uniform sentencing and penalties for those involved in the drug trade on the local, national and international level, but it compels us to stand up and take responsibility for the life we must live in spite of external impositions;

i. continuing and expanding our support for African-centered independent schools through joining their boards, enrolling our children, being concerned and active parents, donating time, services and monies to them and working in various other ways to insure that they provide the highest level of culturally-rooted education; and intensifying and broadening the struggle for quality public education through heightened parental concern and involve-ment and social activism which insist on a responsible administration, professional and committed teachers, continuing faculty and staff development; safe, pleasant, encouraging and fully-equipped campuses and an inclusive and culture-respecting curriculum which stresses mastery of knowledge as well as critical thinking, academic excellence, social responsibility and an expanded sense of human possibility;

j. continuing and reinforced efforts to reduce and eliminate negative media approaches to and portrayals of Black life and culture; to organize a sustained and effective support for positive models, messages and works; to achieve adequate and dignified representation of Blacks in various media and in various positions in these media; to expand support for and development of independent Black media; and to challenge successful and notable African Americans in various media to support all these efforts.

k. strengthening and supporting organizations and institutions of the Black community con-cerned with the uplifting and liberation of our people by joining as families and persons, volunteering service, giving donations and providing and insisting on the best leadership possible;

l. building appropriate alliances with other peoples of color, supporting their liberation strug-gles and just demands and engaging in mutually supportive and mutually beneficial activ-ities to create and sustain a just and good society;

m. standing in solidarity with other African peoples and other Third World peoples in their struggles to free themselves, harness their human and material resources and live full and meaningful lives;

n. reaffirming in the most positive ways the value and indispensability of the spiritual and ethical grounding of our people in accomplishing the historical tasks confronting us by freeing and renewing our minds and reaffirming our commitment to the good, the proper and the beneficial, by joining as families and persons the faith communities of our choice, supporting them, living the best of our traditions ourselves and challenging other members and the leadership to do likewise and constantly insisting that our faith communities give the best of what we have to offer to build the moral community and just society we strug-gle for as a people;

o. and finally, embracing and practicing a common set of principles that reaffirm and strengthen family, community and culture, The Nguzo Saba (The Seven Principles): Umoja (Unity); Kujichagulia (Self- Determination); Ujima (Collective Work and Responsibility); Ujamaa (Cooperative Economics); Nia (Purpose); Kuumba (Creativity) and Imani (Faith).

VIII. CONCLUSION

We stand in Washington conscious that it's a pivotal point from which to speak to the country and the world. And we come bringing the most central views and values of our faith communities, our deepest commitments to our social justice tradition and the struggle it requires, the most instructive lessons of our history, and a profoundly urgent sense of the need for positive and productive action. In standing up and assuming responsibility in a new, renewed and expanded sense, we honor our ancestors, enrich our lives and give promise to our descendants. Moreover, through this historic work and struggle we strive to always know and introduce ourselves to history and humanity as a people who are spiritually and ethically grounded; who speak truth, do justice, respect our ancestors and elders, cherish, support and challenge our children, care for the vulnerable, relate rightfully to the environment, struggle for what is right and resist what is wrong, honor our past, willingly engage our present and self-consciously plan for and welcome our future.

MILLION MAN MARCH
"A HOLY DAY OF ATONEMENT AND RECONCILIATION"
NATIONAL ORGANIZING
COMMITTEE

PACKET

Contents:

- Vision Statement by the Honorable Minister Louis Farrakhan
- Million Man March Fact Sheet
- List of Endorsements to Date
- Women's Statement of Support
- Messages from Mother Rosa Parks, Dr. Maya Angelou, and Dr. Dorothy Height
- Message to Incarcerated Persons
- Fund-raising Appeal
- Declaration of "Holy Day of Atonement and Reconciliation"
- Spiritual Theme

145 KENNEDY STREET, NW • WASHINGTON, DC 20011 • TEL: (202)726-5111 • FAX: (202)726-8112

THE VISION
FOR
THE MILLION MAN MARCH

By: Minister Louis Farrakhan

WHY A MILLION MAN MARCH?

There is an increasingly conservative and hostile climate growing in America towards the aspirations of Black people and people of color for justice. The "Contract with America," proposed by the Republicans and thus far agreed to by the Congress is turning back the hands of time, depriving the Black community of many of the gains made through the suffering and sacrifice of our fellow advocates of change during the '50s and '60s.

The recent Supreme Court decision on Affirmative Action has set the stage in the U.S. for closing the doors, thereby impeding the progress made in Black enrollment in, and graduation from, colleges and universities; and minimizing business opportunities and the hiring of Black Americans in the public and private sectors.

Each day, somewhere in this nation, the Black community witnesses and falls prey to an increased rate of crime and violence. Aspects of the "Crime Bill" suggest that Black males will be filling the jails of America and will spend the rest of their lives working for little or no pay in the new prison industrial coalition. The unfair use of the death penalty to punish the Black male is in fact a systematic genocidal tool being institutionalized to significantly decrease the Black population.

The proliferation of drugs and gun-related violence in the Black community, and the escalation of Black male fratricide has diminished the positive role and attributes of Black men, and instead has elevated ugly images of Black men as thieves, criminals, and savages projected through movies, music and other communications technologies throughout the world.

The epitome of these major challenges to the Black male and our community is this mounting force of hate being built against our people, particularly Black men. We, therefore, have deemed it necessary in this critical hour to call for one million disciplined, committed, and dedicated Black men, from all walks of life in America, to march in Washington, D.C.—showing the world a vastly different picture of the Black male.

PURPOSE OF THE MILLION MAN MARCH

We recognize October 16th as **"A Holy Day of Atonement and Reconciliation."** As the sons of proud people, we are coming together and moving forward to chart the course for our future as responsible heads of our families; to reclaim and build our neighborhoods; to unify our families; and to save our children who will lead us into the next millennium. We believe that it is only when we are at one or at peace with ourselves and our Creator that we are fortified with the ability and the capacity to successfully reconcile our differences with each other, and accelerate the upward mobility of the Black community.

We believe that as men, we must recognize and praise our brothers that work hard everyday to protect family values, unify and improve the quality of life for the Black man, woman and child. And yes—we as Black men must Atone, take responsibility—open the eyes, teach and embrace our brothers who need to achieve their unfulfilled potential. As strong and worthy Black men, nation builders, fathers, husbands, sons, leaders, we must appreciate and support the very essence and strength of the Black woman. We will not—we will not stand for the abuse or misuse of the Black woman by anyone. No, not anyone.

Our presence in Washington, D.C.—the capital of the United States—is a day set aside to reconcile our spiritual inner beings and to redirect our focus to developing our communities, strengthening our families, working to uphold and protect our civil and human rights, and empowering ourselves through the Spirit of God, more effective use of our dollars, and through the power of the vote.

We are asking all religious leaders of the various denominations of Christianity and the various Faith Traditions within the Black community to declare October 16, 1995, as a **Holy Day of Atonement and Reconciliation**—a day of fasting and prayer for those who are able. This will be the first time since the institution of slavery that Black people would have declared a **Holy Day** for our people.

We are asking all members of college, high school, and professional sports teams to observe the **Holy Day** and to not engage in sports activities. We are asking our musicians and entertainers not to perform on this day, as a show of solidarity. We are asking on this declared Holy Day that none of us go to work or school; none of us participate in shopping; and none of us engage in drinking alcohol, drugs, or any unclean or illegal act during the **Holy Day**. We must designate and recognize this day in accordance with the Word of our Creator.

We are asking the Black woman, particularly our mothers, to be with our children teaching them the value of home, self-esteem, family, and unity; and to work with us to ensure the success of the March and our mission to improve the quality of life for our people.

We take this historical moment to recognize the major contributions that the Black woman has made, and continues to make, toward the advancement of our people. Bonded under the guise of leadership and strength, we, as one people must come together to improve the quality of life for our children and for the Black family. For, the long and winding road that we must travel to define our future shall be determined by the depth of our unification.

We are asking that the church doors be opened and that all those who have differences within the congregation go to their house of worship to reconcile their differences. Parents, our children, and members of our community should come together by the end of the day, at a religious temple of any denomination to pray for the success and well-being of the Black man, woman, and child, and our community.

We are asking all those who have not registered to vote to go to a house of worship on October 16th, to get registered. There are approximately eight million Black persons in the U.S. eligible to vote, but who remain unregistered. Our goal is to have a registrar in as many churches as possible. There will be teachers present to provide guidance, instructions, and information. The most critical election of this century will be held in 1996. This will be the last presidential election of the century. We are determined that never again shall any political party take the Black vote for granted.

We are asking that you join many of our leaders who have gathered together to develop a national agenda for our people, as a follow-up to the Million Man March. Religious, political, civic, and youth leaders will be called to come together to incorporate sound ideas and recommendations; and to amend and finalize this national platform of action. We shall take this platform of action to various communities in America to hold town meetings to encourage the Black community's input and secure our people's approval and active support of this agenda. In turn, every presidential candidate will receive our platform of action and will be invited to address the Black community, based on our agenda. We shall emphasize in our actions and in the written word that the Black community shall not give our vote to anyone who is against, or is not willing to represent, the best interests of our people.

We believe that by the grace and goodness of our Creator, the success we envision for the Million Man March, and beyond October 16, 1995—our first declared Holy Day of Atonement and Reconciliation— will be captured in the annals of history as a landmark period in which Black people came together to effect the greatest promise of change for Black people in America, and throughout the world.

MILLION MAN MARCH

FACT SHEET

WHAT IS THE MILLION MAN MARCH?

The Million Man March is a Holy Day of Atonement and Reconciliation for, and by, Black men in the United States of America, who will March in Washington, D.C., to convey to the world a vastly different picture of the Black male, and to publicly proclaim to the global community that the Black man is prepared and moving forward to unify our families and build our communities.

WHAT IS THE PURPOSE OF THE MILLION MAN MARCH?

The purpose of the Million Man March is to enable and encourage Black men in the U.S. to take a greater responsibility and play a greater role in caring for, and uplifting the status of, the Black family. Heretofore, Black women have disproportionately carried the burden of caring for our families. The Million Man March is calling for at least one million Black men to pledge their commitment to the restoration of their roles as sustainers and providers for the Black family and community.

WHAT IS THE MILLION MAN MARCH GUIDING PRINCIPLE?

"If my people, which are called by my name, shall humble themselves, and pray, and seek my face, and turn from their wicked ways; then will I hear from heaven, and will forgive their sin, and will heal their land." II Chronicles 7:14

WHERE AND WHEN WILL THE MILLION MAN MARCH TAKE PLACE?

The Million Man March will be held on Monday, October 16, 1995, and will take place in Washington, D.C.

WHAT ARE THE MAIN ISSUES TO BE ADDRESSED?

There are three key issue areas that will be addressed:

1. The Black Family and Community Development

This includes self-responsibility, loving, nurturing, and caring for the Black family; and working to end self-destruction, Black-on-Black crime and the epidemic of drug and other substance abuse. Coming together and being at one with God, and with one another.

2. Affirmative Action and Voting Rights Support

We support affirmative action and are opposed to the dismantling of policies and regulations which uphold and protect our civil and human rights. We support Representative Cynthia McKinney and other policy-makers in the restoration of voting rights.

3. Corporate America's Reinvestment in the Black Community

We are asking Corporate America to reinvest in the Black Community. Economic viability is a sound and effective means to minimize the incidence of violence and crime, to provide business and employment opportunities, and to improve the quality of life in the Black Community. According to recent figures from the *Wall Street Journal*, the Black Community in America spends $433 billion annually in disposable income.

WHO SUPPORTS THE MILLION MAN MARCH?

To date, the Million Man March has received many endorsements and enjoys a strong broad-base level of support from a long list of major national Black organizations. (See attached list)

MILLION MAN MARCH, INC. NATIONAL HEADQUARTERS

> 145 Kennedy Street, N.W.
> Washington, D.C. 20011
> TELEPHONE NO.: 202-726-5111
> TOLL FREE NO.: 1-800-324-9243
> FAX NO.: 202-726-8112

KEY CONTACT PERSONS FOR THE MILLION MAN MARCH, INC.
NATIONAL HEADQUARTERS

Reverend Dr. Benjamin F. Chavis, Jr.
National Director of the Million Man March, Inc.

Sister Claudette Marie Muhammad
Chief of Protocol to the Honorable Minister Louis Farrakhan
National Assistant to Rev. Dr. Benjamin F. Chavis, Jr. for the Million Man March, Inc.

Brother Bob Brown
National Field Director and National Director of Logistics and Operations

Sister Linda Greene
National Director of Fundraising

Brother Zaheer Ali
Special Assistant to Rev. Dr. Benjamin F. Chavis, Jr.

Sister Donna Ellis
Office Manager

Sister Angela 6X Boné
Director of Public Relations

Sister Stacey 3X
Assistant Office Manager

Sister Brenda Parker
Deputy Director of Public Relations

Brother Gary Foster
National Youth Organizing Committee Coordinator

MILLION MAN MARCH
"A HOLY DAY OF ATONEMENT AND RECONCILIATION"

PARTIAL LISTING OF ENDORSEMENTS TO DATE, SEPTEMBER 30, 1995

African Sisterhood Exchange, University of Missouri (St. Louis & Forrest Park)
Afrikan National Rites of Passage United Kollective
All African People's Revolutionary Party
Alpha Phi Alpha Fraternity, Inc.
Amy Jacques Garvey Institute
Association of Black Political Scientists
Black Firefighters of Memphis
Black Graduate Students Association, University of Memphis
Black Student Association, Long Beach State
Black Student Association, University of Missouri - Forrest Park
Blacks in Government
Caribbean American Chamber of Commerce
Coppin State College
District of Columbia Baptist Minister's Conference
Improved Benevolent Protective Order of the Elks of the World
International Association of Black Professional Fire Fighters
International Black Student Alliance, Inc.
Iota Phi Theta Fraternity, Inc.]
Kappa Alpha Psi Fraternity, Inc.
Las Amigas, Inc.
Liberian Support Group
Maryland State Missionary Baptist Convention
Nation of Islam

National African American Leadership Summit
National African American Student Leadership Association
National Association for Black Veterans
National Association of 2500 Positive Black Men
National Association of Black Psychologists
National Association of Black Social Workers
National Association of Blacks in Criminal Justice
National Bar Association
National Black Chamber of Commerce
National Black Police Officers Association
National Black Student Government Association
National Coalition of Blacks for Reparations in America
National Conference of Black Lawyers
National Conference of Black Mayors
National Council of Negro Women
National Newspaper Publishers of America
National Pan-Hellenic Council
National Political Congress of Black Women
National Society of Black Engineers
National United Black Front
Pan-African Association of Tennessee, Inc.
Pan-African Research Organization, University of Missouri - Forrest Park
Pan-African Student Research Collective, Long Beach State
Pan-African Student/Youth Movement
Phi Beta Sigma Fraternity, Inc.
Provisional Government of the Republic of New Africa
Provisional Student Government Association, University of the District of Columbia
Student Government Association, University of Missouri - Forrest Park
Toledo Public School System
Universal Negro Improvement Association & African Communities League, Woodson-Banneker
    Division 330
Zeta Phi Beta Sorority, Inc.

THE BLACK WOMAN'S STATEMENT OF SUPPORT
FOR
THE MILLION MAN MARCH

Recognizing the historical contributions that Black women have made, and continue to make, toward the advancement of Black people in America, we are proud to endorse and actively support the **Million Man March**. Joining our brothers in the development, planning, and implementation of this landmark event, we embrace their position that:

• October 16, 1995, must be established and recognized as a **"Holy Day of Atonement and Reconciliation."**

• There is an increasingly conservative and hostile climate growing in America towards the aspirations of Black people and people of color for justice.

• The recent Supreme Court decision on Affirmative Action has set the stage in the U.S. for closing the doors, thereby impeding the progress made in Black enrollment in, and graduation from, colleges and universities; and minimizing business opportunities and the hiring of Black Americans in the public and private sectors.

- The proliferation of drugs and gun-related violence in the Black community, and the escalation of Black male fratricide has diminished the positive role and attributes of Black men, and instead has elevated ugly images of Black men as thieves, criminals, and savages—projected through movies, music and other communications technologies throughout the world.

- The time and the hour has come for the world to see a vastly different picture of Black men, and for Black men to convey to the world that they are the sons of a proud people who are coming together and moving forward with Black women, to chart the course of our future as responsible heads of our families; to reclaim and build our neighborhoods; and to save our children.

- The Black man must recognize and unconditionally **Atone** for the absence, in too many cases, of the Black male as the head of the household, positive role model and builder of our community.

- The Black man must **Atone** for and establish positive solutions to the abuse and misuse of Black women and girls.

- Together, we must redirect our focus to developing our communities, strengthening our families, working to uphold and protect our civil and human rights, and empowering ourselves through the power of the vote.

- We encourage Corporate America to reinvest in the Black Community. We agree that economic viability is a sound and effective means to minimize the incidence of violence and crime, to provide business and employment opportunities, and to improve the quality of life in the Black Community.

- The most critical election of this century will be held in 1996. We agree, and are equally determined, that never again shall any political party take the Black vote for granted.

- We shall emphasize in our actions and in the written word that the Black community shall not give our vote to anyone who is against, or is not willing to represent, the best interests of our people.

- We believe the success envisioned for the Million Man March, and beyond October 16, 1995—the first Holy Day of Atonement and Reconciliation—will be captured in the annals of history as a landmark period in which Black people came together to effect the greatest promise of change for Black people in America, and throughout the world.

MILLION MAN MARCH
National Black Women's Endorsement Roster

Mother Rosa Parks

Dr. Dorothy I. Height, President/Chief Executive Officer
The National Council of Negro Women, Incorporated

Mrs. Cora Masters Barry
First Lady of the District of Columbia

Dr. C. Delores Tucker, National Chair
The National Political Congress of Black Women

Dr. Maya Angelou

Reverend Barbara Skinner
Skinner Farm Leadership Institute

Mrs. Wilma Harvey
President of the District of Columbia School Board

Dr. Louise White
Community Activist

Marianne Niles, Secretary
The Government of District of Columbia

Attorney Faye Williams, Co-Convener
Local Organizing Committee - Washington, D.C.

Dr. Mabel Phifer, President
Black College Satellite Network

Dr. Niara Sudarkasa, President
Lincoln University

Mrs. Nadine Winters
Former District of Columbia Council Member

Reverend Rosetta Bryson, Deputy Director
Religious Affairs for the Nation's Capital

Mrs. Marilyn Merry, President
District of Columbia Council of Labor Union of Women

"The Million Man March in October of this year will be the first effort in my lifetime of that many men getting together. It sends a strong message to our government and our families that men want the responsibility and will accept it to lead us into the next century. I think it is a great symbol of courage and I will support it by sending our 'Pathways to Freedom' male students, ages 11 to 17, of the Rosa and Raymond Parks Institute for Self-Development.

"I wish the March all the success and I pray that our men will renounce all negativity and return to their various homes with enthusiasm and a renewed commitment to life."

—Mother Rosa Parks
September 6, 1995

"The promise of the Million Man March is a lever which has lifted century old stones from my soul.

"I am also overjoyed at the title of the march: 'A Holy Day of **Atonement** and Reconciliation.' My rapture comes from my reading of that as a Holy Day of At one ment. I know that when we are at one with each other, all differences can be reconciled."

—Dr. Maya Angelou
September 18, 1995

"If this March does nothing else but to bring one million Black men together to express their commitment to themselves, to their family, and to convey to the whole world the strength of the Black man, then this would be tremendous."

—Dr. Dorothy Height

157

FUNDRAISING COMPONENT

We are embarking on one of the greatest events in history - The Million Man March. Over one million disciplined, sober, committed, dedicated black men will assemble in Washington, D.C. for the most historic march ever.

The first step in this historic event is that we, as Black people, accept responsibilities for the financial support of this march. Our financial support of the March will demonstrate that we have accepted the responsibility of this call.

In order to secure the financial support for the Million Man March and guarantee our success, your backing is required.

How can you help underwrite the costs for this monumental task?

• Corporate/Individual Solicitation - there are over 400,000 black- owned businesses in this country, of which the top 100 generated over 6.7 billion in 1994 (Minority Supplier Development Council).

• Solicit contributions from your mosque, church or temple.

• Ask your family members, friends, neighbors and co-workers for contributions.

• Reach out to those persons with whom you do business, schools & universities your children attend, associations and organizations of which you are affiliated.

• Host fundraisers through your mosque, church or temple, professional associations or organizations, schools, neighborhood associations.

Every dollar contributed will aid in the rebuilding of our communities.

MILLION MAN MARCH
Official Program
October 16, 1995

West Front, U.S. Capitol Grounds
Washington, DC

6:00AM - 7:30AM   **EARLY MORNING GLORY**

Master of Ceremonies
Minister Rasul Muhammad

Invocation/ Adan . . . . .Sheik Ahmed Tijani Ben-Omar
Accra, Ghana

Rev. Fred Haynes
Friendship West Baptist Church
Dallas, TX

Salute To Our Ancestors. . . . . Melvin Deal & The Heritage
(Libation Ceremony)   African Dancers & Drummers
and others

Opening Song . . . ."Victory Is Mine"
Million Man March Ensemble

Welcome To The March . . . . .Minister Arief Muhammad
Washington, DC

Call To Purpose . . . ⁚ . . . . Rev. Benjamin F. Chavis, Jr.
National Director
Million Man March

Litany of Prayers

Prayer For The March . . . . .Rev. Donald Hunter
Sunshine Baptist Church
St. Louis, Missouri

Prayer Of Thanksgiving . . . . .Rev. Jonathan Grier
Cathedral of Faith, COGIC
Atlanta, GA

Prayer For Leaders . . . . .Rev. C. V. Smith
St. Louis, MO

Prayer For Children & Families . . . . .Rev. Kojo Nantambu
Missionary Baptist Church
Charlotte, NC

Community Song . . . . "I Got A Feeling"
                                                      Million Man March Male Chorus

Prayer For Direction & Responsibility . . . . Rev. Robert Smith
                                                      New Bethel Church
                                                      Detroit, Michigan

Prayer For Atonement & Reconciliation . . . . .Rev. John Wright
                                                      United Missionary Baptist
                                                      Conference of Maryland

Closing Musical Selection . . . . .Brother Ah and The Sounds Of
                                                      Awareness

8:00AM -10:30 AM   SANKOFA: LESSONS FROM THE PAST LINKAGES TO THE FUTURE

Section Leader: Matsemela Mfumo
Founder, Umojo Party
Washington, DC

SANKOFA Prayer . . . . .Rev. Wayne Gadie
                                                      Emanuel Baptist Church
                                                      Maiden, MA

Ancestral Salute . . . . Kankouran West African
                                                      Dancers and Drummers

Opening Song . . . ."Kumbaya My Lord"
                                                      Million Man March Male Chorus

Statement of Sankofa . . . . Dr. Oba T'Shaka
                                                      National Black United Front
                                                      Chicago, IL

Greetings From The African Diaspora

Africa . . . . .Imam Malick Sylla, Grand Imam,
                                                      Dakar, Senegal

Caribbean . . . . .Mr. Roy Hastick
                                                      Caribbean American Chamber of
                                                      Commerce

Performance . . . . .African Boot Dancers/Step Show

Greetings From Black American Leaders

Fraternities & Sororities . . . . .Mr. Carter Womack,
                                                      President, Panhellenic Council

Labor . . . . Mr. Oscar Eason,
Blacks In Government

Henry Nicholas
Health & Hospital Workers Union
Philadelphia, PA

Musical Selection . . . . Million Man March Male Chorus

Business . . . . Mr. Willie Wilson
Entrepreneur
Chicago, IL

Mental Health . . . . Dr. Niam Akbar
Florida State University
Tallahassee, FL

Health . . . . Dr. Thurman Evans
Health Practitioner
Philadelphia, PA

(Addiction) . . . . .Mr. Earl King
No Dope Express Foundation
Chicago, IL

African Centered Education . . . . .Mwalima Shujaa
Council Independent Black
Institutions
Buffalo, IL

Youth . . . . .Mr. Zachery McDaniels
National African American
Leadership Summit
Baltimore, MD

Prayer . . . . .Archbishop George A. Stallings
Founder, African American
Catholic Congregation
New Orleans, LA

Musical Selection . . . . .Monk Family Youth Singing Ensemble

10:30 AM - 10:40AM	**READY FOR THE MARCHERS**

Brother Leonard Muhammad
Chief of Staff, Nation of Islam
Chicago, IL

Musical Selection. . . . . The Million Man March Songs
Bill Crews, Chicago, IL

11:00AM - 200PM   **AFFIRMATION/RESPONSIBILITY**

Masters of Ceremonies: Rev. Willie P. Wilson
Union Temple Baptist Church
Washington, DC

Minister Ishmael Muhammad
Mosque Maryam
Chicago, IL

Prayers. . . . . Brother Ahmed Tijani Ben-Omar
Accra, Ghana

Bishop W. C. Walker
4th Episcopal Dist., AME Zion

Liturgical Dance . . . . .”GOD IS” . . . . .Performed by Mr. Tony Powell
Choreographed by Linda Boyd

Raising Of The Flags . . . . The Christian Flag
The Star and the Crescent
The Black Liberation Flag
The Star of David

Opening Song . . . . *"Lift Every Voice and Sing"*
Conducted by Dr. Dexter Allgood
Canaan Baptist Church, NY, NY

A Declaration of Purpose. . . . . Rev. Al Sampson
Fernwood United Methodist Church
Chicago, IL

Greetings From:

The African Diaspora Connection . . . . Mr. Boubacar Joseph Ndiaye
Chief Curator, Goree Island
Senegal, West Africa

Minister Akbar Muhammad
International Representative
Nation of Islam and The
Honorable Louis Farrakhan
Ghana, West Africa

Senator Adelbert M. Bryan
Virgin Island
Resolution In Support Of The
March

The Congress . . . . The Honorable Congressman
Donald J. Payne, Chair
Congressional Black Caucus

162

The Statesman . . . . Former Congressman Gus Savage

The Cities . . . . The Honorable Kurt Schmoke
Mayor, Baltimore

Mayor's Welcome & Official Statement . . . . The Honorable Marion Barry
Mayor of Washington, D. C.

Musical Selection . . . . Million Man March Male Chorus

AFFIRMATION OF OUR BROTHERS

Mrs. Cora Masters Barry
First Lady, District of Columbia

NO GREATER LOVE: A TRIBUTE TO . . .

Booker T. Washington, W.E. B. DuBois, Marcus Garvey, Noble Drew Ali
Paul Robeson, Martin Luther King, Jr., Elijah Muhammad
Medger Evers, Malcolm X, Mary McLeod Bethune
Sojourner Truth, Harriett Tubman

Remarks by:
Dr. Betty Shabazz
Mr. Martin Luther King, III
Ms. Tynetta Muhammed

Prayer *(Courage)* . . . . Rev. Wyatt T. Walker
Canaan Baptist Church,
New York, NY

MOTHERS OF THE STRUGGLE -BEHOLD THY SONS
Attorney Faye Williams
Washington DC Coordinator
Million Man March

Rosa Parks, Dr. Dorothy I. Height
(Introduction of Queen Mother Moore)

APPEAL TO OUR BROTHERS
Dr. Maya Angelou

Prayer (Love) . . . . Rev. Wendell Anthony
Fellowship Chapel
Detroit, MI

Musical Selection . . . . Boys Choir Of Harlem

SAVE THE CHILDREN

Mr. Leonard Dunston
National Association Black Social Workers

163

Father George Clements

Appeal To Our Fathers

Ms. Tiffany Jamille Mayo
Arthur Middleton Elementary School
Waldorf, Maryland

Masters Milton Boyd and Bashiri Wilson
Jefferson Junior High School, Washington, D.C.

Alleynde Baptiste, Chicago, IL
Whitney Young High School

Prayer (Hope) . . . . Rev. Jeremiah Wright
Trinity Baptist Church
Chicago, IL

Musical Selection. . . . .

RESPONSIBILITY
<u>Section Leaders:</u>
Mr. Bob Laws, Talk Radio Host, WLIB/AM, NY,
NY
Rev. Frank Madison Reid, III
Bethel AME Church, Baltimore, MD

Opening Statement . . . . Dr. Conrad Worrill
National Black United Front
Speakers
Economic Empowerment . . . . Danny Bakewell, Black United Front
Los Angeles, California

Rock Newman
Promoter, Manager

Prayer . . . . Rev. William Revely, Jr.
Messiah Baptist Church
Detroit, MI

Youth Empowerment . . . . Ron Sailor, NAACP Youth

Jawanza Kunjufu
Educator, Author

Carl Upchurch
Urban Peace & Social Justice
Movement
Newark, Ohio

Shawn Barney
President, Howard University
Student Body

Chuck D & The Rappers

Prayer . . . . Rev. Johnny Youngblood
St. Paul Community Baptist Church
Brooklyn, NY

Musical Selection . . . . Million Man March Male Chorus

Public Policy . . . . Dr. Alim Muhammad
Minister of Health Nation of Islam

Mr. Damu Smith
Greenpeace,U.S.A.

Political Empowerment . . . . Congressman Kweisi Mfume

Mr. Ron Daniels
Campaign For A New Tomorrow

Cultural Empowerment . . . . Haki Madhubuti, Third World Press
Chicago State University

Musical Selection . . . . *"It's Time To Make A Change"*
Union Temple Men's Chorus
Washington, DC

Rev. Al Sharpton, New York City

National Action Network
Brief Remarks & Introduction

Rev. Jesse Jackson
National Rainbow Coalition

Prayer Of Inspiration . . . . Rev. Clay Evans
Fellowship Missionary
Baptist Church
Chicago, IL

National Entertainment Artist

~~~CHARITY~~~

**Special
Acknowledgements**

2:30PM, 4:00PM   **ATONEMENT & RECONCILIATION**

<u>Masters of Ceremonies</u>
Rev. Willie F. Wilson
Brother Ishmael Muhammad

MISSION STATEMENT
Dr. Maulana Karenga

Prayer For Atonement . . . . Bishop H. H. Brookins
5th Episcopal District, AME
Los Angeles, CA

Theological Foundation For Atonement . . . . Rev. James Bevel
Chicago, IL

Statements Of Atonement & Reconciliation . . . . Dr. Cornel West
Professor, Harvard University

Rev. Joseph Lowery
Southern Christian
Leadership Conference

Musical Selection . . . . Million Man March Male Chorus

TOWARD A PEOPLE HEALED

Introduction of Rev. Ben Chavis. . . . . Brother Ishmael Muhammad

Rev. Benjamin F. Chavis, Jr.
National Coordinator
Million Man March

THE MESSAGE . . . THE VISION
Introduction of Minister Louis Farrakhan . . . . .

THE HONORABLE MINISTER LOUIS FARRAKHAN
National Representative Of
The Honorable Elijah Muhammad
and The Nation Of Islam

Black Men's Pledge . . . . All Assembled

"To God Be The Glory"
Led By Gregory Hopkins and The Million Man March Male Chorus

AFRICAN AMERICAN FATHER'S PLEDGE

I WILL WORK TO BE THE BEST FATHER I CAN BE. FATHERING IS A DAILY MISSION, AND THERE ARE NO SUBSTITUTES FOR GOOD FATHERS. SINCE I HAVE NOT BEEN TAUGHT TO BE A GOOD FATHER, IN ORDER TO MAKE MY "ON THE JOB" TRAINING EASIER, I WILL STUDY, LISTEN, OBSERVE AND LEARN FROM MY MISTAKES.

I WILL OPENLY DISPLAY LOVE AND CARING FOR MY WIFE AND CHILDREN. I WILL LISTEN TO MY WIFE AND CHILDREN. I WILL HUG AND KISS MY CHILDREN OFTEN. I WILL BE SUPPORTIVE OF THE MOTHER OF MY CHILDREN AND SPEND QUALITY TIME WITH MY CHILDREN.

I WILL TEACH BY EXAMPLE. I WILL TRY TO INTRODUCE MYSELF AND MY FAMILY TO SOMETHING NEW AND DEVELOPMENTAL EACH WEEK. I WILL HELP MY CHILDREN WITH THEIR HOMEWORK AND ENCOURAGE THEM TO BE INVOLVED IN EXTRACURRICULAR ACTIVITIES.

I WILL READ TO OR WITH MY CHILDREN AS OFTEN AS POSSIBLE. I WILL PROVIDE OPPORTUNITIES FOR MY CHILDREN TO DEVELOP CREATIVELY IN THE ARTS: MUSIC, DANCE, DRAMA, LITERATURE AND VISUAL ARTS. I WILL CHALLENGE MY CHILDREN TO DO THEIR BEST.

I WILL ENCOURAGE AND ORGANIZE FREQUENT FAMILY ACTIVITIES FOR THE HOME AND AWAY FROM HOME. I WILL TRY TO MAKE LIFE A POSITIVE ADVENTURE AND MAKE MY CHILDREN AWARE OF THEIR EXTENDED FAMILY.

I WILL NEVER BE INTOXICATED OR "HIGH" IN THE PRESENCE OF MY CHILDREN, NOR WILL I USE LANGUAGE UNBECOMING FOR AN INTELLIGENT AND SERIOUS FATHER.

I WILL BE NONVIOLENT IN MY RELATIONSHIPS WITH MY WIFE AND CHILDREN. AS A FATHER, MY ROLE WILL BE TO STIMULATE AND ENCOURAGE MY CHILDREN RATHER THAN CARRY THE "BIG STICK."

I WILL MAINTAIN A HOME THAT IS CULTURALLY IN TUNE WITH THE BEST OF AFRICAN AMERICAN HISTORY, STRUGGLE AND FUTURE. THIS WILL BE DONE, IN PART, BY DEVELOPING A LIBRARY, RECORD/DISC, VIDEO AND VISUAL ART COLLECTIONS THAT REFLECT THE DEVELOPMENTAL ASPECTS OF AFRICAN PEOPLE WORLDWIDE. THERE WILL BE LOVE, SHARING, ORDER AND PREDICTABILITY IN OUR HOME.

I WILL TEACH MY CHILDREN TO BE RESPONSIBLE, DISCIPLINED, FAIR AND HONEST. I WILL TEACH THEM THE VALUE OF HARD WORK AND FRUITFUL PRODUCTION. I WILL TEACH THEM THE IMPORTANCE OF FAMILY, COMMUNITY, POLITICS AND ECONOMICS. I WILL TEACH THEM THE IMPORTANCE OF THE NGUZO SABA (BLACK VALUE SYSTEM) AND THE ROLE THAT OWNERSHIP OF PROPERTY AND BUSINESSES PLAY IN OUR STRUGGLE.

AS A FATHER, I WILL ATTEMPT TO PROVIDE MY FAMILY WITH AN ATMOSPHERE OF LOVE AND SECURITY TO AID THEM IN THEIR DEVELOPMENT INTO SANE, LOVING, PRODUCTIVE, SPIRITUAL, HARD-WORKING, CREATIVE AFRICAN AMERICANS WHO REALIZE THEY HAVE A RESPONSIBILITY TO DO WELL AND HELP THE LESS FORTUNATE OF THIS WORLD. I WILL TEACH MY CHILDREN TO BE *ACTIVISTS* AND TO *THINK* FOR THEMSELVES. I WILL BE A LOVING EXAMPLE FOR MY CHILDREN.

Excerpted from **Black Men: Obsolete, Single, Dangerous?**
by Haki R. Madhubuti

A Proposal To Establish
The African American Development Fund

Submitted To:

Minister Louis Farrakhan
and the
Million Man March
Organizing Committee

Reverend Ben Chavis
and the
African American
Leadership Summit

Submitted By:
The African American Development Fund Task Force

HAKI MADHUBUTI • RON DANIELS • ROY HASTICK

Prepared by **NATIONAL BLACK UNITED FUND, INC.**
Danny J. Bakewell, Sr., Chairman; William T. Merritt, President

In Collaboration with:
Charles D. Craig, Esq., Chief National Legal Counsel, NBUF
The Executive Committee, National Board of Directors, NBUF

November 14, 1995

National Black United Fund
and the Proposed
African American Development Fund

With the announcement of the Million Man March (MMM) its leaders, Minister Louis Farrakhan and Ben Chavis, suggested that a primary goal coming out of the MMM would be the establishment of an African American Development Fund (AADF). Other leaders within the National African American Leadership Summit (NAALS) recognized, immediately, the need to include the National Black United Fund (NBUF) as an organization in this process. NBUF has a proven history of success in providing the African American community with an instrument of economic development for non profit social welfare and social action organizations. NBUF recognized its responsibility to both the MMM and the AADF concept and immediately passed a resolution of support . NAALS established the AADF Task Force. Task Force members, Haki Madhubuti, Ron Daniels and Roy Hastick, began a series of meetings with William T. Merritt, president /CEO and Danny J. Bakewell Sr. chairman and cofounder of NBUF. The meetings were structured to prepare a strategy for implementing AADF as an immediate follow-up to the Million Man March.

A BRIEF HISTORY OF NATIONAL BLACK UNITED FUND

Twenty-three years ago the **National Black United Fund** was incorporated in the State of New York. The organization grew out of the perceived need for the African American community to provide for itself as it had done throughout its history. With the Civil Rights and African American Liberation Movements serving as inspiration, the future founders of NBUF organized the Brotherhood Crusade in Los Angeles in 1968. Their leader, Walter Bredmond, spearheaded the Black United Fund (BUF) movement at the Brotherhood Crusade and headed BUF nationally from 1972 until his death in 1982. Bremond was followed by Garland L. Jaggers (1982-83), Dana Alston (1984 -86) and William T. Merritt, a former president of the National Association of Black Social Workers, who in 1987 became NBUF's fourth President and Chief Executive Officer.

The National Black United Fund's mission is to create, support and sustain African American social, economic, cultural and educational initiatives through the enhancement of African American philanthropy. NBUF participates in community enrichment by helping local leaders organize and develop the vehicles for accessing new dollars and expanding philanthropy. NBUF is a coordinating and planning body established to assist local Black United Funds, and other national Black organizations, with developing and implementing successful fund drives. It has grown from four local BUFs raising a few hundred thousand dollars in the 1970's to 15 BUFs raising over $8 million in 1992. Currently, 20 BUF affiliates are in operation in 18 states. Self-help and volunteerism remain the cornerstones of its founding mission.

The BUF movement has proven itself as a mechanism by which African Americans can invest in their communities, primarily by charitable giving through payroll deduction. The organization has been the leader in democratizing the workplace for combined employee charitable fund-raising campaigns. It took over eight years of litigation and Congressional and regulatory hearings before NBUF prevailed over the Civil Service Commission (which was joined by the United Way of America as co-plaintiff). NBUF won admission to the Combined Federal Campaign (CFC) in 1980. This effort led to the admission of some 800 national organizations into the CFC and set the precedent for formerly excluded local organizations to participate in municipal and state employee campaigns. NBUF now participates in almost 500 CFCs nationwide. Contrary to some predictions, especially among United Way enthusiasts, overall giving increased among employees due to diversity of charity options.

From its present offices in Newark, New Jersey, NBUF provides financial and administrative management, fund raising, advocacy and other forms of technical assistance to its local BUF affiliates . These supportive services help to ensure compliance with high standards of accountability and effectiveness. Affiliate BUFs provide yearly grants to some 600 agencies and organizations which offer services to African Americans and people of color throughout the U.S. and in the international community. While all funded agencies reflect the needs and priorities of their local communities, all must meet guidelines and standards put forth through the national office. Over the past 20 years, more than 2000 different organizations have been funded at the local level.

Further recognizing its capacity to provide support services to national organizations, NBUF established a subsidiary, the National Black United Federation of Charities (NBUF/C) in 1990. NBUF/C began with 15 organizations and qualified to participate in the CFC in the fall of 1991. During its first three years of operation, the Federation received $4.5 million dollars in pledges from federal employees. To date, NBUF/C has collected 85% of pledges to its members. NBUF/C has grown to a 40-member association and continues to expand. In addition, in the last two years NBUF has organized eleven (11) local federations in tandem with BUF affiliates across the country, further strengthening the capacity of locals to raise new dollars for priority community causes. We stand firm in our belief that the success of NBUF is inextricably linked to the continued social and economic development of the African American community.

For over 25 years NBUF has struggled to ensure that the African Americans have an independent infra structure that would provide a vehicle to participate in building and supporting institutions and programs for its own well being. Therefore, the call for an African American Development Fund to further enhance our community's capacity for self sufficiency and self determination is a compelling one. NBUF's approach to supporting social welfare services and institutions is essential to the Black community's capacity to move forward. Social prosperity for the entire community is based on a comprehensive approach to economic development.

The Million Man March called for a new beginning. It put forth the vision of bringing together a broad-based leadership cadre to work together in a concerted, comprehensive, coordinated action like never seen before. It calls for a new spirit of cooperation, one that would find new ways to involve all, regardless of position, in the building of a stronger and more viable community. Therefore it is NBUF's responsibility to offer its hand as a partner with the National African American Leadership Summit in its movement toward a more comprehensive economic development program.

A Proposal To Establish
The African American Development Fund

In order to immediately capture the overriding spirit of goodwill and unity generated by the Million Man March, and to facilitate the collection of monies which persons nationwide wish to contribute to the African-American Development Fund (AADF), the Task Force for the AADF suggests the establishment of a Trust Fund, pursuant to a Trust Agreement between the National Black United Fund (NBUF) and the National African American Leadership Summit (NAALS) /African American Development Fund Task Force or their authorized designee. This Trust Fund will help to insure the longevity of the new spirit of hope, commitment and involvement in the economic growth and development of the nationwide African American community.

Assuming agreement, the Trust Fund would be the repository of all funds collected beginning the day the Trust Agreement is signed. NBUF proposes and will agree to assume responsibility as the Trustee/fiscal agent for the funds and their management. Within 48 hours of authorization, a Trust Account will be opened by NBUF in City National Bank, an African-American owned institution in Newark, New Jersey and will be ready to receive funds. As an indication of its good faith, NBUF will contribute the first account deposit of $1,000. The NAALS may, at its discretion, authorize transfer of Trust funds to another or additional financial institutions as deemed appropriate. All monies collected in the Trust Account will remain untouched until an authorizing document (consisting of three (3) to five (5) signatures) requires that NBUF the Trustee, write a check or checks to access funds. Any and all checks written would require the same authorizing document procedure. Monies in the Trust Account will remain tax-exempt until such time as decisions are made by the NAALS regarding its investment goals and objectives.

As a further demonstration of NBUF's commitment to the NAALS, and in the spirit of service to the African-American community, which was the challenge of the Million Man March, NBUF will bear the initial administrative expenses associated with the establishment of the Fund. NAALS will agree to bear the expense of legal fees or other third party costs, associated with preparation of the Trust Agreement.

The two parties will negotiate an annual management fee. NBUF will not require any management-administration fee until the Fund reaches $25,000. After the Fund is established and a management fee set, any and all costs related to Fund maintenance will be borne by NBUF except for legal, auditing and other third party costs.

As Fund Trustee, the responsibilities of NBUF include: receiving and acknowledging all contributions, developing and maintaining a database of contributors, preparing and providing quarterly financial reports and maintaining financial ledgers and records.

What is proposed is not an economic development plan, rather is a vehicle to implement receipt of funds. Together, NBUF and AADF will form a unique and strong partnership. AADF will for the first time be the vehicle to bring a sense of order, planning and execution to investment in business development, for the economic health and strength of our people and our communities. NBUF has, over the past twenty-five years, assumed a leadership position in the area of fundraising by providing funding to meet the health and welfare needs our people, through projects that strengthen and enrich our people and our communities. We have created confidence and credibility in our organization and in our willingness to be accountable to our community. We can assure the integrity that we all know our people want and deserve.

The role of trustee for the African American Development Fund is an opportunity of historic importance. NBUF humbly submits its experience and expertise to fulfill the obligations of the role of Trustee of the African American Development Fund. It will be an honor and privilege to bring this demonstrated experience and service into partnership with the AADF.

—National Black United Fund